Praise fo

We hear far too often that the doctrine of forensic justification through faith was an invention of the Protestant Reformers, as if the church had never before heard of any such thing. This unbalanced judgment has been challenged strongly, and in my opinion very successfully, by Nathan Busenitz in this well-researched and accessible contribution to Reformation scholarship. I commend it to Protestants and Roman Catholics alike. No future conversations or polemics between the two should ignore what Busenitz has here achieved.

Nick Needham
Church History Tutor, Highland Theological College
Author of *2000 Years of Christ's Power*

In this carefully researched and well-written book, Busenitz deconstructs the myth that salvation by faith alone through grace alone was invented by the Reformers. Here we see how the true gospel has been the faithful church's central proclamation through the centuries. Yet this is not merely history. This is a clarion call for the church today to get the gospel right.

Stephen J. Nichols
President, Reformation Bible College, and Chief Academic Officer, Ligonier Ministries
Author of *The Reformation: How a Monk and a Mallet Changed the World*

One question that Protestants are often asked—and that, if they are honest, they probably ask themselves—is where was the gospel before the Reformation? Did the church merely languish in darkness for over a millennium while nobody truly understood the apostle Paul? Answering this, of course, requires careful study of the great theologians of the early church and the Middle Ages, something that few of us have the time to do for ourselves. Therefore, we should be grateful that Busenitz has made available the fruits of his doctoral research in such an accessible and helpful form. Readers of this book will find that question answered and their own confidence in the Protestant tradition on salvation strengthened.

Carl R. Trueman
William E. Simon Fellow in Religion and Public Life, Princeton University
Author of *Grace Alone—Salvation as a Gift of God: What the Reformers Taught and Why It Still Matters*

This book is a balanced, winsome, easy-to-read, biblical and historical defense of the Reformation doctrine of *sola fide*. With meticulous documentation from primary patristic and medieval sources, Nathan Busenitz has convincingly debunked the notion that the Reformation teaching of justification by faith alone was a sixteenth-century novelty unknown to the prior 1500 years of church history.

William Webster
Pastor, Grace Bible Church, Battleground, WA
Author of *The Church of Rome at the Bar of History*

We have long needed a book that helps us clearly understand who held to the essential gospel truths, recovered in the Reformation, before the Reformation exploded onto the scene. We now have such a book, *Long before Luther* by Nathan Busenitz. In every generation, God has had a remnant of faithful believers that held to the core doctrine of justification by faith alone. Here is a book—carefully researched, precisely documented, and skillfully written—that will help you discover who laid this theological landmark from the second to the fifteenth centuries. You need to know what is contained in these pages.

Steven J. Lawson
President, OnePassion Ministries, Dallas, TX
Author of *Pillars of Grace: AD 100–1564*

LONG BEFORE LUTHER

TRACING THE HEART OF THE GOSPEL FROM CHRIST TO THE REFORMATION

NATHAN BUSENITZ

MOODY PUBLISHERS
CHICAGO

THE MASTER'S SEMINARY PRESS
LOS ANGELES

Edited by Kevin P. Emmert
Author photo: Kevin Ford
Interior and Cover design: Erik M. Peterson

Library of Congress Cataloging-in-Publication Data

Names: Busenitz, Nathan, author.
Title: Long before Luther : tracing the heart of the Gospel from Christ to the Reformation / Nathan Busenitz.
Description: Chicago : Moody Publishers, 2017. | Includes bibliographical references. |
Identifiers: LCCN 2017028668 (print) | LCCN 2017035114 (ebook) | ISBN 9780802496355 () | ISBN 9780802418029
Subjects: LCSH: Justification (Christian theology)--History of doctrines--Early church, ca. 30-600. | Justification (Christian theology)--History of doctrines--Middle Ages, 600-1500. | Theology, Doctrinal--History--Early church, ca. 30-600. | Theology, Doctrinal--History--Middle Ages, 600-1500. | Catholic Church--Doctrines. | Reformation. | Reformed Church--Doctrines.
Classification: LCC BT764.3 (ebook) | LCC BT764.3 .B87 2017 (print) | DDC 234/.709--dc23
LC record available at https://lccn.loc.gov/2017028668

ISBN: 978-0-8024-1802-9

We hope you enjoy this book from Moody Publishers. Our goal is to provide high-quality, thought-provoking books and products that connect truth to your real needs and challenges. For more information on other books and products written and produced from a biblical perspective, go to www.moodypublishers.com or write to:

Moody Publishers
820 N. LaSalle Boulevard
Chicago, IL 60610

1 3 5 7 9 10 8 6 4 2

Printed in the United States of America

To my dad.

CONTENTS

FOREWORD

Along with all those who have been gathered up by the power of Scripture and the Spirit into the recovery of Reformation theology, I have been shaped by the Reformers. I understand the massive spiritual transformation that they launched, but I have long been curious about a nagging question: where was the witness to the true gospel during the dark centuries before the Reformation? Nathan Busenitz has provided the answer to this crucial matter of church history.

Nothing is more important than a right understanding of the gospel. It is the difference between truth and error, life and death, heaven and hell. The issue is so critical, in fact, that the Bible pronounces a curse on anyone who would preach a false version of it. The apostle Paul told his readers, "If any man is preaching to you a gospel contrary to what you received, he is to be accursed" (Gal. 1:9).

That is severe language. It is as harsh as the Word of God ever gets, pronouncing eternal condemnation on anyone who distorts the gospel. In a day of postmodern tolerance, those words may sound disturbing or divisive. But they are critically necessary because salvation is at stake. If sinners are to be forgiven and reconciled to God, they must have the true gospel preached to them. The good news of salvation by grace alone through faith alone in Christ alone is the only way anyone can escape hell and enter heaven.

In the sixteenth century, Martin Luther and his fellow Reformers rallied against the corruption that dominated Roman Catholicism. Chief among their concerns was Rome's distortion of the gospel. Roman Catholicism had subverted the gospel of grace by setting up a sacramental system of works-righteousness in its place. Luther's study of the New Testament, and especially the phrase "the just shall live by faith" (Rom. 1:17; Gal. 3:11; Heb. 10:38; see Hab. 2:4) NKJV, launched his understanding of the gospel and emboldened his stand against the false system of his day. And God used Luther as a key part of the great recovery of the gospel known as the Reformation.

But before Luther was a clear-headed theologian, he was a confused monk. Before he was a powerful force for gospel advancement, he was a tormented failure who lived in constant spiritual pain. Even after joining a monastery, he was profoundly depressed and overwrought with so much guilt that he lived in constant anxiety and fear.

Like many in the sixteenth century, Luther believed the road to salvation depended on his own self-effort. He found that road to be impossibly difficult. No matter what he did, he could not overcome the reality of his own sinfulness. Convinced that he had to reach a certain point of worthiness to receive God's grace, Luther went to extremes—starvation, asceticism, sleeplessness. He punished himself in an effort to pay for his sins and appease God's wrath. Even so, he had no peace—and no salvation.

Because he understood the reality of divine judgment, he desperately wanted to be right with God. The fear of God drove him to seek reconciliation and forgiveness. He longed for a way to escape hell and enter heaven. Yet even as a monk doing everything he could possibly do, he could not find relief for his fear and guilt. "How can I be right before God?" That was the question that tormented Luther. It is a question that every sinner must ask. But it is a question to which only the gospel provides the true answer.

False religion invariably gives the wrong answer: "Be good. Work harder. Go about to establish your own righteousness." The apostle Paul critiqued that perspective in Romans 10:3–4: "For not knowing about God's righteousness and seeking to establish their own, they did not subject themselves to the righteousness of God. For Christ is the end of the law for righteousness to everyone who believes." False religion emphasizes human effort and establishes its own superficial standard of righteousness.

By contrast, the true gospel emphasizes the bankruptcy of human effort. Salvation comes only by believing in the Lord Jesus, who puts an end to the tyranny of the law. Sinners, therefore, are saved by grace through faith, apart from their own works. They are forgiven, not because of what they have achieved, but only because of what God accomplished through Christ—once for all.

That is Paul's gospel, and that is what Luther found when he began teaching through Romans and Galatians. When the gospel of grace broke on Luther's soul, the Holy Spirit gave him life, and peace and joy flooded his heart. He was forgiven, accepted, reconciled, converted, adopted, and justified—solely by grace through faith. The truth of God's Word illuminated his mind, and the chains of guilt and fear fell off him.

Luther was saved the same way any sinner is saved. Like the tax collector in Luke 18, he recognized his utter unworthiness and cried out to God for mercy. Like the thief on the cross, his sins were forgiven apart from any works he had done. Like the former Pharisee named Paul, he abandoned his reliance on self-righteous efforts, resting instead on the perfect righteousness of Christ. Like every true believer, he embraced the person and work of the Lord Jesus in saving faith. And having been justified by faith, for the first time in his life, he enjoyed peace with God.

Importantly, the issue of the gospel was not settled 500 years ago in church history. It was settled long before Luther. The Reformers were responding to the clarion truth of Scripture, submitting to the gospel message articulated on the pages of the New Testament. Following in the footsteps of Christ and the apostles, they proclaimed the biblical gospel with courage and conviction.

But were Luther and his fellow Reformers the first in church history to understand the biblical gospel accurately? The answer is no, as Nathan Busenitz demonstrates with resounding clarity in this thoroughly researched volume.

For those who have ever wondered where the gospel was before the Reformation, this book provides a welcome answer. More importantly, in a day when the church is in danger of compromising the purity of the biblical message, this book serves as a timely reminder of the gospel that true believers in every generation have cherished, proclaimed, and fought to defend.

My prayer for you, as you read this book, is that your heart would resonate with the words of Paul in Romans 1:16–17: "For I am not ashamed of the gospel, for it is the power of God for salvation to everyone who believes, to the Jew first and also to the Greek. For in it the righteousness of God is revealed from faith to faith; as it is written, 'But the righteous man shall live by faith.'"

John MacArthur
The Master's Seminary

INTRODUCTION

It was Mother's Day 2007. I remember it well because of what happened a few days earlier. On May 5, Francis Beckwith, then-president of the Evangelical Theological Society, officially resigned his presidency and publicly announced that he was leaving evangelicalism to become a Roman Catholic. By going home to Rome, he claimed, he was returning to the mother church.

Beckwith's reasons, as he explained them, were largely due to his belief that the early church was more Roman Catholic than Protestant. Specifically, he claimed the Roman Catholic understanding of salvation—and the doctrine of justification in particular—was closer to "the church's historical understanding of salvation prior to the Reformation all the way back to the ancient church of the first few centuries."[1] To return to the Roman Catholic Church was, in his estimation, to return to the church of history.

Beckwith's announcement sent shockwaves through the evangelical world, due both to its suddenness and the rationale behind it. In response, a few days before Mother's Day, my colleague Jesse Johnson published a critical assessment of

Beckwith's statement. The article—titled "Mother Church?" —took Beckwith to task. Though it was only a short blog post, its publication would change the course of my studies.

As provocative blog posts often do, Johnson's response generated numerous comments from a wide variety of perspectives. But one commenter stands out in my memory. A staunch defender of Roman Catholic teaching, he identified himself only as Gerry. He entered the online conversation with one primary assertion—that the key doctrines of the sixteenth-century Reformation were entirely without historical warrant. He put it this way: "As far as 'Protestant Christianity' goes it did not exist until the 1500s. I challenge anyone to find the current Protestant beliefs and practices before the 1500s." When asked what beliefs and practices he had in mind, Gerry narrowed his focus to the Reformation doctrines of *sola Scriptura* (that "Scripture alone" is the church's highest authority) and *sola fide* (that sinners are justified by God's grace through "faith alone" in Jesus Christ).[2]

Having just begun my doctoral studies in church history, I felt compelled to respond to Gerry's challenge. For the next seven days, using the comments section of the blog as our forum, we discussed the pre-Reformation evidence for these core Protestant doctrines. The conversation was direct, but gracious. It was also fairly expansive. The combined comments, when pasted into a Word document, came out to more than 300 pages single-spaced. When it was over, I knew this was a topic I wanted to continue studying, both to satisfy my own curiosity and to help evangelicals answer similar questions.

It might seem odd to write an entire book in response to a

challenge issued by a solitary blog commenter. But Gerry's perspective represents a popular Roman Catholic assertion—that the Reformers' understanding of the gospel was novel, absent from the first 1,500 years of church history. For evangelicals, that allegation constitutes a serious charge and is one we need to be able to answer.

As I write this, many Protestants are celebrating the 500th anniversary of the Reformation. Like them, I am grateful for the courage and faithfulness of the sixteenth-century Reformers. Yet our enthusiasm for this transformational period of church history can have an unintended effect: Protestants can unwittingly give the impression that our theological heritage is only 500 years old. Such an impression is neither helpful nor accurate, as the following pages will demonstrate.

Join me in exploring how the cherished Protestant doctrine of justification by faith alone—which is at the heart of the gospel—can be traced all the way back to Christ, our Lord and Savior.

PART ONE

THE REFORMERS AND JUSTIFICATION

CHAPTER ONE

AN INVENTION OR A RECOVERY?

The doctrine of justification by grace through "faith alone" (expressed by the Latin phrase *sola fide*) is central to a right understanding of the gospel. Stated negatively, it denies any notion that forgiveness for sin and a right standing before God can be attained through human effort or moral virtue on the part of the sinner. Stated positively, it affirms that God's gift of salvation is based completely on the finished work of Christ, which is received solely by grace through faith in Him. Salvation is not predicated, even in part, on the sinner's good works. That is why when the Philippian jailer asked Paul and Silas, "What must I *do* to be saved," the appropriate response was simply, "*Believe* in the Lord Jesus, and you will be saved" (Acts 16:30–31, emphasis added).

"Faith alone" was one of the main rallying cries of the Protestant Reformation. The Reformers recognized that it stands at the heart of the gospel, which is why Martin Luther famously said of this doctrine, "If this article [of justification] stands, the church stands; if this article collapses, the church collapses."[1] Along with "grace alone" (*sola gratia*), "Christ alone" (*solus Christus*), and "for the glory of God alone" (*soli Deo Gloria*), *sola fide* expressed the Reformers' conviction that salvation is entirely by God's grace through faith in the person and work of Jesus Christ. Through faith in Him, believers receive both pardon from sin (because He bore their punishment on the cross) and justifying righteousness (because His righteousness is credited to their account). As a result, they can take no credit for their salvation. All the glory goes to God.

It is important to note that in their emphasis on "faith alone," the Reformers did not deny the importance of good works in the lives of believers. They taught that saving faith is a repentant faith and they stressed obedience to the commands of Christ. Nonetheless, they insisted that good works ought to be viewed only as the *fruit* or *consequence* of salvation, rather than the *root* or *cause* of it. Thus, they could assert that although believers are saved by grace through faith alone, saving faith is never alone. True faith always gives evidence of itself through fruits of repentance and obedience.[2]

In the sixteenth century, the Protestant understanding of *sola fide* stood in contrast to the Roman Catholic emphasis on sacramental works and good deeds as being necessary for justification. Catholicism viewed justification as a lifelong process that depended, at least in part, on how a person lived. Reformers like Martin Luther, Philip Melanchthon, and John Calvin rejected the Catholic view, teaching instead that justification was the sole work of God in which He declared believers to be instantly righteous, not because of their good deeds, but because they were clothed with the perfect righteousness of Christ.

In response to the Reformers' teaching, Roman Catholics in the sixteenth century accused Protestant theologians of inventing a new version of the gospel. The Council of Trent (1545–1563) anathematized any who taught justification through faith alone. Since that time, numerous Roman Catholic writers have denounced *sola fide* as a heretical novelty.[3] Popular Roman Catholic apologist Dave Armstrong provides one such example. He writes, "Distinctively Protestant tenets such as *sola fide* ('faith alone') . . . were virtually nonexistent through Church history."[4] He goes on to assert, "Protestantism per se didn't exist until 1517 A.D."[5] Further, "Radically new doctrines such as *sola fide* . . . were sheer novelties, rather than reforms, supposedly harkening back to the alleged state of affairs in the early Church. But they simply cannot be found in the early Church."[6]

By contrast, Protestant scholars have defended *sola fide* as representing a return to both biblical and historic Christian orthodoxy. The doctrine of justification by faith, then, was not an *invention* but a *recovery* of theological truth that had been obscured. R. C. Sproul summarizes the traditional Protestant view: "The sixteenth-century Reformers were not interested in creating a new religion. They were interested, not in innovation, but in renovation. They were reformers, not revolutionaries."[7] The Reformers themselves would have agreed with Sproul's assessment.[8] The sole authoritative basis for their teachings was the Word of God (the idea captured by the phrase "Scripture alone"). Yet, they also appealed in a secondary sense to the church fathers—the Christian leaders of earlier centuries—to demonstrate historical affirmation for their views. As John Calvin (1509–1564) explains in the 1536 preface to his *Institutes of the Christian Religion*, "We do not despise the fathers; in fact, if it were to our present purpose, I could with no trouble at all prove that the greater part of what we are saying today meets their approval."[9] Martin Luther's colleague, Philip Melanchthon (1497–1560), likewise argued that the Reformation represented a return to the pure teachings of earlier generations. He denied any allegation that he and his fellow Reformers had departed from the teachings of the early church, insisting instead that he was defending "just that which Ambrose and Augustine have taught."[10]

Later Protestant works on justification by theologians like Martin Chemnitz (1522–1586),[11] John Owen (1616–1683),[12] Jonathan Edwards (1703–1758),[13] George Stanley Faber (1773–1854),[14] and James Buchanan (1804–1870)[15] echoed those same Reformation claims. Of these, Buchanan is perhaps the most dogmatic in his assertions "that the Protestant doctrine of Justification was not a 'novelty' introduced for the first time by Luther and Calvin,—it was held and taught, more or less explicitly, by some in every successive age,—and that there is no truth in the allegation that it had been unknown for fourteen hundred years before the Reformation."[16]

Some modern Protestant scholars, however, have challenged such claims made by previous generations. In response to Buchanan, Anthony Lane objects that "no historically qualified writer would make any such claim today."[17] Others, like Matthew C. Heckel, are far more dogmatic. He writes, "The Reformation understanding of justification *sola fide* was unheard of in the pre-Reformation church and thus not believed until Luther."[18] He continues, "Luther's doctrine of justification *sola fide* was not a recovery but an innovation within the Western theological tradition."[19] Those kinds of statements bring us back to the question at hand: was the Reformation understanding of justification through faith alone an invention or a recovery?

ALISTER MCGRATH AND FAITH ALONE

Alister McGrath is one of broader evangelicalism's foremost thinkers. The Oxford professor and Anglican priest is perhaps most well known for his robust defense of Christian theism against the attacks of atheists such as Richard Dawkins. Having taught historical theology at Oxford, McGrath is certainly qualified to trace the history of doctrinal discussions throughout the centuries. His book on the history of justification—entitled *Iustitia Dei,* which means "The Righteousness of God"—is widely regarded as one of the most comprehensive treatments of the subject. Yet it is McGrath's distinguished pedigree and theological acumen that make his assertions about the Reformers' understanding of justification so disappointing. In a number of his books, including *Iustitia Dei,* McGrath claims the Reformation doctrine of justification by faith alone was a sixteenth century novelty unknown in the prior 1,500 years of Christian thought.[20] McGrath is arguably the most distinguished Protestant to affirm the basic charge that Roman Catholics have leveled against Protestantism for the past 500 years—that Luther and his fellow Reformers invented a new understanding of justification. Because the doctrine of justification lies at the heart of the gospel, the implications of this charge are serious (see Gal. 1:6–9).

In making his case, McGrath identifies three primary characteristics of the Reformation doctrine of justification.[21]

1. Forensic Justification

First, the Reformers taught that justification was *forensic* rather than *formative*. In other words, they understood justification in terms of a divine declaration of righteousness, like a judge issuing a full pardon to a defendant in a courtroom. This was different from the medieval Roman Catholic understanding in which justification was viewed as a process by which sinners would become righteous over an extended period of time.

2. Justification Distinguished from Regeneration

Second, the Reformers distinguished the doctrine of justification from the doctrines of regeneration and progressive sanctification. In justification, God declares sinners to be *positionally* righteous, because they have been clothed in the righteousness of Christ. In regeneration, God renews sinners so that they can begin to grow in *practical* holiness. This distinction had been lost in medieval Catholicism. As a result, people confused justification with sanctification, which is why they thought their justification before God was dependent, at least in part, on their own personal holiness.

3. The Imputed Righteousness of Christ

Third, the Reformers insisted on the *imputed righteousness of Christ* rather than some sort of *infused righteousness*. Roman Catholicism taught that believers were infused with righteousness from God, which enabled them to live holy lives and then be progressively justified. By contrast, the Reformers taught that good works contribute nothing to one's justification before God. Instead, He justifies sinners solely on the basis of Christ's perfect righteousness, which is credited to them. Thus, salvation is by grace alone through faith alone in Christ alone, apart from any good works that believers might perform (see Eph. 2:8–9).

Up to this point, McGrath's analysis is helpful—since these three distinctives enable us to think more precisely about what the Reformers taught. In fact, we will return to these characteristics throughout this book. But problems arise when McGrath asks whether any pre-Reformation Christians taught these same doctrines.[22] In his survey of the first fifteen centuries of church history, McGrath claims no such theologian or writer can be found who taught these distinctives. On that basis, he concludes that no one, either in the patristic age (the era of the church fathers) or the medieval age, anticipated the Reformers' understanding of justification. According to McGrath, the Reformation doctrine of *sola fide* was a theological innovation introduced in the sixteenth century.

THE IMPLICATIONS OF MCGRATH'S POSITION

McGrath is aware that his conclusions raise troubling questions about the historical orthodoxy of the Protestant teaching on justification.[23] Yet he ultimately dismisses such questions as having "little relevance today."[24] However, we cannot dismiss this issue easily. The Reformers recognized the critical importance of what was at stake, because they understood that the doctrine of *sola fide* stands at the heart of the gospel. As a result, when their Roman Catholic opponents charged them with heretical innovation, they treated those allegations seriously and took time to respond carefully.

The challenges created by McGrath's claim can be seen in the way he is favorably cited by critics of the Reformation. Contemporary Roman Catholic apologists often point to McGrath's work as an example of a Protestant scholar who acknowledges the novelty, and nonhistorical nature, of *sola fide*.[25] Francis Beckwith, for example, notes that the writings of Alister McGrath featured prominently in convincing him that the Reformation understanding of justification lacked authentic historical roots. As Beckwith recounts, "The idea, that the Reformation's view of forensic justification was a virtual theological innovation, is put forth even more strongly by none other than the great theologian and Oxford professor, Alister McGrath."[26] Convinced that the Reformers introduced a new understanding of justification into church history, Beckwith rejected Protestantism in favor of a Roman Catholic position that, he claims, better fits the writings and teachings of the pre-Reformation church.[27] Though Beckwith's reasons for returning to Rome were broader than just a rejection of justification by faith alone, it is evident that McGrath's arguments served as an important catalyst in his thinking.

LOOKING FOR THE GOSPEL BEFORE THE REFORMATION

The notion that "faith alone" is a sixteenth-century innovation raises significant questions, especially for those who embrace the Reformation principle of *sola fide*. If the evangelical understanding of the gospel is only 500 years old, on what grounds can Protestants defend their belief in forensic justification, the distinction between justification and regeneration, or the imputed righteousness of Christ? Further, what are Protestants to conclude about those who lived during the first 1,500 years of church history, before the Reformation? Answering such questions becomes difficult if the Protestant understanding of the gospel only dates back to the sixteenth century.

However, if it can be shown that the Reformation understanding of justification was in fact *articulated* by the biblical authors and subsequently *anticipated* by pre-Reformation church leaders, the challenges raised by various opponents quickly evaporate. McGrath has boldly asserted that, in church history, there are no forerunners to the Reformation—not even a single theologian "who can be shown to have anticipated one or more of the characteristic and distinctive features of the Reformation doctrines of justification."[28] It is our goal to investigate that claim, using the very criteria he provides regarding the primary doctrinal distinctives of *sola fide*: forensic justification, a distinction between justification and sanctification, and the imputed righteousness of Christ.

CHAPTER TWO

REGAINING BIBLICAL CLARITY

The year was 1505 when a young Martin Luther, then a student in law school, was nearly struck by lightning while walking through the German countryside. Panicked, he cried out, "Saint Anne, spare me and I will become a monk." True to his word, Luther left his pursuit of law and joined the Augustinian monastery in Erfurt.

The fear of death had prompted Luther to become a monk, and for the next decade, the fear of divine judgment would continue to haunt him. In an attempt to calm those fears, Luther tried fervently to earn God's favor through good works and acts of penance. Yet the harder he worked, the more frustrated he became because he recognized he could never be good enough to atone for his sin and appease God's wrath. He later recounted that he came to hate the phrase "the righteousness of God" because in it he saw nothing but his own condemnation. Luther understood that God's righteous standard is perfection (see Matt. 5:48), and he knew that he fell far short of it (see Rom. 3:23).

It wasn't until a number of years later, as he lectured through the books of Psalms, Romans, and Galatians, that Luther's eyes were opened to the truth of the gospel. He came to understand that the righteousness of God revealed in the gospel (Rom. 1:16–17) speaks not only of God's perfect standard, but also of His righteous provision—in which the righteousness of Christ is accounted to those who embrace Him in saving faith (Rom. 3:21–4:5). For the first time in his life, this desperate monk realized that forgiveness for sin and a right standing before God depended not on his own self-effort, but solely on the finished work of Christ. In that moment, through the working of the Holy Spirit, Luther experienced the glorious truth and transforming power of God's saving grace.

Luther's testimony vividly illustrates the reality that for him and his fellow Protestants, the Reformation was deeply personal. It was not an esoteric discussion about irrelevant philosophical musings. Rather, it concerned the means by which sinners might be reconciled to God by grace through faith in Christ. The heart of gospel itself was at stake (see Gal. 2:5). Having been personally transformed by the truth of the gospel, the Reformers took a bold stand to defend the good news and preach it to others.

THE BIBLE: THE REFORMERS' STARTING POINT

More than anything else, the Reformers[1] wanted their teachings to be grounded in the Bible. Their theological conclusions were driven by an unwavering commitment to the authority of Christ and His Word above any other authority.

In this regard, the *Geneva Confession* of 1536 is representative: "We affirm that we desire to follow Scripture alone as the rule of faith and religion."[2] Though they appreciated and used the writings of the church fathers, the Reformers viewed the Bible as their final authority. As Luther explained in 1519 to his Catholic opponent Johann Eck, all nonbiblical writers must be evaluated "by the authority of the canonical books" of Scripture.[3]

It was the Reformers' commitment to Scripture as the ultimate authority that compelled them to teach the doctrine of *sola fide*. In other words, they taught justification by faith alone because they were convinced it was revealed clearly in Scripture. After providing an extensive survey of biblical passages regarding justification, Martin Chemnitz—known as the second "Martin" of Lutheranism—declares, "The doctrine of justification itself will be plain and clear, if only we are allowed to seek and judge it from the divine oracles and not from the philosophical opinions of reason."[4] John Calvin similarly addresses the topic by amassing "many clear testimonies of Scripture to confirm" his assertions in his *Institutes*.[5]

Although the Reformers sought secondary affirmation from the writings of the church fathers, it was Scripture that served as the ultimate foundation for their theological claims.[6] Convinced that the purity of the church was at stake,[7] and that the gospel they preached was overwhelmingly supported by the biblical text, they proclaimed it with bold confidence, regardless of whether it departed from medieval Roman Catholic tradition. Commenting on Galatians 1:6–9, for instance, Luther noted that "everyone must obey, and be subject to" the Scriptures. He stated further,

> The pope, Luther, Augustine, [or even] an angel from heaven—these should not be masters, judges or arbiters, but only witnesses, disciples, and confessors of Scripture. Nor should any doctrine be taught or heard in the church except the pure Word of God. Otherwise, let the teachers and the hearers be accursed along with their doctrine.[8]

It was to Scripture that the Reformers repeatedly turned in defending their understanding of justification, and it is there that we must begin.

SALVATION BY GRACE THROUGH FAITH

The fact that believers are saved by grace through faith apart from works is reiterated in many places throughout the New Testament. Near the beginning of His ministry, Jesus says of Himself that "whoever believes will in Him have eternal life" (John 3:15; see also 20:31). Later, He tells a story about a Pharisee and a tax collector to demonstrate that the grace of justification is given not to those who look religious on the outside but to those who recognize their utter unworthiness and cry out to God for mercy (Luke 18:10–14). The fact that salvation is not contingent upon good works is seen perhaps most vividly at the cross, when Jesus tells the thief who believed, "Today you shall be with Me in Paradise" (Luke 23:43). The thief on the cross was saved even though he had no opportunity to perform good deeds.

If good works were the basis for justification, the apostle Paul would have had much to boast about (Phil. 3:4–6). Yet, he recognized that his self-righteous efforts were all worthless and that the only righteousness that mattered was that given to him through faith in Christ. As he explains to the believers in Philippi, "I count all things to be loss in view of the surpassing value of knowing Christ Jesus my Lord . . . not having a righteousness of my own derived from the Law, but that which is through faith in Christ, the righteousness which comes from God on the basis of faith" (Phil. 3:8–9).

In his missionary journeys, Paul boldly preached the good news of divine forgiveness freely extended to sinners by grace through faith in Christ. To an audience at the synagogue in Psidian Antioch, he declares, "Therefore let it be known to you, brethren, that through this Man [Jesus] is preached to you the forgiveness of sins; and by Him everyone who believes is justified from all things from which you could not be justified by the law of Moses" (Acts 13:38–39 NKJV). When false teachers threatened the purity of that gospel message, by insisting that certain religious works were necessary for salvation (Acts 15:1, 5), Paul refused to yield to them for even a moment (Gal. 2:5). The issue came to a head at the Jerusalem Council in Acts 15, where the apostle Peter defended Paul by publicly affirming that the hearts of sinners are cleansed "by faith" and that believers are saved solely "through the grace of the Lord Jesus" (Acts 15:9–11).

For the rest of Paul's missionary career, the gospel of grace through faith alone, apart from works, was a repeated theme. The former Pharisee was clear in his teaching: those seeking to add legalistic works to the gospel were guilty of frustrating grace (Gal. 2:21; Rom. 11:6) and preaching another gospel (Gal. 1:6–9). Conversely, salvation is God's free gift to those who believe. As Paul tells the Ephesians, "For by grace you have been saved through faith; and that not of yourselves, it is the gift of God; not as a result of works, so that no one may boast" (Eph. 2:8–9). He similarly explains to the church in Rome, "For we maintain that a man is justified by faith apart from works of the Law. . . . To the one who does not work, but believes in Him who justifies the ungodly, his faith is credited as righteousness" (Rom. 3:28; 4:5). Near the end of his life, Paul reiterates these truths to Titus, who was ministering on the island of Crete, "[God] saved us, not on the basis of deeds which we have done in righteousness, but according to His mercy, by the washing of regeneration and renewing by the Holy Spirit, whom He poured out upon us richly through Jesus Christ our Savior, so that being justified by His grace we would be made heirs according to the hope of eternal life" (Titus 3:5–7).

As these and similar passages demonstrate, the New Testament presents salvation as being freely given to those who embrace the Lord Jesus in saving faith. Their sins are forgiven not on account of their good deeds, but solely on the basis of Christ's redemptive work. It was from these texts, and others like them, that the Reformers derived their commitment to preach the good news of salvation by grace alone through faith alone in Christ alone, so that all glory may be given to God alone.

At this point, we are ready to dig deeper into the writings of some of the leading Reformers, to learn more about their understanding of the doctrine of justification. In the previous chapter, we learned about three characteristics of their position: (1) forensic justification, (2) a distinction between justification and sanctification (or regeneration), and (3) the imputed righteousness of Christ. In the remainder of this chapter, we will consider the writings of men like Martin Luther, Philip Melanchthon, and John Calvin to see how they defined and defended these three aspects of Protestant doctrine. In particular, we will pay close attention to the biblical arguments they used to make the case that sinners are justified by grace through faith alone.

THE FORENSIC NATURE OF JUSTIFICATION

When we consider the writings of these leading Reformers, we see that they understood justification to be the forensic declaration of God in which He, as the supreme Judge, pardons sinners by forgiving their sin and declaring them to be righteous. The assertion that "to be justified" means "to be declared righteous" stood in sharp contrast to the prevailing Roman Catholic teaching of the sixteenth century. Most Roman Catholics viewed justification as a formative process that involved sinners being "made righteous" over the course of their entire lives. Consequently, in the Roman Catholic view, believers contributed to their justification through the acts of penance and good works they performed. The Reformers rejected that notion, arguing instead that justification is an immediate change in the sinner's status before God, to which believers contribute nothing. It is entirely a work of God.

The term *forensic* refers to the law court. God as Judge declares sinners to be righteous because Jesus' righteousness has been credited, or imputed, to them. Though they deserve condemnation on account of their guilt, God views them as righteous because they are clothed in the perfect righteousness of His Son. They receive this righteousness not because of anything they have done, but because they have been united to Christ through faith in Him.

A forensic understanding of justification is particularly clear in the writings of Philip Melanchthon and John Calvin. Melanchthon pictured the sinner standing before a divine tribunal. He writes, "Certainly no man in God's court is without sin. . . . All men must come before God through the Mediator Jesus Christ, and must first receive forgiveness of sins and acceptance for the sake of the Lord Christ."[9] Although worthy of condemnation on account of their own works, believers are forgiven by the divine Judge and declared to be righteous. This is possible because they are "accounted just by God on account of Christ when [they] believe."[10]

In his *Institutes,* Calvin also used law court imagery to describe justification. He writes, "Our discourse is concerned with the justice not of a human court but of a heavenly tribunal, lest we measure by our own small measure the integrity of works needed to satisfy the divine judgment."[11] He later adds that everyone must admit their guilt before "the Heavenly Judge."[12] Like Melanchthon, Calvin understood that, in themselves, sinners can do nothing to earn God's favor or appease His wrath. For believers, their righteous standing before the divine Judge is possible only because they are covered by the perfect righteousness of Christ. As Calvin explains, "Justified by faith is he who, excluded from the righteousness of works, grasps the righteousness of Christ through faith, and clothed in it, appears in God's sight not as a sinner but as a righteous man."[13]

Melanchthon and Calvin give us two clear examples of a Reformation understanding of the forensic nature of justification.[14] In the court of heaven, sinners are guilty and worthy of condemnation. Even their self-righteous works are like filthy rags in the sight of a holy God (see Isa. 64:6). Yet by grace through faith in Christ, sinners are pardoned by the heavenly Judge and declared to be righteous. Being justified, therefore, means to be acquitted of sin and accepted by God as if we were righteous, because we are clothed in the perfect righteousness of Christ.[15]

DEFENDING FORENSIC JUSTIFICATION

Now that we understand that the Reformers saw justification as a forensic declaration of righteousness, we are ready to explore the biblical underpinnings of their teachings. The Reformers insisted that "to be justified" meant "to be declared righteous" in terms of a person's status before God. In order to support their doctrinal position, they put forward a number of Scripture-based arguments. Let's consider several of them briefly.

First, the Reformers looked to the Old Testament, asserting that the New Testament authors based their understanding of justification on what was previously revealed in the Hebrew Scriptures. They noted the forensic nature of the justification language in the Old Testament, where forms of the word *ṣādaq* (meaning "to be just" or "righteous"), refer to a declaration of righteousness. As Melanchthon explains, "According to the Hebrew usage of the term, *to justify* is *to pronounce* or *to consider just*."[16] Calvin similarly notes that the phrase "to be justified" derives its meaning "from legal usage" in the Old Testament.[17] Chemnitz uses the same argument by appealing to the Septuagint—the ancient Greek translation of the Hebrew Old Testament—looking specifically at instances where the translators used the Greek word *dikaioō* ("to justify") to translate *ṣādaq* in terms of a forensic declaration of righteousness (in passages like Gen. 44:16; Deut. 25:1; 2 Sam. 15:4; 1 Kings 8:32; Job 13:18; 27:5; 32:2; 40:8; Ps. 51:4; Prov. 17:15; and Isa. 5:23; 43:9, 26).[18] Chemnitz observed in the New Testament the "earnest care the apostles bestowed, lest the Hebrew character of the word 'justify' which is less well known in other languages, should either disturb or obscure the doctrine."[19] He also cited examples from Acts 13:38–39; 15:11; Romans 3:24; 4; 5:10–11, 19; Galatians 2:16; and Ephesians 2:5 to demonstrate that the New Testament writers fully understood—and preserved—the forensic quality of the Hebrew terms.[20] According to the Reformers, the apostles' use of the verb "to justify" in the New Testament reflected their understanding of the parallel concept from the Hebrew Old Testament.

Second, the Reformers defended a forensic understanding of justification by noting places in the New Testament where *justification* is directly contrasted with *condemnation*. In Romans 8:33–34, for example, Paul asks rhetorically, "Who will bring a charge against God's elect? God is the one who justifies; who is the one who condemns?" Paul's use of the courtroom metaphor here is evident, with an imaginary accuser bringing legal charges against God's elect. Yet the accusations carry no weight because no one can condemn those whom God has justified. The direct contrast between the terms *justifies* and *condemns* indicates that both should be understood as legal declarations.

In his *Institutes*, Calvin uses this Pauline antithesis to

argue that justification is forensic since the apostle contrasts acquittal with accusation.[21] Commenting on Romans 5:17, Luther states, "As the sin of the one [Adam] becomes known through our condemnation without any actual sin of our own, so the grace of the other is made known by this that His [Christ's] righteousness is granted to us without our merit."[22] As sinners are condemned (declared guilty) through Adam, believers are justified (declared righteous) through Christ. In this way, justification (acquittal) is accurately defined in light of its opposite (condemnation).

Third, the Reformers supported their understanding that "to justify" means "to declare righteous" and not "to make righteous" by pointing to places in Scripture where God is said to be justified. Clearly, God cannot be "made righteous," since He is already morally perfect. But He can be "declared righteous" by those who recognize and praise Him for His absolute holiness. In 1 Timothy 3:16, Paul applies the language of justification to the Lord Jesus: "Great is the mystery of godliness: God was manifested in the flesh, justified in the Spirit, seen by angels, preached among the Gentiles, believed on in the world, received up in glory" (NKJV). Calvin understood that here the point is that Jesus was *shown* or *declared* to be righteous, not *made* righteous.[23] Luke 7:29 communicates something similar. Luke writes, "And when all the people heard Him, even the tax collectors justified God, having been baptized with the baptism of John" (NKJV). Calvin points out that the tax collectors did not make God righteous, but rather declared His righteousness.[24]

Fourth, the Reformers pointed to 1 Corinthians 4:3–4 for further evidence of the declarative, forensic nature of justification. In that passage, Paul writes, "But with me it is a very small thing that I should be judged by you or by a human court. In fact, I do not even judge myself. For I know of nothing against myself, yet I am not justified by this; but He who judges me is the Lord" (NKJV). Paul can declare himself to be righteous and even seek to be vindicated by a human court, but the only declaration of righteousness that truly matters is that which comes from God on the behalf of sinners. That Paul will be "examined" by the divine Judge, and "justified" by Him, indicates that he understood justification in forensic terms.[25] Rather than basing his confidence in the opinions of men, he appeals to the only opinion that matters: God's verdict.

Fifth, the Reformers believed the whole of Paul's teaching in the book of Romans necessitates a forensic understanding of justification.[26] As the epistle of Romans explains, both Jews and Gentiles stand condemned before the law of God, the standard of which is perfection.[27] If sinners are to avoid the punishment they rightly deserve, they must seek His pardon. Such assumes a forensic understanding of justification in which sins are forgiven and the guilty acquitted by the divine Judge. Paul's argument hinges on the fact that justification is granted by faith apart from works. But that is incompatible with the notion that justification consists of a gradual moral transformation that includes works.[28]

Based on these lines of evidence, the Reformers built a biblical case for a forensic understanding of justification, asserting that it must be understood as *declarative* rather than *transformative*.[29] Their appeal to history (addressed in the next chapter) was secondary to the arguments they derived from the Word of God. Whether or not their position was in agreement with the church fathers (a point they debated with their Roman Catholic opponents), their primary concern was to set their interpretations squarely in line with the teachings of Paul and the rest of Scripture.

But what about the distinction they made between justification and sanctification, and about the imputed righteousness of Christ? What passages of Scripture did the Reformers use to define and defend these doctrines? Turn the page, and we will continue our exploration.

CHAPTER THREE

CLOTHED IN CHRIST'S RIGHTEOUSNESS

In the previous chapter, we considered the teachings of some of the leading Reformers regarding justification by faith alone. We saw their commitment to God's Word as their highest authority, noting their desire to define and defend their theological views first and foremost from Scripture itself. From their study of the biblical text, they concluded that justification is a forensic declaration of righteousness, rather than a gradual process by which sinners become righteous. We will build on that theme in this chapter as we consider what they taught about the distinction between justification and sanctification, and the imputation of Christ's righteousness.

JUSTIFICATION DISTINGUISHED FROM SANCTIFICATION

In keeping with their forensic understanding of justification, the Reformers were careful to distinguish between justification ("the external act by which God declares the sinner to be righteous") and regeneration or sanctification ("the internal process of renewal within humans").[1] This distinction is vital, because it means that believers are counted as righteous in God's sight, not on account of their own good works, but only because of the righteousness of Christ, which is credited to them by grace through faith. When justification and sanctification are confused, the inevitable conclusion is that the believer's personal holiness contributes, at least in part, to his or her right standing before God. This legalistic notion was something the Reformers passionately sought to guard against.

The Reformers taught that justification occurs at the moment of salvation, which means the believer is immediately declared righteous and restored to God's favor. Sanctification, by contrast, takes place progressively over a believer's entire life, and results in his or her growth in personal holiness through the power of the Holy Spirit. The regenerated heart, having received new life in Christ, is able to respond in obedience to God and grow in godliness. Thus, regeneration results in a lifetime of progressive sanctification that flows out of it.[2]

While recognizing that all true believers are in the process of being sanctified, the Reformers insisted that sanctification is not the basis of one's justification. Luther emphasizes this point in his *Commentary on Galatians*: "Christians are not made righteous in doing righteous things, but being now made righteous by faith in Christ, they do righteous things."[3] Luther identified two distinct kinds of righteousness that result from saving faith in Christ. The first is a positional righteousness, which includes the "forgiveness of sins, and imputation of righteousness, because of our faith in Christ."[4] Of this justifying righteousness, Luther states,

> Through faith in Christ, therefore, Christ's righteousness becomes our righteousness and all that he has becomes ours; rather, he himself becomes ours. . . . This is an infinite righteousness, and one that swallows up all sin in a moment, for it is impossible that sin should exist in Christ. On the contrary, he who trusts in Christ exists in Christ; he is one with Christ, having the same righteousness as he.[5]

Luther referred to this righteousness as an "alien righteousness" because it comes from a source outside of the believer, namely from Christ Himself.[6]

Yet Luther also recognized a second kind of righteousness, which is the practical righteousness of personal holiness. This righteousness flows from hearts that have been regenerated by the Holy Spirit and enables believers to exhibit the fruit of obedience and good works.[7] Thus, he can say,

> The second kind of righteousness is our proper righteousness, not because we alone work it, but because we work with that first and alien righteousness. This is the manner of life spent profitably in good works. . . . This righteousness is the product of the righteousness of the first type, actually its fruit and consequence.[8]

In this way, Luther distinguished between justification (the imputed righteousness of Christ received by faith in Him) and sanctification (the practical righteousness made possible by the regenerating power of the Holy Spirit).

Yet, distinguishing between these two kinds of righteousness does not imply that believers can possess one without the other. The two are inseparably linked. Luther insisted that those covered with Christ's justifying righteousness will subsequently exhibit personal holiness by living in obedience to His commands. He explains, "Now, when we are appareled with Christ as with the robe of righteousness and our salvation, then we must put on Christ also by example and imitation."[9]

Philip Melanchthon similarly distinguished between the righteousness of faith (in justification) and the fruit of good works (in sanctification). Commenting on Romans 3:24, he asserts that to be "justified means that we obtain forgiveness of sins, and are received by God into grace." But he is quick to mention "the renewal that follows, which God effects in us, [which] he calls sanctification, and these two words [*justification* and *sanctification*] are clear and distinct."[10] In response to his opponents who pointed to passages like 1 Corinthians 13:2 and 1 John 3:14 to assert that justification was partially based on love and obedience, Melanchthon answers,

> These and similar passages say that love and a new obedience must be in us; that is true. However, love and new obedience do not merit forgiveness or cause a person to be pleasing to God. A person has forgiveness and is pleasing to God for the sake of the Mediator alone, whom one appropriates only by faith, and Christ gives his Holy Spirit who is the flame of true love and joy in God. This single true answer explains many passages.[11]

In this way, Melanchthon was careful to explain that God's gracious gift of justification, which is received by faith, is founded entirely on the righteousness of Christ, and not the obedience of believers.

Like Luther and Melanchthon, Calvin also distinguished between justification and sanctification, explaining "that the benefits of Christ—sanctification and righteousness [justification]—are different,"[12] that "they are things distinct,"[13] and that "Scripture, even though it joins them, still lists them separately in order that God's manifold grace may better appear to us."[14] Yet Calvin also emphasized that the two cannot be separated.[15] In his *Institutes*, after citing 1 Corinthians 1:30—"Christ Jesus . . . became to us wisdom from God, and righteousness and sanctification, and redemption"—Calvin demonstrates both the distinctiveness and inseparability of justification and sanctification. He writes, "Therefore Christ justifies no one whom he does not at the same time sanctify. . . . How true it is that we are justified not without works yet not through works, since in our sharing in Christ, which justifies us, sanctification is just as much included as righteousness."[16] In other words, the righteousness of justification is given freely on account of faith in Christ. But those who receive Christ also receive His Holy Spirit, through whom they are regenerated and sanctified.[17] For Calvin, believers' union with Christ means they are partakers of His righteousness—both in justification, through the imputation of Christ's righteousness, and in sanctification, through the impartation of righteousness by the Holy Spirit, who conforms believers to the image of Christ.[18]

The writings of the Reformers demonstrate a clear distinction between the positional righteousness of justification and the personal holiness of sanctification. While their Roman Catholic opponents viewed regeneration and sanctification as part of justification, such that believers' good works contributed to their righteous standing before God, the Reformers insisted that the two must not be conflated or confused.

DEFENDING THE DISTINCTION

The Reformers pointed to a number of biblical texts to maintain their distinction between justification and sanctification, such as 1 Corinthians 1:30; 6:11; and Revelation 22:11.[19] For them, a key New Testament passage demonstrating the distinction between justification and sanctification is Romans 6:15–23. Having established that justification is by grace through faith apart from works in chapters 3–5, Paul transitions his focus in chapter 6 to discuss the ethical implications of the gospel. Commenting on that transition, Calvin observes,

> Paul maintains here that we cannot receive righteousness in Christ [justification] without at the same time laying hold on sanctification. . . . It follows, therefore, that no one can put on the righteousness of Christ without regeneration. Paul uses this as the basis of exhortation to purity and holiness of life.[20]

In focusing on the doctrine of sanctification in Romans 6, Paul insists that grace does not give believers a license to sin (vv. 1–2). Rather, those who belong to Christ now walk in newness of life (v. 4), being dead to sin (vv. 6, 11) and freed from its bondage (v. 16). Consequently, their lives are marked by active righteousness and obedience to the Lord (vv. 17–18). As Paul states, "But now having been freed from sin and enslaved to God, you derive your benefit, resulting in sanctification, and the outcome, eternal life" (v. 22; see also v. 19).

Melanchthon, Calvin, and Chemnitz affirmed that Paul's description of sanctification in verses 19 and 22 distinguishes it from the forensic act of justification that he described in the previous chapters of the epistle.[21] They understood Paul to be teaching that those who have been justified and are positionally righteous on account of Christ have also been regenerated by the power of the Spirit, which enables them to demonstrate practical righteousness through acts of virtue and obedience. Though justification and sanctification are distinct, they are also inseparable in the lives of the redeemed.

At the same time, because sanctification is a lifelong process, believers still struggle in the fight against sin. The Reformers looked to Romans 6 to illustrate that reality in a vivid way. Reflecting on Paul's teaching in verses 15–23, Melanchthon explains,

> The saints always need the forgiveness of sins. Our fulfillment of the Law, our love, and our works are not good enough for us to be righteous because of them, that is, accepted [by God]; neither are they worthy of eternal life. But we receive remission of sins by faith because of Christ, the mediator, and life eternal by imputation of righteousness.[22]

Paul's testimony in Romans 7 exemplifies the reality that believers are simultaneously righteous yet still sinners,[23] thereby demonstrating that justification and sanctification represent two distinct realities. Though believers have been justified and forgiven in Christ (see Rom. 8:1) so that they are *positionally* righteous before God, in *practice* they still sin because the sanctification process is not yet complete (see Rom. 6:15–23).

THE IMPUTED RIGHTEOUSNESS OF CHRIST

If sinners stand guilty and condemned before the law of God, and if their works can make no contribution to their justification, the question naturally arises: How can they be pardoned and declared righteous by the holy Judge of heaven? To state the question another way, if God is perfectly just (and therefore cannot arbitrarily ignore sin), and if sinners fall woefully short of God's perfect standard (which everyone does; Rom. 3:23), how then can those who deserve to be punished be acquitted? The Reformers answered this by pointing to the substitutionary atonement and imputed righteousness of Jesus Christ. In other words, the sins of believers are imputed (or credited) to Christ, who paid the penalty for them on the cross.[24] Conversely, the righteousness of Christ is imputed to believers who are reckoned righteous by God on account of Christ. Luther expressed how this marvelous exchange took place:

> So making a happy change with us, He took upon Him our sinful person and gave unto us His innocent and victorious person; wherewith we being now clothed, are freed from the curse of the law. . . . By faith alone therefore we are made righteousness, for faith lays hold of this innocence and victory of Christ.[25]

Elsewhere, he contrasted the cursed inheritance received from Adam with the gracious gift received through faith in Christ, stating,

> As Adam became a cause of death to his descendants, though they did not eat of the forbidden tree, so Christ has become a Dispenser of righteousness to those who are of Him, though they have not earned any righteousness; for through the Cross He has secured righteousness for all men.[26]

Because of Adam's sin, all of Adam's descendants stand condemned before God and are worthy of eternal death (see Rom. 5:12–21). But in Christ, believers receive both the forgiveness of sins and the imputation of His righteousness.[27] Rather than being punished, they are promised the free gift of eternal life.

Melanchthon similarly emphasizes both the negative and positive sides of justification; namely, that sins are forgiven and righteousness is imputed. Referring to Romans 5, he explains,

> If we believe on the Son of God, we have forgiveness of sins; and Christ's righteousness is imputed to us, so that we are justified and are pleasing to God for the sake of Christ. . . . And we have all this only on account of the Lord Christ, by grace, without merit, through faith alone.[28]

Consequently, the righteousness that covers believers is not their own inherent righteousness. Rather, they are covered by the righteousness of Christ. In Melanchthon's words,

> We are clothed with a strange righteousness [namely, a righteousness outside of ourselves]. Although our nature itself is still not uniform with God, nevertheless, as

> the Mediator Christ in his complete obedience is uniform with God and covers our sins with his righteousness, so we are justified, have forgiveness of sins, and are pleasing to God, for Christ's sake, whose righteousness is accepted on our behalf.[29]

Calvin echoes this, declaring that "we are justified before God solely by the intercession of Christ's righteousness. This is equivalent to saying that man is not righteous in himself but because the righteousness of Christ is communicated to him by imputation."[30] Because Christ's righteousness is the sole basis for justification, believers enjoy the forgiveness of all sins—past, present, and future. Calvin teaches that both the initial pardon and ultimate glorification of every believer is guaranteed by the righteousness of Christ: "Furnished with this righteousness [of Christ], we obtain continual forgiveness of sins in faith. Covered with this purity, the sordidness and uncleanness of our imperfections are not ascribed to us but are hidden as if buried that they may not come into God's judgment."[31] Because believers are covered by the perfect righteousness of Christ, they are spared from God's wrath against sin.

DEFENDING IMPUTED RIGHTEOUSNESS

As with the other aspects of their understanding of justification, the Reformers appealed to Scripture as their primary defense for the doctrine of Christ's imputed righteousness. To anyone who might accuse them of inventing this doctrine, Chemnitz's reply still applies:

> We do not ourselves devise this teaching, that Christ the Mediator has fulfilled the Law for us by the fullest satisfaction of the punishments and by the most perfect obedience and that this righteousness of the Mediator is imputed to the believers, that by it they may be justified before God to life eternal. But this is the specific and perpetual doctrine of the Gospel.[32]

A host of biblical passages were used by the Reformers to illustrate and defend this doctrinal tenet, including Acts 13:38–39; Romans 3:21–4:25; 5:18–19; 10:4; and 1 Corinthians 1:30.[33] Arguably, the two primary texts to which the Reformers appealed were 2 Corinthians 5:21 and Philippians 3:7–9, so we will concentrate our discussion on those two passages.

2 Corinthians 5:21

If the doctrine of imputation is implicit in other passages, the Reformers found it taught explicitly in 2 Corinthians 5:21, where Paul writes, "He made Him who knew no sin to be sin on our behalf, so that we might become the righteousness of God in Him." The Reformers recognized that Jesus did not actually become a sinner on the cross; yet God punished Him as if He were a sinner so that, in Christ, believers might be treated as if they were righteous. The sins of believers were imputed to Christ at the cross so that, because He bore the punishment for those sins, His righteousness might be imputed to those who believe in Him. Chemnitz summarized that principle by simply asking, "How was Christ made sin? Certainly by imputation. And thus we are made the righteousness of God in Him."[34] Calvin articulated that same perspective in his commentary on 2 Corinthians:

> How can we become righteous before God? In the same way as Christ became a sinner. For He took, as it were, our person, that He might be the offender in our name and thus might be reckoned a sinner, not because of His own offences but because of those of others, since He Himself was pure and free from every fault and bore the penalty that was our due and not His own. Now in the same way we are righteous in Him, not because we have satisfied God's judgment by our own works, but because we are judged in relation to Christ's righteousness which we have put on by faith, that it may become our own.[35]

The parallel Paul draws in 2 Corinthians 5:21 caused Calvin to regard that verse as the clearest passage on imputation in Scripture. As he stated in his *Institutes*, "The best passage of all on this matter is the one in which he [Paul] teaches that the sum of the gospel embassy is to reconcile us to God, since God is willing to receive us into grace through Christ, not counting our sins against us [2 Cor. 5:18–21]."[36]

Philippians 3:7–9

If 2 Corinthians 5:21 was one of the Reformers' favorite texts for defending the doctrine of imputation, Philippians 3:7–9 provided a vivid illustration of that truth in the life of Paul. Having once been a Pharisee in pursuit of works-righteousness, the apostle declares, as a believer,

> But whatever things were gain to me, those things I have counted as loss for the sake of Christ. More than that, I count all things to be loss in view of the surpassing value of knowing Christ Jesus my Lord, for whom I have suffered the loss of all things, and count them but rubbish so that I may gain Christ, and may be found in Him, not having a righteousness of my own derived from the Law, but that which is through faith in Christ, the righteousness which comes from God on the basis of faith.

Here Paul explains that his righteous standing before God was not based on law-keeping or his own merits, but rather on a righteousness given by God through faith in Christ.[37] The Reformers were quick to point out the implications of Paul's testimony. Calvin exclaims that this is "a remarkable passage, if anyone desires to have a good description of the righteousness of faith, and to understand its true nature. . . . For whereas the law employs works, faith presents man naked before God, that he may be clothed with the righteousness of Christ."[38] Calvin goes on to explain that justifying righteousness is received solely as a gift of God's grace through faith.

These and other texts[39] were used to defend the imputed righteousness of Christ as the sole grounds for justification. Armed with a doctrinal conviction drawn from Scripture, the Reformers boldly denounced any teaching that made the believer's justification partly dependent on his or her own good works. To base justification on personal merit, they insisted, would subvert the gospel by succumbing to legalism.

THE REFORMERS' APPEAL TO CHURCH HISTORY

Up to this point, we've seen that the Reformers defended their doctrinal positions, first and foremost, by appealing to Scripture. Convinced that God's Word presents justification as a forensic declaration of righteousness, based on the imputed righteousness of Christ, they carefully distinguished it from regeneration. Moreover, they identified justification through faith alone as the heart of the gospel. They asserted that the position of their Roman Catholic opponents was wrong because it ran contrary to clear biblical teaching.

But the Reformers' commitment to the primacy of Scripture did not stop them from also appealing to the writings of theologians of previous generations. Though the Reformers grounded their arguments primarily in the Bible, they maintained that their case had historical support as well.

Martin Luther's appreciation for the church fathers, especially Augustine (354–430) and Bernard of Clairvaux (1090–1153), has been well documented.[40] Melanchthon cites similar sources,[41] though not uncritically.[42] For example, in the introduction to his commentary on Romans, Melanchthon appeals to Augustine, Chrysostom, and Bernard as witnesses to the truth that believers receive the forgiveness of sin by grace through faith alone.[43] Elsewhere, Melanchthon contends that he espouses truths that faithful theologians had always taught "ever since the time of the apostles."[44]

Calvin is equally dogmatic in his insistence that evangelical principles can be defended from church history.[45] As with Luther and Melanchthon, his favorite church father was unquestionably Augustine, whom he cites some 1,708 times.[46]

Other pre-Reformation writers also received significant attention in his writings.[47] While not all of these were cited favorably, Calvin viewed some—such as Chrysostom, Augustine, and Bernard—as theological allies.[48] Consequently, he asserted that his Protestant views could be defended by appealing to historical sources.[49]

In his *Examination of the Council of Trent*, after a thorough examination of Scripture, Chemnitz likewise appeals to the witness of the church fathers. While recognizing that the Latin fathers sometimes used the verb *to justify* in a broader sense than the Reformers did,[50] he remains convinced that the thrust of their teaching about salvation harmonizes with Protestant doctrine.[51] Accordingly, he cites Origen, Hilary, Basil, Ambrose, Jerome, Augustine, Gregory, Anselm, and Bernard to support his claims.[52] After concluding his historical survey, he declares, "I have noted down these in order to show that our teaching concerning justification has the testimony of all pious men of all times."[53]

The Reformers undoubtedly held the writings of church fathers (and medieval writers like Bernard of Clairvaux) in high regard. Though they were willing to part with the fathers when the teaching of Scripture compelled them to do so, they nonetheless sought affirmation from prior generations of Christian theologians. As McGrath observes, Reformers like Melanchthon, "asserted that the Reformation represented a long-overdue return to the truly catholic teaching of the church, which had become distorted and disfigured through the questionable theological methods of later medieval theology."[54] The Reformers were well aware of the charge of novelty levelled at them by their Roman Catholic opponents, and they sought to answer that charge with an appeal to church history.

The question remains, however, as to whether that appeal to church history was warranted. Is there historical precedence for the Reformation doctrine of justification *sola fide*? It is that specific issue to which this study now turns, to see whether there exists any evidence from pre-Reformation theologians to support the distinctive tenets of the Reformation understanding of justification by grace through faith alone.

PART TWO

THE CHURCH BEFORE AUGUSTINE

CHAPTER FOUR

SAVED BY GRACE

The Reformers looked primarily to Scripture to establish their understanding of justification by grace through faith alone, yet they also claimed secondary affirmation for their position from the writings of Christian leaders throughout church history. Were they right to make such a claim? In the next few chapters, we will consider the writings of early Christian leaders—known as church fathers—who lived up to the time of Augustine, who died in the year AD 430. Our goal is to examine what ancient writers and theologians said about the doctrine of justification.

Evangelicals should be encouraged to know that, in recent years, a number of early church scholars have noted significant levels of continuity between the patristics and the Reformers with regard to the doctrine of justification. (The word *patristic* refers to the church fathers.) Foremost among them is Thomas Oden, who contended that "there are in patristic texts clear anticipations of the Reformers' teaching on justification."[1] D. H. Williams agrees that "there is evidence that Latin theology before Augustine promulgated the tenets of unmerited grace and the necessity of righteousness that come only through justifying faith."[2] If such assertions are correct, they indicate the Reformers were right to look for affirmation and support from early Christian leaders. But before we simply accept those statements, we need to investigate the writings of the church fathers to see if such assertions are warranted.

SALVATION BY GRACE THROUGH FAITH

To what degree did the church fathers believe that sinners are justified by grace through faith apart from works? A brief survey of early Christian writers produces a chorus of affirming voices.[3] For example, Clement of Rome (who died around 100) explains that Christians, like the Old Testament patriarchs before them, are justified through faith apart from works. In his *Epistle to the Corinthians* 32.4, Clement writes,

> And so we, having being called through his will in Christ Jesus, are not justified through ourselves or through our own wisdom or understanding or piety, or works that we have done in holiness of heart, but through faith, by which the Almighty God has justified all who have existed from the beginning; to whom be the glory for ever and ever. Amen.[4]

Though Clement does not use the term *alone,* his statement makes it clear that the faith that justifies stands apart from any contribution of wisdom, understanding, piety, works, or personal holiness by the believer. Noting the parallels between Clement and Martin Luther, Jordan Cooper concludes, "For both Clement and Luther, the Pauline polemic against works does not refer only to Jewish boundary markers, but to good works in general. If Clement were asked what works a man must perform to achieve justification, he would likely respond as did Luther: 'Nothing at all.'"[5]

Writing more than a century later, Origen (182–254) says of Paul's teaching in Romans 3:28, "He is saying that the justification of faith alone suffices, so that the one who only believes is justified even if he has not accomplished a single work."[6] Origen subsequently finds an example of justification apart from works by looking to the thief on the cross:

> Who has been justified by faith alone without works of the law? Thus in my opinion that thief [who] was crucified with Christ should suffice for a suitable example. He called out to him from the cross, "Lord Jesus, remember me when you come into your kingdom!" In the Gospels, nothing else is recorded about his good works, but for the sake of this faith alone Jesus said to him, "Truly I say to you, today you will be with me in paradise."[7]

In light of such statements, Thomas P. Scheck observes that "Origen recognizes that *sometimes* Scripture says that human beings are justified by faith *alone*."[8]

In the fourth century, Hilary of Poitiers (ca. 300–368) produced a commentary on Matthew in which he differentiated between the wages of good works and the gift of grace. He writes, "Wages cannot be considered as a gift, because they are due to work, but God has given free grace to all men by the justification of faith."[9] Commenting on the hostility of the

Pharisees, he remarks, "It disturbed the scribes that sin was forgiven by a man (for they considered that Jesus Christ was only a man) and that sin was forgiven by Him whereas the Law was not able to absolve it, since faith alone justifies."[10] Elsewhere Hilary adds, "Because faith alone justifies . . . publicans and prostitutes will be first in the kingdom of heaven."[11] For Hilary, sinners are not justified on the basis of law-keeping or personal merits, otherwise justification would be a wage and not a gift. Rather, they are justified by faith alone. This truth was so prominent in Hilary's mind that, in his commentary on Matthew, he uses variations of the phrase "faith justifies" some twenty times.[12]

The fourth-century writer Marius Victorinus (who converted to Christianity around 355), says of Paul's teaching in Galatians: "Therefore righteousness is not from the law; that is, justification and salvation come not from the law but from faith, as is promised."[13] Commenting on the book of Ephesians, he says of God's grace, "He did not give back to us what was merited, since we did not receive this by merits but by the grace and goodness of God."[14] Later he adds, "The fact that you Ephesians are saved is not something that comes from yourselves. It is the gift of God. It is not from your works, but it is God's grace and God's gift, not from anything you have deserved."[15] And again, "Only faith [*sola fides*] in Christ is salvation for us."[16] Commenting on the work of Victorinus, Robert Eno concludes, "It is quite clear that Victorinus teaches salvation by grace through faith."[17] Along similar lines, Ian Christopher Levy, Philip D. W. Krey, and Thomas Ryan note that Victorinus "emphasized terms like 'justification' and 'by faith alone' (*sola fide*) to such an extent that he was seen as a proto-Reformer and Adolf von Harnack [1851–1930] called him an 'Augustine before Augustine.'"[18]

Ambrose (337–397), the famous preacher of Milan, Italy, similarly states of salvation, "It is not because of your efforts, but because of the grace of Christ. 'By grace you are saved,' says the apostle. Therefore, it is not a matter of arrogance, but faith."[19] Elsewhere, he declares, "We are not justified by works, but by faith, because the weakness of the flesh is a hindrance to works, but the brightness of faith puts the error that is in man's deeds in the shadow and merits for him the forgiveness of his sins."[20] Philip Melanchthon, the chief writer of the Augsburg Confession (1530), believed the Reformation teachings on justification were in accord with those of Ambrose, which is why he is referenced in the Augsburg Confession as someone who anticipated Protestant teaching.[21]

The fourth-century Pauline commentator known as Ambrosiaster[22] makes numerous statements affirming justification by grace through faith apart from works. In his commentary on Romans, he writes, "For the mercy of God had been given for this reason, that the law should cease, as I have often said, because God, taking pity on our weaknesses, decreed that the human race would be saved by faith alone, along with the natural law."[23] Commenting on Romans 3:24, he explains, "They are justified freely because, while doing nothing or providing any repayment, they are justified by faith alone as a gift of God."[24] Reflecting on verse 27, he adds, "Paul tells those who live under the law that they have no reason to boast basing themselves on the law and claiming to be of the race of Abraham, seeing that no one is justified before God except by faith."[25] His remarks on Romans 4:6 are even more explicit: "Those are blessed of whom God has decreed that, without work or any keeping of the law, they are justified before God by faith alone."[26] Such statements have led patristic scholars like Gerald Bray to declare,

> Ambrosiaster did not have to face the complex issues surrounding justification by faith alone that confronted Martin Luther, but there can be no doubt that the two men are on the same wavelength. . . . This is Luther *avant la lettre* [before his time], and shows incidentally just how deeply rooted in patristic thought the German Reformer's theology was.[27]

One of the greatest early sources of justification by faith is the renowned preacher of Constantinople, John Chrysostom (ca. 347–407), who often speaks of justification in the context of grace, faith, and even "faith alone."[28] Many examples from his *Homilies* demonstrate this reality. Commenting on Peter's words in Acts 15:9, that God cleanses the hearts of Gentiles by faith, Chrysostom explains, "From faith alone, he says, they obtained the same gifts [as the Jews]. This is also meant as a lesson to those [objectors]; this is able to teach them that faith alone is necessary, and not works or circumcision."[29] In answer to the Philippian jailor's question, "What must I do to be saved?" Chrysostom's response is clear, "What does Paul answer? 'Believe in the Lord Jesus, and you will be saved,' he says, 'you and your household' . . . 'And he rejoiced,' it says. And yet it [namely, the means of his salvation] was nothing but words alone and good hope."[30]

In a sermon on Romans 3:27, Chrysostom declares that believers are "saved by grace," noting that God "has not only saved, but has even justified, and led them to boasting, and this too without needing works, but looking for faith only."[31] Later, in expositing Romans 5:1–2, he emphasizes that the sinner contributes nothing in salvation and that God accomplishes everything. As Chrysostom explains, "He died for us, and further reconciled us, and brought us to Himself, and gave us grace unspeakable. But we brought faith only as our contribution."[32] On the one hand, Chrysostom can say that the only thing we supply is our faith.[33] Yet he is clear that faith itself is not regarded as a work, but rather is a gift from God.[34]

In a homily on Galatians 3:8, Chrysostom contrasts the Judaizers' insistence on law-keeping with Paul's emphasis on salvation by grace: "They said that he who kept not the Law was cursed, but [Paul] proves that he who kept it was cursed, and he who kept it not blessed. Again, they said that he who adhered to faith alone was cursed, but he shows that he who adhered to faith alone, is blessed."[35] Later, commenting on verse 12, Chrysostom draws a clear distinction between the Law, which requires works, and grace, which "saves and justifies by faith."[36] Elsewhere, he reflects on the truth of Ephesians 2 with these words: "For by faith alone He saved us. . . . Instead of a certain manner of life, He brought in faith."[37] And in another place: "[God] has justified our race not by right actions, not by toils, not by barter and exchange, but by grace alone. . . . The justice [or, righteousness] of God comes through faith in Jesus Christ and not through any labor and suffering."[38]

Chrysostom was aware that salvation by grace through faith alone sounded almost too good to be true, especially for those who came from a legalistic background. In a sermon on 1 Timothy 1:15–16, he addressed this concern:

> For as people, on receiving some great good, ask themselves if it is not a dream, as not believing it; so it is with respect to the gifts of God. What then was it that was thought incredible? That those who were enemies and sinners, justified by neither the law nor works, should immediately through faith alone be advanced to the highest favor.[39]

He continues, speaking of those who had a background in Judaism, "It seemed to them incredible that a person who had misspent all his former life in vain and wicked actions should afterwards be saved by his faith alone. On this account [Paul] says, 'It is a saying to be believed.'"[40] When taking into account all these statements from Chrysostom, it is no wonder that Reformers like Calvin held him in high esteem.[41]

A final father to consider is the well-known Bible translator Jerome (347–420), who articulated justification by grace through faith. While Jerome did not always articulate the doctrine consistently, glimpses of it are nevertheless found in his writings.[42] In his commentary on Ephesians, Jerome explains that "we are saved by grace rather than works, for we can give God nothing in return for what he has bestowed on us."[43] Elsewhere, in response to the fourth-century heresy of Pelagianism—the teaching that original sin did not taint humans after Adam and that humans could choose to live righteously without divine grace—he adds "[Paul] shows clearly that righteousness depends not on the merit of man, but on the grace of God, who accepts the faith of those who believe, without the works of the Law."[44] And again, "We are righteous when we confess that we are sinners, and our righteousness depends not on our own merits but on the mercy of God, as the holy Scripture says."[45] Safeguarding the fact that faith is God's gift, not man's work, Jerome comments on Ephesians 2:8, "Paul says this in case the secret thought should steal upon us that 'if we are not saved by our own works, at least we are saved by our own faith, and so in a way our salvation is of ourselves.' Thus he added the statement that faith too is not in our own will but in God's gift."[46]

THE EXAMPLE OF ABRAHAM

In making such statements about justification by faith, the church fathers frequently looked to Abraham as the primary example of one who was reckoned righteous apart from works. They understood that Christians, as the spiritual descendants of Abraham, are likewise justified by faith. In the words of the second-century apologist Justin Martyr (ca. 100–165),

> For Abraham was declared by God to be righteous, not on account of circumcision, but on account of faith. . . . And we, therefore, in the uncircumcision of our flesh, believing God through Christ, and having that circumcision which is of advantage to us who have acquired it—namely, that of the heart—we hope to appear righteous before and well-pleasing to God.[47]

Irenaeus of Lyons (ca. 130–202) similarly looks to Abraham as the paradigm for the justification of believers, noting that "all who, following the example of his faith, trust in God, should be saved. . . . For he [Abraham] learned from the Word of the Lord, and believed Him; wherefore it was accounted to him by the Lord for righteousness. For faith towards God justifies a man."[48] Elsewhere Irenaeus is equally explicit, noting that "our faith was also prefigured in Abraham" so that "his faith and ours are one and the same."[49] Thus, Irenaeus can say of believers, "They who are of faith shall be blessed with faithful Abraham, and these are the children of Abraham . . . that is, those who are justified by faith."[50]

Nearly two centuries later, John Chrysostom similarly stated that Abraham, who preceded the giving of the Law, "was justified by faith."[51] Elsewhere he declares, "The patriarch Abraham himself before receiving circumcision had been declared righteous on the score of faith alone: before circumcision, the text says, 'Abraham believed God, and credit for it brought him to righteousness.'"[52] Noting the difficulty this concept might pose for some people, Chrysostom explains,

> Now since the Jews kept turning over and over the fact, that the Patriarch, and friend of God, was the first to receive circumcision, he wishes to show, that it was by faith that he too was justified. . . . For a person richly adorned with good deeds, not to be made just from hence, but from faith, this is the thing to cause wonder, and to set the power of faith in a strong light.[53]

As the above survey demonstrates, a number of pre-Augustinian church fathers used the language of "justification by faith alone" to describe the salvation of sinners.[54] Following the pattern of Paul in Romans 4–5, they looked to Abraham as the archetype of one who was justified by faith apart from works. In at least some of these instances, distinct elements of continuity between them and the later teachings of the sixteenth-century Reformers can be seen.[55] Thus, the claim that there was no patristic precedent for the Reformation doctrine of *sola fide* fails to hold.

But our investigation is far from complete. In order to explore fully the parallels between the church fathers and the Protestant Reformers, we need to examine what early Christian leaders believed about justification in greater detail.

CHAPTER FIVE

JUSTIFICATION: A DIVINE DECLARATION

In the previous chapter, we surveyed a number of church fathers with respect to the doctrine of justification by faith alone. We found numerous instances in which early Christian leaders use language that generally parallels the teachings of the Protestant Reformers. But we still need to dig deeper before reaching any definite conclusions. Our goal in this chapter is to examine whether we can find anticipations of the forensic nature of justification and a distinction between justification and sanctification.

THE FORENSIC NATURE OF JUSTIFICATION

Did the early church fathers view justification in a forensic sense—that is, as a declaration of righteousness and acquittal rendered by the divine Judge? In a chapter-length treatment on the subject, historian Nick Needham provides compelling evidence to show that the majority of them in fact did.[1] Needham states, "We have, then, in the fathers of the first four centuries, this major strand of justification teaching where the meaning is forensic: a not-guilty verdict, an acquittal, a declaration of righteousness, a nonimputation of sin, an imputation of righteousness."[2] He continues, "The evidence for justification language bearing a forensic meaning in this major strand in the fathers is parallel to the evidence for its having this meaning in the Bible."[3] Joel C. Elowsky concurs, noting that Athanasius of Alexandria, Basil of Caesarea, Gregory of Nyssa, Chrysostom, Cyril of Alexandria, and John of Damascus all spoke, at times, in forensic terms.[4] The forensic nature of justification in the patristic literature can be seen in at least two ways: through the use of law court terminology and through the contrast drawn between justification and condemnation.[5]

The Use of Law Court Imagery

In places, the church fathers either define or describe justification using legal (or forensic) language. John Chrysostom is perhaps the most explicit in this regard. In a homily on Romans 3:4, he addresses the definition of justification directly:

> What does the word "justified" mean? It means, that if there could be a trial and an examination of the things God had done for the Jews, and of what had been done on their part toward him, the victory would be with God, and all the right on his side.[6]

Needham observes, "Chrysostom understands clearly that justification means a verdict in which right is pronounced to lie with one party in a dispute."[7] Elsewhere, Chrysostom employs imagery from the law court to illustrate justification in practice. Commenting on Paul's statement in Romans

8:33–34 ("God is the one who justifies; who is the one who condemns?"), he writes,

> Paul does not say, it is God who forgave our sins, but what is much greater, "It is God who justifies." For when the Judge's sentence declares us just—and he is a Judge such as the one we have here—what can the accuser say? And so, we should not be afraid of trials either, because God is for us and has shown he is for us by what he has done. Nor should we fear Jewish triflings [about the law], for he has both elected and justified us.[8]

Chrysostom similarly uses forensic language when he describes justification in terms of a divine verdict: "There is no human being on earth who could come to judgment in the face of precepts from You and be justified; so the verdicts are overwhelmingly in Your favor."[9] In another place, he compares salvation by grace to "a person who after committing great sins was unable to defend himself in court, but was condemned and going to be punished, and then [was] forgiven by royal pardon."[10] Elsewhere, Chrysostom applies the same analogy to Paul's description of himself as the chief of sinners in 1 Timothy 1:15–16:

> Suppose there was a populous city in which all of its inhabitants were wicked, some more so and some less, but all deserving condemnation. Then suppose that there is one among that multitude who is more deserving of punishment than all the rest, and guilty of every kind of wickedness. Now, if it were declared that the king was willing to pardon everyone, nobody would believe it.

> But if this person who was the wickedest wretch among them were actually pardoned, there could then be no doubt any longer. This is what Paul says, that God, who wanted to fully assure humanity that he pardons all their transgressions, chose as the object of his mercy one who was more of a sinner than any of them were. . . . Thus Paul shows that he himself, even though he was unworthy of pardon, first obtained that pardon so that others could be assured of their own salvation.[11]

In his *Homilies on 2 Corinthians,* Chrysostom again illustrates salvation by comparing God to a king who transfers the death and guilt of a robber to his son so that he might "save the condemned man and clear him from his evil reputation."[12]

Chrysostom is not alone in using courtroom terminology to describe justification. Hilary of Poitiers, for example, describes justification in terms of the believer's acquittal at the tribunal of God. Paul's teaching in Romans 8:33–34 causes Hilary to ask,

> Is He who rose again other than He who died? Is He who died other than He who condemns us? Lastly, is not He who condemns us also God who justifies us? Distinguish, if you can, Christ our accuser from God our defender [literally, "justifier"]; Christ who died from Christ who condemns. . . . All is one and the same Christ.[13]

As Needham observes, "The law court framework is particularly clear in Hilary of Poitiers as he reflects on our position before the judgment seat, arguing, in this context, for the oneness of Christ the Savior-Judge against any splitting up of his natures."[14]

Ambrose likewise connects justification to the declaration of divine pardon. He asks, "Why do you fear to confess your sins to our good Lord?" The answer: "that you may be justified." He continues, "The rewards of justification are set before him who is guilty of sin, for he is justified who voluntarily confesses his own sin; and lastly, 'the just man is his own accuser in the beginning of his speaking.' The Lord knows all things, but He waits for your words, not that He may punish, but that He may pardon."[15]

Finally, Rufinus (ca. 340–410), like Chrysostom, describes salvation in terms of a pardon:

> As to the forgiveness of sins, it ought to be enough simply to believe. For who would ask the cause or the reason when a prince grants a pardon? When the liberality of an earthly sovereign is not a fit subject for discussion, shall people's impudence discuss God's generosity? For the pagans are likely to ridicule us, saying that we deceive ourselves, imagining that crimes committed in deed can be purged by words. And they say, "Can he who has committed murder be no murderer, and he who has committed adultery be accounted no adulterer? How then shall one guilty of crimes of this sort all of a sudden be made holy?" But to this, as I said, we answer better by faith than by reason. For he is a King of all who has promised it: he is Lord of heaven and earth who assures us of it. Would you have me refuse to believe that he who made me a man of the dust of the earth can of a guilty person make me innocent? And that he who when I was blind made me see, or when I

was deaf made me hear, or lame walk, can recover for me my lost innocence?[16]

As these examples demonstrate, leading church fathers did not shy away from using forensic language and law court metaphors to describe the nature of justification.[17]

The Contrast between Justification and Condemnation

The church fathers not only used law court terminology to describe justification, but also contrasted it with legal concepts like guilt and condemnation. As Needham explains, "The fathers frequently set 'justify' and 'condemn' antithetically against each other, as equal and opposite verdicts or judgments. Justification thus becomes the positive judgment, a declaration of approval."[18] Examples of this contrast can be found in various patristic authors. For example, Origen explains, "The judgment on Adam was that through his one sin *condemnation* came to all men. But in sharp contrast to this, through Christ *justification* is given to all for the many sins in which the entire human race [was] bound up."[19] Methodius (d. 311) prays, "Set me free from the yoke of *condemnation*, and place me under the yoke of *justification*."[20] Reflecting on the consequences of Adam's sin and the reversal of those consequences in Christ, Gregory of Nazianzus (330–390) writes, "For where sin abounded, grace did much more abound; and if a taste *condemned* [us], how much more does the passion of Christ *justify* us?"[21]

Ambrose similarly contrasts the ramifications of Adam's sin with what Christ has done: "In Adam I fell, in Adam I was cast out of Paradise, in Adam I died. How shall the Lord call me back, unless He finds me in Adam, so that as I was liable to guilt and owing death in him, so now in Christ I am justified?"[22] Ambrosiaster, commenting on Paul's teaching in Romans, similarly asserts that "there is an obvious difference between the fact that those who have sinned in imitation of Adam's transgression have been *condemned* and the fact that the grace of God in Christ has *justified* men not from one trespass but from many sins, giving them forgiveness of sins."[23] John Chrysostom, reflecting on Galatians 2:17, makes the same distinction: "If faith in Him, [Paul] says, avails not for our justification, but it is necessary again to embrace the law, and if, having forsaken the law for Christ's sake, we are not *justified* but *condemned* for such abandonment, then we shall find Him, for whose sake we forsook the law and went over to faith, the author of our condemnation."[24]

By contrasting condemnation with justification, the church fathers demonstrate that they understood them to be antithetical concepts of declaration—one negative, one positive. Insofar as condemnation involves a legal status based on the divine declaration of guilt, it follows that justification involves the opposite legal status based on the divine declaration of righteousness. A survey of the patristic *corpus*, then, reveals that a forensic conception of justification can in fact be found in the church fathers before Augustine.

JUSTIFICATION DISTINGUISHED FROM SANCTIFICATION

Not only did many of the church fathers understand justification in forensic terms; many of them also distinguish justification from sanctification. This distinction is evidenced in at least two ways.

First, there are instances in which the church fathers distinguished between justification and sanctification as distinct components of salvation. Victorinus separates them when he writes, "A man is not justified by the works of the law but through faith and the faith of Jesus Christ. . . . It is faith alone that gives justification and sanctification."[25] Ambrosiaster similarly distinguishes between them:

> Therefore, whether it is because we have been redeemed, or because we have been sanctified (i.e., purged from the works of the flesh and the filthiness of idols), or because we have been justified (for it is just to worship only the Creator and spurn everything else) or because we are wise, having learned that worldly people are unwise—all this is a gift of God through Christ.[26]

Chrysostom likewise lists justification and sanctification as distinct blessings that are part of God's work of salvation. Commenting on 2 Corinthians 8:9, he says, "By riches here [Paul] means the knowledge of godliness, the cleansing away of sins, justification, sanctification, the countless good things which He bestowed upon us and purposes to bestow."[27]

A second way in which the church fathers differentiate justification from sanctification is found in the distinction they make between the *root* of salvation (the faith that justifies and brings divine forgiveness) and the *fruit* of salvation (the good works of sanctification that follow justification). The apostolic father Polycarp (ca. 69–160) does this in his letter to the Philippians, where he writes, "I also rejoice because your firmly rooted faith, renowned from the earliest times, still perseveres and bears fruit to our Lord Jesus Christ, . . . knowing that by grace you have been saved, not because of works, but by the will of God through Jesus Christ."[28] Ignatius of Antioch (ca. 35–ca. 110) articulated a similar dichotomy in his letter to believers in Ephesus, describing the beginning (root) of the Christian life as faith and the evidence (fruit) of it as love. He states, "None of these things escapes your notice, if you have perfect faith and love toward Jesus Christ. For these are the beginning and the end of life: faith is the beginning and love is the end. . . . The tree is known by its fruit; thus those who profess to be Christ's will be recognized by their actions."[29] Origen also makes the root-fruit distinction explicit:

> And this faith, when it is has been justified, is firmly embedded in the soil of the soul like a root that has received rain, so that when it begins to be cultivated by God's law, branches arise from it that bring forth the fruit of works. The root of righteousness, therefore, does not grow out of the works, but rather the fruit of works grows out of the root of righteousness, that root, of course of righteousness that God also credits even apart from works.[30]

Cyprian (ca. 200–258) looks to Abraham as an example of one whose salvation was rooted in faith and yet adorned with the fruit of obedience. He writes, "Thus Abraham, believing God, and first of all instituting the root and foundation of faith, when tried in respect of his son, does not hesitate nor delay, but obeys the commands of God with all the patience of devotion."[31] Ambrosiaster also makes such a distinction in his commentary on Titus 3:4–8: "This good which is seen to flourish in Christians stems from the root of divine godliness. God in his mercy has saved us through Christ, by whose grace we have been born again and now receive the Holy Spirit in abundance, so that we may excel in good works."[32]

THE INSEPARABILITY OF JUSTIFICATION AND SANCTIFICATION

Time and again, we find the church fathers distinguishing between the moment of salvation (a past event in which divine pardon for sin is granted by faith alone) and the post-conversion pursuit of holiness (an ongoing process in which the believers' life is characterized by the fruit of good works). Yet, like the Reformers, they insisted that faith without works is dead—meaning that although justification is by grace through faith, saving faith always evidences itself in the fruit of good works.[33] A mere profession of faith unaccompanied by a transformed life was considered empty and dead. As Justin Martyr explains, "Let those who are not found living as He taught, be understood to be no Christians, even though they profess with the lip the precepts of Christ; for not those who make profession, but those who do the works, shall be saved."[34] Didymus the Blind (ca. 313–398) also saw good works as proof or evidence of true faith. After stating that one is saved by faith and not by works, he explains, "There should be no doubt but that faith saves and then lives by doing its own works, so that the works which provide evidence of salvation by faith are not those of the law but of grace—a different kind of thing altogether."[35] John Chrysostom likewise teaches that good works should be done in loving response to what God has done for us in Christ. Commenting on Romans 11:6, he says, "Let us then give thanks, that we belong to them that are being saved, and not having been able to save ourselves by works, were saved by the gift of God. But in giving thanks, let us not do this in words only, but in works and actions."[36]

Commenting on Christ's statement, "Your faith has saved you," Origen acknowledges that "the faith of the believer is the cause of his salvation" and that Paul "is correct to hold that that person is justified through faith without works of the law." Yet he is quick to offer a warning to those tempted to think that God's grace is a license to sin:

> Perhaps someone who hears these things should become lax and negligent in doing good, if in fact faith alone suffices for him to be justified. To this person we shall say that if anyone acts unjustly after justification, it is scarcely to be doubted that he has rejected the grace of justification. For a person does not receive the forgiveness of sin in order that he should once again imagine that he has been given a license to sin.[37]

Elsewhere, Origen emphasizes that those who claim to be Christians but continue to walk in sin are not truly justified. He explains,

> If we have risen together with Christ, who is our justification, and we now walk in newness of life and live according to righteousness, then Christ has risen for the purpose of our justification. But if we have not yet cast off the old man with all his works but instead live in unrighteousness, I dare to suggest that Christ has not

> yet risen for our justification, nor has he been sacrificed for our sins.[38]

Ambrosiaster reiterates that same expectation, asserting that those who seek eternal life must not only believe correctly, but also live correctly.[39] Further, while faith alone is necessary for justification, "faith must be fortified with brotherly love for the perfection of the believer."[40]

Some of the most forceful statements in this regard come from John Chrysostom,[41] who says of professing believers living in unrepentant sin (like the unworthy wedding guest of Matthew 22:13 who was cast out), "Let not us either expect that faith is sufficient to us for salvation; for if we do not show forth a pure life, but come clothed with garments unworthy of this blessed calling, nothing hinders us from suffering the same as that wretched one."[42] Elsewhere Chrysostom expands on this concept, using the language of James:

> Faith without works is dead, and works without faith are dead also. For if we have sound doctrine but fail in living, the doctrine is of no use to us. Likewise if we take pains with life but are careless about doctrine, that will not be any good to us either. It is therefore necessary to shore up the spiritual edifice in both directions.[43]

According to Chrysostom, those who initially profess faith in Christ but later fall away must not think their profession of faith, standing by itself, is sufficient to save. True faith is evidenced by perseverance in good works.[44] Thus, he urges, "Let us give thanks, let us glorify Him, not by our faith alone, but also by our very works, that we may obtain the good things that are to come, through the grace and lovingkindness of our Lord Jesus Christ."[45] Though such statements could be interpreted to suggest that works contribute to our salvation, they are better understood—especially in light of Chrysostom's strong statements elsewhere affirming "faith alone"—as a warning against a faith that is dead (see James 2:26).[46]

Like the later Reformers, the church fathers emphasized that saving faith was a repentant faith.[47] Those who demonstrate genuine repentance can be assured of their right standing before God.[48] Thus, Justin Martyr could tell Trypho, "For the goodness and the lovingkindness of God, and His boundless riches, hold righteous and sinless the man who, as Ezekiel tells, repents of sins; and reckons sinful, unrighteous, and impious the person who falls away from piety and righteousness to unrighteousness and ungodliness."[49]

The church fathers viewed justification and sanctification as inseparably linked—meaning that those who have been justified are also being sanctified. Yet that does not mean they were unable to distinguish between the two.[50] As Needham observes, only "a minor strand of patristic teaching" would conflate justification with "moral transformation, what Protestant theology calls 'regeneration' or 'sanctification.'"[51]

As this chapter has demonstrated, many of the church fathers viewed justification as a forensic declaration of righteousness, not as a process in which believers are made increasingly righteous. As a result, they distinguished it from sanctification and the fruit of good works that flows from a regenerated heart. To be sure, they insisted that faith without works is dead. Yet they were equally clear that sinners are saved by grace through faith in Christ, not as a result of works.

CHAPTER SIX

THE GREAT EXCHANGE

So far in our survey of the church fathers, we have seen that they speak of justification by faith using language that parallels the Reformers. They affirm a forensic understanding of justification and a distinction between justification and sanctification. But did they affirm the notion that Christ's righteousness is imputed to believers? In answering that question, we will consider four points.

THE SINNER'S NEED FOR RIGHTEOUSNESS

The church fathers speak of the sinner's need for a righteousness that cannot be found in either his own merits or the law. Speaking of the unattainable standard of God's perfect righteousness, Origen explains that to be justified before people is different from being justified before God. "In comparison with other people," he writes, "one person can be deemed just if he has lived relatively free from faults; but in comparison with God, not only is a person not justified, but even as Job says, 'But the stars are not pure before him.'"[1] Origen explains that while we may seem pure in comparison to other people, and vice versa, we can never be pure in comparison to God, who is perfectly pure. Chrysostom similarly notes,

> As a man that has acquired wealth, with respect to himself appears rich, but upon a comparison with the treasures of kings is very poor and the chief of the poor; so it is in this case. Compared with angels, even righteous men are sinners; and if Paul, who wrought the righteousness that is in the law, was the chief of sinners, what other man can be called righteous? For he says this not to condemn his own life as impure, let not this be imagined; but comparing his own legal righteousness with the righteousness of God, he shows it to be nothing worth, and not only so, but he proves those who possess it to be sinners.[2]

Going a step further, Basil of Caesarea (330–379) notes that eternal life is a gift of God's grace that cannot be earned on the basis of human merit. "An eternal rest awaits those who have rightly contended in this life," he writes, "not because of the merits of their works but from the grace of a most bountiful God, in which they have hoped."[3] Ambrose concurs,

> By what human merit, in short, can we deserve that this perishable flesh should put on imperishability, and this mortal put on immortality? By what labours, by what harshness inflicted on ourselves, can we take away our sins? The sufferings of this present age are unworthy toward the gaining of future glory. Not in keeping with

> our merits, therefore, but in keeping with God's mercy, the rule of heaven's judgments reaches down to mortal humans.[4]

Statements like these affirm the need for a righteousness outside of the sinner. If the unredeemed person is to be justified, it must be on the basis of something other than self-righteousness.

THE IMPUTATION OF SIN TO CHRIST

In explaining how unworthy sinners could be forgiven, the church fathers taught that the believer's sin was imputed (or reckoned) to Christ, who atoned for it on the cross.[5] As Polycarp explains,

> Let us, therefore, hold steadfastly and unceasingly to our hope and the guarantee of our righteousness, who is Christ Jesus, who bore our sins in his own body upon the tree, who committed no sin, and no deceit was found in his mouth; instead, for our sakes he endured all things, in order that we might live in him.[6]

Using the language of cancelled debt, Irenaeus speaks of the "remission of sins which follows upon [Christ's] advent, by which 'He has destroyed the handwriting' of our debt, and 'fastened it to the cross,' so that as by means of a tree we were made debtors to God, [so also] by means of a tree we may obtain the remission of our debt."[7] The debt of sin incurred by Adam when he ate from the tree in Eden was paid for by the second Adam when He died on the tree at Calvary. For believers, their debt has been transferred to Christ who paid it in full on the cross. The Lord Jesus is the perfect substitute for all who trust in Him, as Origen explains: "God is just, and therefore he could not justify the unjust. Therefore he required the intervention of a propitiator, so that by having faith in him those who could not be justified by their own works might be justified."[8]

In a similar vein, Cyprian declares that God the Son became man, "although He Himself was not a sinner, to bear the sins of others. His immortality being in the meantime laid aside, He suffers Himself to become mortal so that the guiltless may be put to death for the salvation of the guilty."[9] Athanasius likewise says regarding the death of Christ,

> He assumed a body capable of death, in order that it, through belonging to the Word Who is above all, might become in dying a sufficient exchange for all. . . . For naturally, since the Word of God was above all, when He offered His own temple and bodily instrument as a substitute for the life of all, He fulfilled in death all that was required.[10]

That the Lord Jesus died as a substitute for sinners is also highlighted by Gregory of Nazianzus who says of Christ, "For my sake He was called a curse, who destroyed my curse, and was called sin, who takes away the sin of the world. . . . He was in His own Person representing us. For we were the forsaken and despised before, but now by the sufferings of Him who could not suffer, we were taken up and saved."[11] Consequently, the believer can rejoice in the work of the Savior, through whom forgiveness is offered on the basis of His atoning death. Ambrose articulates that joy in a particularly poignant passage:

> Nevertheless, the law was of help to me. I began to confess what I used to deny, I began to know my sin and not to cover over my injustice. I began to proclaim my injustice to the Lord against myself, and you forgave the impurities of my heart. But this too is of help to me, that we are not justified by the works of the law. Thus, I do not have the wherewithal to enable me to glory in my own works, I do not have the wherewithal to boast of myself, and so I will glory in Christ. I will not glory because I have been redeemed. I will not glory because I am free from sins, but because sins have been forgiven me. I will not glory because I am profitable or because anyone is profitable to me, but because Christ is an advocate in my behalf with the Father, because the blood of Christ has been poured out in my behalf. My guilt became for me the price of redemption, through which Christ came to me. On account of me, Christ tasted death.[12]

The Reformers would have gladly echoed Ambrose's perspective. Believers can take no credit for their salvation. Consequently, they can glory only in the fact that Christ died as the perfect substitute on their behalf, bearing their sin so that they might be freed from it.

THE RECEPTION OF IMPUTED RIGHTEOUSNESS

The church fathers taught that, in addition to having their sins forgiven, believers receive the gift of divine righteousness at the moment of salvation.[13] This righteousness can be variously described as being imputed, credited, or reckoned by God to the believer. After discussing Abraham—as an archetype of one who was justified by faith—Tertullian (ca. 155–240) responds to the false teachings of Marcionism by noting that only the true God can "impute righteousness to those who believe in him, and make the just live [through him], and declare the Gentiles to be his children through faith."[14]

Marius Victorinus uses the language of *reckoning* when he writes, "God prefigured and foretold that man would be justified from faith. Therefore, just as it was reckoned as righteousness to Abraham because he had faith, so we too, if we have faith in Christ and every mystery of his, will be sons of Abraham. Our whole life will be accounted as righteous."[15] In the same vein, Ambrosiaster says of Romans 4:5,

> He says, that without the works of the law, to an impious person (that is, a Gentile) believing in Christ, his faith is imputed for righteousness, as it was to Abraham. How then can the Jews imagine that through the works of the law they are justified with Abraham's justification, when they see that Abraham was justified not from the works of the law, but by faith alone? Therefore there is no need of the law, since an impious person is justified with God through faith alone.[16]

Noting the relationship between man's faith and the bestowal of divine righteousness, Ambrosiaster comments on Romans 1:17, "God freely justifies the ungodly by faith, without the works of the law. . . . This same righteousness is revealed in the gospel when God grants faith to man, through which he may be justified."[17] Elsewhere he states, "What else comes through faith in Jesus Christ except the righteousness of God which is the revelation of Christ? For it is through faith in the preaching of Christ [e.g., the gospel] that the gift of long ago is known or received."[18]

In his homily on Romans 3:25, John Chrysostom identifies the righteousness of God as that which is declared by God and which makes the sinner instantly righteous: "The declaring of his [God's] righteousness also means that not only is he himself righteous but that he also makes those who are filled with the putrefying sores of sin instantaneously righteous. And in order to further explain what he means by this 'declaring,' he has added, 'That he might be just, and the justifier of him who believes in Jesus.' Have no doubt, then, for it is not of works but of faith."[19]

Speaking of Paul's testimony in Philippians 3:7–10, where the apostle acknowledges that he is dependent on a righteousness other than his own, Chrysostom writes,

> If then he who was so excellent is saved by grace, much more are you. For since it was likely they would say that the righteousness which comes from toil is the greater, he shows that it is dung in comparison with the other. For otherwise I, who was so excellent in it, would not have cast it away, and run to the other. But what is that other? That which is from faith in God, i.e. it too is given by God. This is the righteousness of God; this is altogether a gift. And the gifts of God far exceed those worthless good deeds, which are due to our own diligence.[20]

Chrysostom makes the same point in a sermon on Romans, where he says,

> Whoever has become righteous through faith will live, not just in this life but in the one to come as well. . . . This righteousness is not ours but belongs to God, and in saying this Paul hints to us that it is abundantly available and easy to obtain. For we do not get it by toil and labor but by believing. Then, since his statement does not seem credible, if the adulterer and homosexual, the grave-robber and the magician are not only to be suddenly set free from punishment but to be made righteous, and righteous with the righteousness of God, Paul backs up his assertion from the Old Testament . . . showing that both the righteous and the sinners were justified by faith even then.[21]

Chrysostom's point is that even the worst of sinners not only are pardoned from sin, but also receive the righteousness of God by grace through faith, apart from works.

THE RECEPTION OF CHRIST'S RIGHTEOUSNESS

There are instances when the fathers specifically identify the divine righteousness that believers receive as being the righteousness of Christ—or the righteousness of God through Christ. In such cases, the fathers anticipate the Reformation doctrine of Christ's imputed righteousness. Perhaps the clearest example of this is found in the words of the anonymous author of the second-century *Epistle to Diognetus*:

> He gave His own Son as a ransom for us, the holy One for transgressors, the blameless One for the wicked, the righteous One for the unrighteous, the incorruptible

> One for the corruptible, the immortal One for them that are mortal. For what other thing was capable of covering our sins than His righteousness? By what other one was it possible that we, the wicked and ungodly, could be justified, than by the only Son of God? O sweet exchange! O unsearchable operation! O benefits surpassing all expectation! That the wickedness of many should be hid in a single righteous One, and that the righteousness of One should justify many transgressors![22]

Commenting on that text, Michael Haykin expresses that it "sounds like it has been lifted straight from the pages of Luther. . . . What is expressed here is in full accord with the classical Reformed view of the meaning of Christ's death for our salvation."[23] Jordan Cooper similarly concludes, "This language corresponds with Luther's description of the great exchange wherein Christ takes man's [un]righteousness upon himself and attributes his own righteousness to the believer."[24] He continues, "This righteousness, according to the author of *Diognetus*, is transferred from God as the acting subject to man as the recipient. It is put over sin as a covering—not infused causing inward change—and consequently results in the non-imputation of sin to the believer. It would be consistent with the author's language to describe this as 'alien' righteousness."[25]

The fact that believers are justified by the righteousness of Christ, rather than their own righteousness, leads them away from boasting. As Basil of Caesarea explains in his *Sermon on Humility*, "This is perfect and pure boasting in God, when one is not proud on account of his own righteousness but knows that he is indeed unworthy of the true righteousness and is justified solely by faith in Christ. And Paul boasts that he despises his own righteousness, seeking that righteousness that is on account of Christ, which is the righteousness of God by faith."[26] As Michael Haykin explains, "This passage clearly reveals Basil's fundamental opposition to any idea that we can save ourselves by our own good works. . . . Little wonder that when the sixteenth-century Reformers sought to argue that their view of saving grace was not so novel as their Roman Catholic opponents maintained, this Basilian text was one to which they turned."[27]

Speaking of Christ's sacrificial death, John Chrysostom declares, "For the purpose of His dying was not that He might hold us liable to punishment and in condemnation, but that He might do good unto us. For this cause He both died and rose again, that He might make us righteous."[28] Therefore, at the cross "it was not that the sins were done away only, but that righteousness was given. And Christ did not merely do the same amount of good that Adam did of harm, but far more and greater good."[29] In his homily on 2 Corinthians 5:21, Chrysostom expands on this concept:

> "For although Christ was righteous," Paul says, "he was made a sinner so that he might make the sinners righteous." Yes rather, he said not only this, but even something far greater. For the word he employed is not the habit but the quality itself. For he did not say that he made him a sinner, but "sin"—not "he who had not sinned" only, but "who had not even known sin so that we" also "might become"—he did not say "righteous"

> but "righteousness," and "the righteousness of God." For this is [the righteousness] "of God" when we are justified not by works—in which case it would be necessary that not a spot even should be found—but by grace, in which case all sin is done away.[30]

This is the language of the great exchange: Christ takes the guilt of the sinner so that the sinner might receive God's righteousness through Him. Chrysostom's distinction between the "habit" and the "quality" is significant. Jesus was not a sinner by habit. He never sinned, but God treated Him as a sin offering on the cross. Similarly, believers are not righteous by habit. They fall woefully short of God's standard, but God treats them as qualitatively righteous (in terms of their status before Him) on account of Christ.

In a sermon on Romans 5:17, Chrysostom delineates the many blessings of God's superabundant grace. Not only were our sins taken away, but "we were at once freed from punishment, and put off all iniquity, and were also born again from above, and rose again with the old man buried, and were redeemed, sanctified, led up to adoption, justified, made brothers of the Only-begotten, and joint heirs and of one Body with Him, and reckoned as His Flesh, and even as a Body with the Head, so were we united unto Him!"[31] The benefits of God's grace in salvation, as Chrysostom points out, go far beyond the removal of guilt and condemnation. Positively, the believer receives a superabundance of undeserved blessings, including the righteousness of justification. To illustrate this reality, Chrysostom continues,

> As then if any one were to cast a person who owed ten mites into prison, and not the man himself only, but wife and children and servants for his sake; and another were to come and not to pay down the ten mites only, but to give also ten thousand talents of gold, and to lead the prisoner into the king's courts, and to the throne of the highest power, and were to make him partaker of the highest honor and every kind of magnificence, the creditor would not be able to remember the ten mites; so hath our case been. For Christ hath paid down far more than we owe, yea as much more as the illimitable ocean is than a little drop.[32]

Significantly in this passage, Chrysostom teaches that Christ not only paid the debt of sin for the believer, but also credited the believer's account with an "illimitable ocean" of "grace and righteousness" by which believers "may be justified." Such language accords wondrously with the Protestant understanding of imputation—that the immeasurable debts of the sinner were credited to Christ, who paid for them at the cross (see Col. 2:14), while the immeasurable righteousness of Christ was credited to the believer so that God might declare him to be righteous (see 2 Cor. 5:21).

Two other passages from Chrysostom warrant mention in this regard, because each depicts the believer as being clothed by Christ—a concept that closely parallels the Reformation concept of imputation. Regarding the death of Christ, Chrysostom explains that believers are clothed with Him in His redemption: "Christ has purchased us with His blood, and adorned us with His blood. They who share this blood stand with Angels and Archangels and the Powers that are above, clothed in Christ's own kingly robe, and having the armor of the Spirit. Nay, I have not as yet said any great thing: *they are clothed with the King Himself*."[33] The redeemed are those who have not only been purchased by Christ, but are covered by Him like a royal robe.

Having been justified by faith, their sinful cloaks have been removed and replaced with His robes of perfect righteousness. Thus, Chrysostom could say,

> Those who, by their faith in Christ, had put off like an old cloak the burden of their sins, those who had been set free from their error and been illumined by the light of justification, had put on this new and shining cloak, this royal robe. This is why he said: "If any man is in Christ, he is a new creature: the former things have passed away; behold, they are all made new."[34]

Such language is in keeping with the Reformation emphasis on the extrinsic nature of Christ's imputed righteousness, with which the believer is clothed.

In sum, examples from the patristic *corpus* anticipate key Reformation distinctives of justification, including the need for a righteousness outside of the sinner, the imputation of the believer's sin to Christ, and the imputation of an alien righteousness to the believer on account of Christ's death.[35] In cases such as the *Epistle to Diognetus*, the patristic author specifically designates the righteousness of Christ as being that which covers the believer as part of a great exchange. In other cases, such as Chrysostom's discussion of 2 Corinthians 5:21, that exchange results in the believer being declared righteous in terms of *quality* or *status*. Moreover, as Chrysostom explains regarding Romans 5:21, the believer is not merely forgiven his debt at the moment of salvation, but is instantly credited with a limitless supply of righteousness. Thus, believers can be said to be clothed in the royal robes of Christ Himself.

As we have seen, evidence from the writings of the church fathers shows that they were able (1) to speak of justification in forensic terms, (2) to distinguish between justification and sanctification, and (3) to make statements that anticipate the doctrine of imputed righteousness. Accordingly, a compelling case can be made for significant levels of continuity between the pre-Augustinian church fathers and the sixteenth-century Reformers.

Speaking of the earliest centuries of church history, Jordan Cooper concludes, "In the first and second centuries, in a context far different from that of late medieval Europe, the most prominent themes in Luther's Pauline hermeneutic are already present."[36] D. H. Williams agrees. Speaking of the entire pre-Augustinian period, he writes,

> It was all but universally accepted that the work of salvation is completely God's work on our behalf and that without God's initiative toward us in Christ, Adam's race has no hope. . . . While it is hazardous to generalize, we may say that the early Fathers maintained the free and unmerited character of God's grace toward fallen humanity, expressing it sometimes in the terms of justification by faith.[37]

Of course, our historical investigation is not yet complete. More than any other theologian in church history, the Reformers looked back to Augustine. The next question we will consider is whether the Reformer's understanding of justification squares with that of the renowned bishop of Hippo.

PART THREE

AUGUSTINE AND JUSTIFICATION

CHAPTER SEVEN

A FORERUNNER TO THE REFORMERS?

The Reformers looked to Augustine (354–430) more than any other church father in their defense of the doctrine of salvation by grace. Because he was so influential on their thinking, many evangelicals today consider Augustine to be a theological forefather of the Reformation.[1] In particular, the Reformers appreciated Augustine's response to a late fourth-century heretic named Pelagius, who denied the concept of original sin and emphasized human free will and moral effort to the point that salvation could be attained through those things. In refuting Pelagius's teachings, Augustine insisted instead that salvation is by God's sovereign grace alone and cannot be earned by good works or moral achievement.

By the sixteenth-century, medieval Catholicism had become highly moralistic, with its emphasis on asceticism and sacramental works. In significant ways, it had become semi-Pelagian. As McGrath explains,

> Salvation was widely regarded as something which could be earned or merited through good works. The confused and vague theology of forgiveness of the late medieval period lent weight to the suggestion that it was possible to purchase the forgiveness of sins and procure the remission of "purgatorial penalties" through the purchase of indulgences.[2]

In combatting the moralism of their day, the Reformers understandably found a close ally in Augustine.

The Reformers' understanding of salvation demonstrated a number of parallels with what Augustine taught. At least five points of similarity can be identified.[3] First, both Augustine and the Reformers emphasized the priority of God's sovereignty in salvation. Augustine understood election to be anchored in God's eternal decree of predestination.[4] Salvation was grounded in God's choice, not in man's. As he explains, God's elect are "not those who are chosen because they believed, but those who are chosen in order that they may believe."[5] Thus, Augustine notes of believers, "They were chosen before the foundation of the world by that predestination by which God foreknew His future actions."[6]

Second, Augustine, like the Reformers, acknowledged the reality of human depravity, noting that the unbeliever's will is enslaved to sin.[7] Augustine taught that unbelievers are incapable of performing any good works, in the eyes of God, until they have been liberated by God's grace from their bondage to sin.[8] At the moment of justification, the will of the sinner is set free, so that he or she is given the freedom to act righteously.[9] In asserting that unbelievers are unable to perform good works, Augustine distinguishes between external actions and inner motives. Though unregenerate people can perform acts that look good on the outside, they are incapable of doing so from godly motives. Only those who have been redeemed can perform works that are both externally good and internally righteous.[10]

Third, like the Reformers, Augustine taught that although believers do not become sinless at the moment of regeneration, the penalty for their sin is no longer imputed to them. Instead, the debt of their sin is nailed to the cross, such that the punishment due to them is paid by Christ. The guilty sinner is deemed innocent because the weight of his sin is no longer reckoned to his account.[11]

Fourth, both Augustine and the Reformers taught that the divine righteousness with which believers are justified is a gift from God.[12] Such righteousness is received through faith, which also is a gift from God.[13] According to Augustine, the unredeemed sinner, due to the bondage of his will, is not able to desire or attain justification. God must intervene by bestowing the divine gift of faith. He acts on the heart and soul of the person so that the sinner comes to embrace the gospel in faith.[14]

Finally, Augustine, like the Reformers, insisted that the unredeemed sinner can do nothing to merit salvation through good works performed before conversion. Both Augustine and the Reformers reacted strongly against the Pelagian tendencies that existed during their lifetimes, clearly maintaining that no unredeemed person can merit God's saving grace through good works.

SALVATION BY GRACE THROUGH FAITH

A brief survey of Augustine's writings demonstrates the clarity with which he emphasizes the priority of God's grace in salvation. In one of his letters, he explains that "it is grace which justifies the ungodly, that is, the one formerly ungodly thereby becomes just. Hence the receiving of this grace is not preceded by any merits because the ungodly merit punishment, not grace, and it would not be grace if it were awarded as something due and not freely given."[15] In another letter, he similarly states, "No man can say that it is by the merit of his own works, or by the merit of his own prayers, or by the merit of his own faith, that God's grace has been conferred upon him; nor suppose that the doctrine is true which those heretics hold, that the grace of God is given us in proportion to our own merit."[16]

Those convictions are reiterated in his work *On the Spirit and the Letter*, which was a favorite of the Reformers. Therein he explains that "where sin abounded grace might much more abound, not through the merit of the sinner, but by the intervention of his Helper."[17] And again, "We conclude that a man is not justified by the precepts of a holy life, but by faith in Jesus Christ; in a word, not by the law of works, but by the law of faith; not by the letter, but by the spirit; not by the merits of deeds, but by free grace."[18] In other words, justification is received by grace through faith, and not on the basis of self-righteous works.[19]

Commenting on the false teachings of Pelagius and his followers, Augustine writes, "These men however, attribute faith to free will in such a way as to make it appear that grace is rendered to faith not as a gratuitous gift, but as a debt—thus ceasing to be grace any longer, because that is not grace which is not gratuitous."[20] Even Old Testament saints, Augustine argues, were saved by grace and not on account of their good works. "Nothing saved them but belief in the Mediator who shed his blood for the remission of their sins," he explains. "You who are enemies to this grace do not wish this, that the ancients should be believed to have been saved by the same grace of Jesus Christ."[21] Of these Old Testament saints, Augustine looked to Abraham as the prime example of a person saved by grace through faith. As he explains, Abraham "was justified not by his own merit, as if by works, but by the grace of God through faith."[22]

The theme of salvation by grace alone continues in Augustine's *Expositions of the Psalms.* Commenting on Psalm 23, he writes, "He has brought me forth in the narrow ways of His righteousness, wherein few walk, not for my merit's sake, but for His Name's sake."[23] In his remarks on Psalm 56, Augustine declares, "There is another sense in this verse, 'For nothing You will save them:' with none of their merits going before You will save them. . . . All in them is rough, all foul, all to be detested: and though they bring nothing to You whereby they may be saved; 'For nothing You shall save them,' that is, with the free gift of Your grace."[24] Augustine personalizes this truth in his sermon on Psalm 71: "From the time that I have been converted, I have learned that no merits of mine have preceded, but that Your grace has come to me freely, in order that I might be mindful of Your righteousness alone."[25] And on Psalm 86, he states, "For no merits of ours had gone before, for which the Son of God should die: but the more, because there were no merits, was His mercy great."[26] These and other examples[27] demonstrate Augustine's commitment to the doctrine of salvation by grace alone. Sinners can offer nothing to God by which they might merit forgiveness from sin and the gift of salvation. Instead, salvation is solely a work of His grace, which is received by faith in Christ.[28]

It's not difficult to understand why the Reformers would resonate with Augustine's emphasis on God's grace. But important questions remain. Augustine clearly taught salvation by grace alone. But what about justification by faith alone? Is there evidence from Augustine's writings that he anticipated that specific aspect of Reformation doctrine? In the minds of some scholars, the answer to these questions determines whether or not Augustine can rightly be considered a forerunner to the Reformation.[29]

AREAS OF ALLEGED DISAGREEMENT

Those wanting to distance Augustine from the Reformers have suggested that they disagreed about justification in a number of ways. These alleged differences might be summarized under four points. First, Augustine saw justification as a lifelong process in which believers are *made righteous*, whereas the Reformers understood justification as a legal pronouncement in which believers are *declared righteous.*[30] Second, Augustine made no attempt to differentiate between justification and sanctification (or regeneration). By contrast, the Reformers maintained a clear distinction between the two.[31] Third, for Augustine, justifying righteousness is *imparted* to sinners so that it becomes an internal part of them. By contrast, the Reformers taught that justifying righteousness is *imputed* to sinners so that they are covered with the external righteousness of Christ.[32] Finally, the Reformers taught that believers are justified by *faith alone.* Augustine, according to some contemporary scholars, taught something closer to justification by *love alone.*[33] On the basis of these criteria, some assert that Augustine's understanding of justification was fundamentally different than that of Luther, Calvin, and other leading Reformers.[34]

Before responding to such assertions, let's examine these four areas of alleged disagreement in greater detail.

Justification as a Process

First, it is argued that Augustine did not conceive of justification forensically and, therefore, his views are incompatible with later Protestant teaching. Whereas the Reformers understood justification as a *declarative* act, Augustine viewed it as a *transformative* process.[35] Rather than defining justification as "to declare righteous" or "to reckon as righteous," Augustine defined it as "to make righteous." In other words, justification for Augustine encompassed the process of the sinner becoming righteous[36] and was not limited to a divine pronouncement of righteousness at the moment of the sinner's conversion.[37]

A primary reason for this was Augustine's reliance on the Latin translation of the Bible rather than the original languages of Scripture. The Greek word rendered "to justify" (*dikaioō*) means "to declare righteous," but it was translated by the Latin word *iustificare,* which Augustine took to mean "to make righteous." Due to his reliance on the Latin text, he was blinded to the forensic meaning of the Greek—and the Hebrew—terms for justification in Scripture. Consequently, he misinterpreted the precise meaning of justification language in the Bible.[38]

The claim that Augustine defined justification as "to make righteous" or "to become righteous" is supported by several of his writings. In one place, he asks, "What is, 'who justifies the ungodly'?" and answers, "The ungodly is made righteous."[39] Elsewhere, he similarly explains that "the unrighteous man is justified, that is, becomes just instead of impious, and begins to possess that good reward which God will crown when the world shall be judged."[40] In another place, he writes, "What does this mean, 'for our justification'? So that He might justify us; so that He might make us just."[41] Perhaps the most explicit statement in this regard comes from *On the Spirit and the Letter*, where Augustine states, "For what else does the phrase 'being justified' signify than being made righteous—by Him, of course, who justifies the ungodly person so that he may become a godly one instead?"[42] These examples suggest that, at least in places, Augustine understood justification to be transformative.[43]

Conflating Justification and Sanctification

Some also assert that Augustine did not distinguish between justification and sanctification, whereas the Reformers did. This, they believe, is because he viewed justification as a process by which the sinner is made righteous, and not as a finished act in which the sinner is declared righteous.[44] Consequently, he did not distinguish between the initial *act* of justification, in which God's grace is singularly *operative* on the sinner, and the subsequent *process* of sanctification, in which God's grace is *cooperative* with the sinner.[45] They further argue that, because Augustine saw justification as a lifelong process, he granted a place for human merit after conversion in which eternal life, at least in part, is viewed as a reward for good works performed by believers.[46]

Imparted versus Imputed Righteousness

Those who make the previous points also contend that Augustine saw justifying righteousness as only being *imparted* to believers.[47] This imparted righteousness is not extrinsic, but rather intrinsic, meaning it is a righteousness inside the believer that produces moral transformation and growth in personal holiness.[48] That definition of justifying righteousness is quite different from the one espoused by the Reformers, who taught that the justifying righteousness of Christ, which is outside believers, is *imputed* to them by grace through faith so that they are clothed in His perfect righteousness, which is credited to their account.

Following this line of argument: because he saw justifying grace as being imparted to believers, Augustine viewed the good works Christians performed after conversion as being *both* meritorious *and* the result of God's grace.[49] He understood them to be the fruits of God's gracious gift of transformational righteousness in the lives of His people. Though he could speak of meritorious works on the part of believers, Augustine believed the ultimate credit for such acts of obedience goes to God, who graciously enables believers to walk justly in His sight.

Justification through "Love Alone"

Some modern scholars go so far as to suggest that instead of saying Augustine taught justification *sola fide* ("through faith alone"), it is more accurate to say that he taught justification *sola caritate* ("through love alone").[50] After all, Augustine insisted that justifying faith is that which works itself out through love.[51] Though a profession of faith can be made without love, it is useless unless it is accompanied by love.[52] In his writings, Augustine prioritized the necessity of love—and on faith working through love. If his understanding of justification is better expressed as being through "love alone" rather than through "faith alone," a significant difference indeed exists between Augustine and the Reformers.

Based on these four areas of alleged discontinuity, some scholars assert that the Reformation doctrine of *sola fide* was not anticipated in the writings of Augustine.[53] Though they would acknowledge that the basic framework of Reformation soteriology shares some commonality with Augustine's teaching, they would also insist that major differences exist.[54] Some of these differences are so significant that they question whether the Reformers were right to consider Augustine a theological ally.

So, what are we to think about these areas of alleged disagreement? The short answer is that the issues raised in the preceding pages do not tell the whole story about Augustine and his understanding of justification. Our goal in the next chapter is to provide a more balanced picture.

CHAPTER EIGHT

THE DOCTOR OF GRACE

As we saw in the previous chapter, some contemporary scholars argue for major discontinuity between Augustine and the Reformers regarding the nature of justification.[1] Such an assertion, however, greatly overstates the case because it fails to present the entire picture regarding Augustine's thought.[2] We acknowledge, as the Reformers themselves did, that there are places in Augustine's writings where his definition of justification lacks the precision required by the Greek and Hebrew terms found in Scripture. We would further agree that this was primarily due to his reliance on the Latin text. Yet there are also places where Augustine is more careful. In those places, he speaks of justification in ways that closely parallel the teachings of the Reformers.[3]

At the outset, it is important to note that Augustine never addressed the doctrine of justification in a systematic way.[4] While Augustine sometimes speaks of justification in ways that seem congruent with later Roman Catholic teaching, in other places he makes statements with which the Protestant Reformers would agree. Those who overstate the discontinuity between Augustine and the Reformers do so because they read Augustine solely through the lens of later Roman Catholic theology. Such precludes them from fully appreciating the diverse richness of Augustine's writings regarding justification by faith.[5]

In certain contexts, Augustine's teaching aligns clearly with that of Luther's and Calvin's.[6] So let's revisit the areas of alleged disagreement surveyed in the previous chapter, to bring some much needed balance to our analysis of Augustine.

THE FORENSIC NATURE OF JUSTIFICATION

While Augustine is sometimes imprecise, and therefore inconsistent, in the way he defines justification, there are places where he articulates the doctrine of justification in a forensic sense. His exposition of Psalm 31 provides one such example. There Augustine reflects on Romans 4:5 and states,

> When someone believes in him who justifies the impious, that faith is reckoned as justice to the believer, as David too declares that person blessed whom God has accepted and endowed with righteousness, independently of any righteous actions. What righteousness is this? The righteousness of faith, preceded by no good works, but with good works as its consequence.[7]

Augustine describes God's justifying work in this passage in terms of the reckoning of righteousness to the believer. Such language is clearly in line with what the Reformers taught more than a millennium later—that justification is a declarative act.

In his anti-Pelagian work *On the Spirit and the Letter,* Augustine refers to the lawyer in Luke 10:25 and explains that, in some passages, "the term 'they shall be justified' is used in the sense of, they shall be deemed, or reckoned as just, as it is predicated of a certain man of the Gospel, 'But he, wanting to justify himself,' meaning that he wished to be thought and accounted just."[8] Elsewhere, Augustine similarly explains that "faith is counted for righteousness."[9] These instances again demonstrate that, in places, Augustine understood justification in a declarative, forensic sense.

On other occasions, Augustine contrasts the concept of justification with that of condemnation. He asks, "Why, indeed, is the judgment from one offence to condemnation, while the grace is from many offenses to justification?"[10] Elsewhere, he comments on the apostle Paul's teaching in Romans 5:18, "Notice how he emphasizes 'one' and 'one,' that is Adam and Christ, the former for condemnation, the latter for justification."[11] Because *condemnation* is a forensic concept (a declaration of guilt), it follows that when Augustine uses justification in direct contrast to it, he is thinking of justification in a forensic way (as a declaration of righteousness).[12]

Examples like these have led a number of scholars to be more balanced in their approach to Augustine's teaching.[13] They recognize that, at times, he defined justification in forensic terms, as a declaration of righteousness.[14]

JUSTIFICATION DISTINGUISHED FROM SANCTIFICATION

In addition to recognizing the forensic nature of justification, Augustine sometimes distinguishes between the punctiliar past event of being declared righteous and the ongoing process of being made righteous. The Reformers would later distinguish these as justification and sanctification, yet the notion that some distinction exists is anticipated in various Augustinian texts.

David F. Wright highlights passages in which Augustine uses justification language to refer to a past event—as opposed to an ongoing process—in the believer's life.[15] Speaking of the necessity of holiness in the life of a Christian, Augustine explains that "even after he has become justified by faith, grace should accompany him on his way, and he should lean upon it, lest he fall."[16] Notice that the past event of being justified by faith is distinguished from the present reality of continuing on the way of Christian living. Augustine makes this same distinction in other places as well. For example, he asks, "How can a man live justly who has not been justified? . . . Grace justifies so that he who is justified may live justly."[17] Augustine continues, "No one merits justification by his good works, since unless he has been justified he cannot do good works. Nevertheless God justifies the Gentiles by faith."[18] And again, "Christ died for the ungodly not that they should remain ungodly but that, having been justified, they should be converted from their ungodliness, believing in the one who justifies the ungodly."[19] And as he declares in his exposition of Psalm 111, "No one acts justly unless he has been justified:

'to believe in him who justifies the ungodly' starts from faith, so that good works do not by coming first show what a person has deserved, but by following show what he has received."[20] These examples demonstrate that Augustine could speak of justification as a past event in the believer's life—an event that was distinct from the subsequent process of righteous living.

In *Sermon* 158, Augustine again speaks of the believer's justification as a past event. Referring to Romans 8:30, Augustine tells his congregation, "You are among the predestined, the called, the justified. . . . If the faith which works through love is in you, you already belong to the predestined, the called, the justified. . . . We are sons of God, predestined, called, justified; we are sons of God and what we shall be has not yet been revealed."[21] Commenting on that text, Wright concludes, "From *Sermon* 158 and other passages in his works, we must extract as one strand in Augustine's teaching on *justificatio* [justification] a declarative event that warrants a perfect passive verb. . . . Although this is a minor note in his works, it is clearly not an isolated aberration."[22] Such statements contradict the assertion that Augustine never distinguishes between the initial *event* of justification and the subsequent *process* of righteous living. As John Gerstner writes,

> Many historical theologians interpret him as confusing justification with sanctification, of which justification is merely a part. This is not accurate, however. Though Augustine finds justification and sanctification inseparable, they are not indistinguishable. Augustinian justification leads into sanctification, but is not confused with it.[23]

Evidence warrants a final comment regarding Augustine's teaching on merits. It is true that Augustine sometimes emphasizes the concept of merit in addressing the lives of believers. The question is how we should interpret Augustine's theology of merit. Was Augustine implying that eternal life was earned, in some way, by good works? Or was he using merit language in a way that harmonizes with the later Protestant understanding of heavenly rewards?[24] R. C. Sproul writes,

> The way historic Protestantism has spelled it out is that the only way we get into heaven is through the work of Christ, but we are promised rewards in heaven *according to our works*. Saint Augustine said that it's only by the grace of God that we ever do anything even approximating a good work, and none of our works are good enough to demand that God reward them. The fact that God has decided to grant rewards on the basis of obedience or disobedience is what Augustine called God's crowning his own works within us.[25]

In making that claim, Sproul references a repeated theme in Augustine's writings. As Augustine himself said, "What merit, then, does a man have before grace, by which he might receive grace, when our every good merit is produced in us only by grace, and, when God, crowning our merits, crowns nothing else but His own gifts to us?"[26]

Augustine insists that the believer's merits are possible only by the grace of God,[27] so that, although God rewards his good works, he cannot boast in them. "Neither can he that is pardoned glory in any merit of his own," he states, "nor he that is condemned complain of anything but his own demerit. For it is grace alone that separates the redeemed from the lost."[28] In his work *Against Faustus*, Augustine explains that heaven cannot be earned on the basis of good works. Speaking of Old Testament saints, he notes, "For my part, I am ready to join you in the belief that the ancestors reached heaven not by any merit of their own but by that divine mercy that is stronger than sin."[29] Commenting on Romans 6:23, and referring to post-conversion good works, Augustine explains that "God does not, for any merits of our own, but from His own divine compassion, prolong our existence to everlasting life."[30] Even those who produce insignificant works will be saved on the basis of the merits of Christ: "Those who build upon the foundation, Christ, not gold, silver, and precious stones, but wood, hay, and stubble . . . shall be saved, yet so as by fire, *the merit of the foundation saving them.*"[31] In other words, believers are saved based on the merits of Christ, their sole foundation, and not on the basis of their own works. These and similar passages help us see that Augustine's merit language harmonizes with Protestant teaching on rewards.

THE IMPUTED RIGHTEOUSNESS OF CHRIST

Augustine is also able to speak about the justifying righteousness believers receive in a way that accords with the Reformed understanding of imputation. As noted above, Augustine affirmed the merit of Christ as being sufficient for saving the believer.[32] Elsewhere, he used the language of imputation to describe the believer's reception of God's righteousness. He explains,

> The very reason, indeed, why [the apostle Paul] so often declares that righteousness is imputed to us, not out of our works, but our faith, whereas faith rather works through love, is that no man should think that he arrives at faith itself through the merit of his works; for it is faith which is the beginning whence good works first proceed; since (as has already been stated) whatsoever comes not from faith is sin.[33]

Augustine could also speak of justifying righteousness as that which clothes the believer. In his work *On the Spirit and the Letter,* he writes, "The righteousness of God is not that by which God is righteous but that with which he clothes man when he justifies the ungodly. To this the Law and the Prophets bear witness."[34] Later, he compares this righteousness to a garment with which the believer is clothed, calling it the "vestment of the righteousness of faith . . . with which we cannot be found naked."[35] In his *Tractates on the Gospel of John,* Augustine similarly explains that "Christ is for us righteousness" and that God's righteousness is "that which God bestows on human beings so that they may be righteous through God."[36] This is echoed in *The Enchiridion,* where he says of Christ, "He, then, being made sin, just as we are made righteous (our righteousness being not our own, but God's, not in ourselves, but in Him).'"[37]

These and other examples[38] demonstrate clearly Augustine's ability to articulate God's justifying righteousness in an extrinsic or external sense. Such "is right in line with Luther's millennium-later appropriation of him," says Ellingsen.[39] The righteousness given to believers is not their own. It comes from outside them. That is something with which the Reformers would have wholeheartedly agreed. Noting the parallels between Augustine and Luther in particular, Eugene Osterhaven writes, "Augustine did not ask whether justifying faith gives one an *infused* or an *imputed* righteousness from Christ. It would seem that, had he been asked the question which later confronted Luther, he would have answered very much as the Reformer did."[40]

JUSTIFICATION BY LOVE ALONE?

Finally, we need to address the assertion that Augustine's view of justification can be encapsulated in the phrase *sola caritate iustificamur* ("love alone justifies").[41] To be sure, Augustine emphasized the necessity of love (or charity) as the visible evidence or fruit of genuine faith.[42] He often defines saving faith as that which works through love.[43] But that does not substantiate the claim that Augustine's view of justification is best summarized as "love alone justifies."[44] As Wright observes, the teaching that believers are "justified by faith" occurs frequently in Augustine's writings, but never "justified by love."[45] To be sure, Augustine emphasizes that genuine faith will be evidenced by works of love in the life of a believer. But this is hardly the same as claiming that Augustine taught justification through "love alone."

Augustine's emphasis on the fruitfulness of genuine faith is seen repeatedly throughout his writings. Those who make a profession of faith and yet live in disobedience deceive themselves; their faith is dead, being as worthless as the faith of demons (see James 2:19).[46] By contrast, true believers are characterized by a love for God and for others (see Mark 12:30–31).[47] As Augustine preached in one of his sermons, "That person believes in Christ who also hopes in Christ and loves Christ. If he has faith without hope and love, he believes Christ exists but does not believe in Christ."[48]

Augustine affirmed the truth that believers are justified by grace through faith, apart from works.[49] Yet he cautioned his congregants against the error of thinking that God's grace provides a license for sin. As he warned his readers,

> You see that Abraham was justified not by what he did but by his faith. All right then, so I can do whatever I like, because even though I have no good works to show but simply believe in God, that is reckoned to me as righteousness? Anyone who has said this and has decided on it as a policy has already fallen in and sunk. Anyone who is still considering it and hesitating is in mortal danger.[50]

Augustine's point is clear: Those who think they can live in unrepentant sin simply because they profess faith in Christ should think again (see Rom. 6:1–2). Genuine faith is a repentant faith, which manifests itself in the fruit of love and obedience.[51]

Though Augustine emphasizes the necessity of good works, he repeatedly notes that those good works are gifts from God. The righteousness that characterizes the believer is a righteousness bestowed on him by God so that "whatever righteousness a person has, he must not presume that he has it of himself, but from the grace of God who justifies him."[52] Consequently, believers can take no credit for their salvation. If God rewarded human beings according to their just deserts, they would be condemned to hell. Hence, Augustine declares, "The good works which we do after we have received grace are not to be attributed to us but rather to him who has justified us by his grace. For if God had wanted to give us our due reward, he would have given us the punishment due to sinners."[53]

While it is true that Augustine placed a heavy emphasis on the fruit of love and good works that accrues in the life of a believer, that emphasis must be understood in light of his equally forceful insistence that salvation is entirely a gift of God's grace. Even the ability to live righteously, and to respond in love to both God and neighbor, is possible only because of God's unmerited favor toward us (see 1 John 4:19). All the glory goes to Him.

AUGUSTINE AND THE REFORMERS

Any survey of Augustine's teaching on justification ought to acknowledge that he was not as precise or consistent as the Reformers. This appears to be largely due to his reliance on the Latin translation of the Bible, which caused him to miss, at times, the clear meaning of the original Greek and Hebrew terms for justification. Consequently, he sometimes defined justification in terms of being *made* righteous, rather than being *declared* righteous. This has led some modern historians to conclude that, for Augustine, justification and sanctification were virtually indistinguishable.

Yet there are places in Augustine's writings where he articulates the doctrine of justification in such a way that affirms—and anticipates—various aspects of the Reformation doctrine of justification *sola fide*. It was these "more Protestant" statements that Luther and his fellow Reformers embraced as they taught justification by grace through faith alone.[54] As Wright explains, "We should not lose sight of the genuine affinity between Augustine and the sixteenth-century Reformers on justification."[55] Ellingsen concurs: "When they addressed similar contexts, Luther was clearly in line with the Augustinian heritage."[56] Thus, it is only by ignoring these areas of similarity that some scholars overstate the differences between Augustine and the Reformers.[57]

Of course, the Reformers were more concerned with being biblical than being Augustinian. In places where they saw Augustine affirming the teaching of Scripture, they gladly embraced him. They especially applauded his insistence that salvation is by grace alone, and not something sinners can earn through their own good works. That truth served as a powerful rebuke to the works-righteousness that at the popular level could so easily characterize the medieval Roman Catholic system.

At the same time, in places where they found Augustine's teaching muddled or unbiblical, the Reformers did not hesitate to part ways with the esteemed church father.[58] Thus, while claiming the "Doctor of Grace" as a historical ally, their commitment to *sola Scriptura* transcended their commitment to Augustine.[59] For his part, Augustine would have commended their allegiance to Scripture above all else. As he explained in one of his letters,

> For the reasonings of any men whatsoever, even though they be [true Christians], and of high reputation, are not to be treated by us in the same way as the canonical

> Scriptures are treated. We are at liberty, without doing any violence to the respect which these men deserve, to condemn and reject anything in their writings, if perchance we shall find that they have entertained opinions differing from that which others or we ourselves have, by the divine help, discovered to be the truth. I deal thus with the writings of others, and I wish my intelligent readers to deal thus with mine.[60]

The Reformers sought to be intelligent readers of Augustine. Consequently, they evaluated his writings through the lens of Scripture, which led them to disagree with him at times. Nevertheless, as this study has shown, there are significant reasons why they found him to be a mighty theological ally.

Our study now moves to consider the Christian leaders and theologians who lived after Augustine. In the vast expanse known as the Middle Ages, was there anyone who anticipated the doctrine of justification by grace alone through faith alone? The answer to that might seem bleak, considering how critical the Reformers were of certain aspects of medieval Roman Catholicism, but common perceptions must not prevent us from continuing our investigation.

[illegible]

Scriptures are treated. Whereas [illegible] without [illegible] to the respect which these men deserve, to condemn and reject anything in their writings, if perchance we shall find that they have entertained opinions differing from that which others or we ourselves [illegible] by the divine help, discovered to be the truth. I deal thus with the writings of others, and I wish my intelligent readers to deal thus with mine.

[illegible] passage ought to [illegible] intelligent readers [illegible] Constantly, they [illegible] through the [illegible] of Scripture [illegible] led them to disagree with [illegible] [illegible] as is [illegible] shown [illegible] [illegible] theologically.

[illegible] moves to consider the Christian [illegible] and the [illegible] after Augustine. In the vast [illegible] Middle Ages was there [illegible] doctrine of justification by grace alone through faith alone. The answer to that [illegible] consider[illegible] that the Reformers were [illegible] Roman Catholicism, but [illegible] investigation.

PART FOUR

THE CHURCH AFTER AUGUSTINE

CHAPTER NINE

PARDONED FROM SIN

Clear anticipations of the Reformers' understanding of justification can be found in the writings of the church fathers, including statements made by Augustine. But what about those theologians who lived after Augustine into the Middle Ages? Did anyone in the medieval era anticipate a forensic understanding of justification, a distinction between justification and sanctification, or the imputed righteousness of Christ?

SALVATION BY GRACE THROUGH FAITH

As with the early church, there is evidence in the writings of post-Augustinian theologians that salvation is received by grace through faith apart from works. Examples can be found from both the Eastern church and the Western church.[1] In the East, Cyril of Alexandria (ca. 376–444) describes the nature of the gospel this way: "We are justified by faith, not by works of the law, as Scripture says. By faith in whom, then, are we justified? Is it not in him who suffered death according to the flesh for our sake? Is it not in one Lord Jesus Christ? Have we not been redeemed by proclaiming his death and confessing his resurrection?"[2] Elsewhere, he writes, "For truly the compassion from beside the Father is Christ, as he takes away the sins, dismisses the charges and justifies by faith, and recovers the lost and makes [them] stronger than death. . . . For by him and in him we have known the Father, and we have become rich in the justification by faith."[3]

Writing a generation later, Theodoret of Cyrrhus (ca. 393–457) is even more direct in expressing an understanding of salvation by grace through faith alone. In his commentary on Romans, he states, "The doer of righteousness expects a reward, but justification by faith is the gift of the God of all."[4] Earlier in that same work, he explains that Paul quoted Habakkuk in Romans 1:17 to demonstrate that the Old Testament prophets "had predicted that one day there would be salvation by faith alone."[5]

Theodoret's commentary on Ephesians expresses that same perspective, noting that salvation is received only through faith, and even faith is not something for which believers can take credit. He writes,

> All we bring to grace is our faith. But even in this faith, divine grace itself has become our enabler. For [Paul] adds, "And this is not of yourselves but it is a gift of God; not of works, lest anyone should boast" (Eph. 2:8–9). It is not of our own accord that we have believed, but we have come to belief after having been called; and even when we had come to believe, He did not require of us

> purity of life, but approving mere faith, God bestowed on us forgiveness of sins.[6]

Accordingly, Theodoret can use the language of "faith alone" to describe the hope of salvation: "I consider myself wretched—in fact, wretched three times over. I am guilty of all kinds of errors. Through faith alone I look for finding some mercy in the day of the Lord's appearing."[7] Notice that Theodoret emphasizes both the inherent unworthiness of the sinner and the hope of God's mercy, which is received solely through faith. Such statements are clearly in line with later Reformation teaching.[8]

In his treatise entitled "Concerning Those Who Think to Be Justified through Works," Marcus Eremita (fifth century, also known as Marcus the Ascetic) explains that "the kingdom of heaven is not a reward for works, but a gift of grace prepared by the Master for his faithful servants."[9] He goes on to caution his readers against two extremes that must be avoided. On the one hand, some think they are saved yet they continue in unrepentant sin. On the other hand, others think they can earn salvation through good works. Both are incorrect, says Marcus.[10] As he writes: "Some without fulfilling the commandments think that they possess true faith. Others fulfill the commandments and then expect the kingdom as a reward due to them. Both are mistaken."[11] Marcus warns against both the error of legalism (that salvation can be earned through works) and the error of antinomianism (that repentance is not part of saving faith). As we noted in chapter 2, the Reformers would later issue warnings against both of those errors.

In the Western church, a similar emphasis on God's grace in salvation is evidenced in statements made by Augustinian theologians[12] like Prosper of Aquitaine (390–455), Fulgentius of Ruspe (462–533), Ildefonsus of Toledo (ca. 607–657), Julian of Toledo (642–690), and Bede (673–735). For example, Prosper writes that the "faith that justifies a sinner cannot be had except for God's gift, and it is not the reward for previous merits."[13] He goes on to explain that no one is so wicked as to be beyond the reach of God's grace; nor is anyone so good as to be able to earn God's grace:

> And just as there are no crimes so detestable that they can prevent the gift of grace, so too there can be no works so eminent that they are owed in deserved judgment that which is given freely. Would not the redemption of Christ's blood be debased, and would not God's mercy be made secondary to human works, if justification, which is through grace, were owed in view of preceding merits, so that it were not the gift of a Donor, but the wages of a laborer?[14]

Along those lines, Fulgentius observes, "The blessed Paul argues that we are saved by faith, which he declares to be not from us but a gift from God. Thus there cannot possibly be true salvation where there is no true faith, and, since this faith is divinely enabled, it is without doubt bestowed by his free generosity."[15] Ildefonsus similarly observes that justification is given through faith in Christ: "Behold, he [Paul] preached the beginning of faith which, when it is in Christ, is justification for the believer."[16] Elsewhere, he reiterates that this justification is received apart from good works, "God, who makes the unclean clean and removes sins, justifies the sinner apart from works."[17] The Venerable Bede similarly affirms that "the apostle Paul preached that we are justified by faith without works,"[18] yet he is also careful to emphasize that genuine saving faith inevitably produces the fruit of good works in a believer's life.[19]

In the late Middle Ages, no theologian expresses the reality of justification by grace through faith, apart from works, more forcefully than Bernard of Clairvaux (1090–1153).[20] For anyone who might claim to be justified through his own efforts, Bernard responds emphatically, "Nobody will be justified in His sight by works of the law. . . . Conscious of our deficiency, we shall cry to heaven and God will have mercy on us. And on that day we shall know that God has saved us, not by the righteous works that we ourselves have done, but according to His mercy."[21] Speaking of his own Christian conversion, Bernard acknowledges, "Therefore my beginning is solely of grace, and I have nothing which I can attribute to myself in predestination or in calling."[22] Thus, he can exclaim, "Grace freely justifies me and sets me free from slavery to sin."[23] Based on such statements, Nick Needham observes that "one of Augustine's greatest disciples, Bernard of Clairvaux, was teaching a Protestant-type concept of justification as late as the 12th century."[24]

Without doubt, a number of post-Augustinian theologians spoke of justification by grace through faith apart from works.[25] In at least some of these instances, we see clear similarities with the later teachings of the Reformers. It should also be noted that throughout the medieval period, a number of Latin commentators echoed the Pauline language of faith alone (*sola fide*) when commenting on justification in the book of Romans. Examples include Cassiodorus (ca. 485–583),[26] Lanfranc of Bec (ca. 1003–1089),[27] Bruno of Cologne (1032–1101),[28] and Robert of Melun (ca. 1100–1167).[29] A survey of these medieval commentators suggests that they limited their understanding of justification primarily to the remission of past sins only.[30] Nonetheless, it is significant to note that the Reformers were not the first to use the phrase *sola fide* in their interpretation of Romans.[31]

In searching for medieval anticipations of Reformation teaching, it is necessary to devote further consideration to the three distinctives we have been highlighting in our study: the forensic nature of justification, a distinction between justification and sanctification, and the imputed righteousness of Christ. The question before us is whether or not glimpses of these specific distinctives can be found in the writings of post-Augustinian theologians.

THE FORENSIC NATURE OF JUSTIFICATION

In his study *Justification in Earlier Medieval Theology*, Charles P. Carlson concludes that throughout the medieval period, the Western church generally defined justification in forensic terms.[32] Gregory the Great (ca. 540–604), for example, writes, "Therefore our righteous Advocate defends us as righteous in the judgment, because we both know and accuse ourselves as unrighteous. And so let us trust not in our tears or in our works but in the fact that we have an advocate."[33] He is not alone. Bernard of Clairvaux argues that any charges brought against believers are dismissed on account of Christ's righteousness, writing,

> Who shall bring any accusation against the elect of God? To me it is sufficient, for all righteousness, only to have Him propitiated, against whom only I have sinned. Everything, which He will have decreed not to impute to me, is thus as if it had never been. Freedom from all sin is the righteousness of God; the pure indulgence [pardon] of God is the righteousness of man.[34]

Bernard's words picture the courtroom of heaven, where no accusation can be brought successfully against believers because their sins are not imputed to them. Instead, they have been pardoned by God on account of Christ. Believers, therefore, are deemed righteous.

A generation before Bernard, Anselm of Canterbury (1033–1109) articulated salvation in forensic terms through his satisfaction theory of the atonement. In his famous work, *Cur Deus Homo* ("Why God Became Man"), Anselm taught that human beings owe God a debt of honor on account of their sin.[35] As Anselm explains, "Everyone who sins is under an obligation to repay to God the honour which he has violently taken from him, and this is the satisfaction which every sinner is obliged to give to God."[36] Because God is just, He cannot simply overlook the debt of sin that is owed to Him.[37] Consequently, sinners cannot be saved without paying back all that they owe; yet, they are utterly unable to do so. Each sinner is bound "by a debt which he cannot repay, [having] thrown himself into this state of incapacity by his guilt."[38]

Only God is able to make the satisfaction that is required.

Consequently, "since only God can, and only humans ought to, make the necessary satisfaction, it must be made by someone who is both God and human."[39] Thus, God the Son became man so that He might pay humanity's debt and satisfy divine justice.[40] Though He owed God nothing, Jesus Christ gave up His life for the sake of hopelessly indebted sinners. He paid a debt He did not owe in order to save those who owed what they could never repay.[41]

Anselm teaches that the incarnation became a necessity so that God the Son, by becoming the Son of Man, might redeem fallen human beings and reconcile them to God. Consequently, the mercy of God is placed on glorious display through the death of His Son: "What, indeed, can be conceived of more merciful than that God the Father should say to a sinner condemned to eternal torments and lacking any means of redeeming himself, 'Take my only-begotten Son and give him on your behalf,' and that the Son himself should say, 'Take me and redeem yourself.'"[42] Based on this, Anselm appeals to unbelievers to believe in Christ so that they might be saved by grace through faith in Him.[43]

A full evaluation of Anselm's argument in *Cur Deus Homo* is outside the scope of this book. Nonetheless, Anselm clearly articulated a model of the atonement in which a forensic framework can be perceived.[44] Five centuries later, the Reformers built on this forensic foundation.[45] As John W. de Gruchy explains,

> Anselm's theory also prepared the way for the Protestant theory of penal substitution. Not only does Christ pay our debts, he is also punished for our faults. Through

> Christ's death on the cross in our place, the penalty for sin has been fully paid, God's righteousness is imputed to us fully by grace alone, and we are justified by faith alone.[46]

Consequently, the Reformers often looked to Anselm for the proper language to describe the atonement.[47]

Scholars such as F. W. Dillistone have observed that Anselm's view of the atonement is set within the context of civil law, where concepts such as honor, debt, and satisfaction feature prominently. The Reformers, by contrast, set the atonement within the context of criminal law, emphasizing guilt, punishment, and substitution. Yet both systems involve forensic interpretations of the atonement.[48] Accordingly, Anselm can tell a parable in which a king offers to pardon an entire city of rebellious people on account of the reconciling work of one innocent man: "Any people who acknowledge before or after that day that they wish to receive pardon through the act which is to be performed on that day, and that they accede to the agreement concluded on that occasion, will be absolved from all their past guilt."[49] Here Anselm illustrates a forensic understanding of justification by picturing absolution being granted in a royal court to many sinners on account of one person's righteous work.[50]

Anselm's *Prayers* and *Meditations* provide additional evidence that he understood salvation within a forensic framework.[51] In one of his prayers, Anselm compares the sinner's pardon to that of a convicted criminal. In the same way that a prisoner might be acquitted by an angry ruler for the sake of that ruler's son, so sinners are pardoned by God on account of His Son. Anselm writes, "Thus prisoners are to be delivered from dungeons; thus those who have been sold into slavery are to be set free from their chains; thus those who are awaiting the mournful sentence of death are not only to be acquitted, but over and above to obtain unexpected favor, when they plead before angry rulers the love of their beloved offspring."[52] Anselm proceeds to call upon God the Father, asking Him to show mercy and extend grace, not on account of his works—which deserve only death—but on account of His Son:

> Set me free from the bonds of my sins, by Your only co-eternal Son, I implore You; though my own deserts threaten the sentence of death, restore me to life, appeased by the intercession of Your most precious Son, who sits at Your right hand. For I know not what other intercessor I could bring before You for myself, save Him who is the propitiation for our sins, who sits at Your right hand interceding for us.[53]

In another place, Anselm speaks of heavenly judgment using courtroom language:

> On one side will be sins accusing, on the other justice terrifying: beneath, the fearful chaos of hell gaping; above, the Judge angry; within, conscience burning, without, the world blazing. . . . Who is He who is called the Angel of mighty counsel, who is called Savior, that I may call upon His name? Yes it is He, it is He Himself Jesus. He too is the Judge, in whose hands I tremble.[54]

Jesus is the Judge, yet Anselm finds comfort in knowing He is also the Savior. Thus, he comforts himself with these words, "Breathe again then, O sinner, breathe again, despair not, hope in Him, whom you fear. Flee to Him from whom you have fled. . . . For what else is Jesus but Savior?"[55] Though Satan may bring accusations against God's elect, the redeemed have no reason to fear because they have been justified through the death of Christ. Anselm asks the rhetorical question, "How then, being justified by His blood, shall I not be saved from wrath by Him? . . . Who will be my accuser, when His love covers the multitude of my sins?"[56]

At times, Anselm even speaks of Christ's death in ways that parallel Luther's explanation of the "wondrous exchange." Negatively, the sinner's guilt is transferred to Christ:

> O wonderful compact of judgment; O arrangement of unspeakable mystery! The unjust sins, and the Just is punished; the guilty errs, and the Innocent is beaten; the impious offends, and the Pious is condemned; what the evil deserves, the Good suffers; what the slave perpetrates, the Master pays the penalty for; what man commits, God endures. . . . For I have done wickedly, You suffer the penalty: I have committed sin, You are visited with the vengeance; I have been guilty of crimes, and You are subjected to torment; I have been proud, You are humbled; I have been puffed up, You are emaciated; I have shown myself disobedient, You, by being obedient to the Father, pay the penalty of my disobedience.[57]

Positively, repentant sinners receive from Jesus "good for evil, gifts for iniquity, merit for offense, righteousness for guilt, grace for faults."[58] On the cross, Christ endured the penalty for those who would believe in Him so that they might receive His merit, righteousness, and grace. In light of such statements, it is not difficult to draw parallels between Anselm and the Reformers.[59]

As we have seen from the writings of a number of post-Augustinian theologians, the language of "faith alone" continues after Augustine into the medieval period. Moreover, we see examples, especially in the writings of Anselm, in which salvation is described in forensic terms. But what about a distinction between justification and sanctification, and the imputed righteousness of Christ? To those issues we now turn.

CHAPTER TEN

RECKONED AS RIGHTEOUS

A number of significant developments and changes took place during the 1,100 years between Augustine and the Reformers. The fall of Rome, the consolidation of papal power in the west, the split between Roman Catholicism and Eastern Orthodoxy, the crusades, and the rise of scholasticism provide a few examples of these developments—each of which significantly impacted the history of the church. By the sixteenth century, Protestant theologians noted the pervasive corruption in the Roman Catholic system, and expressed a desire to return to the purity of the patristic period—a time in which biblical truth had not yet been eclipsed by man-made tradition.

While they were critical of certain developments within the church that took place during the Middle Ages, the Reformers nonetheless found affirmation for their views in the writings of selected medieval theologians. Chief among these were Anselm of Canterbury and Bernard of Clairvaux. In the previous chapter, we looked at places where post-Augustinian writers spoke about justification by faith alone, apart from works, and places where salvation was presented within a forensic framework. In this chapter, we will continue our survey of medieval writers by looking for both the distinction between justification and sanctification, and the notion of the imputation of Christ's righteousness.

JUSTIFICATION DISTINGUISHED FROM SANCTIFICATION

In his work on "Logic and Argumentation in *The Book of Concord*," Jayson Scott Galler seeks to answer whether any medieval theologians distinguished between the two graces of justification and sanctification.[1] Though a bit technical in places, Galler's response effectively rebuts the claim that the Reformers were the first in history to distinguish between justification and sanctification. Let's briefly consider three of the primary points Galler presents.

First, Galler explains that, in making a notional distinction between justification and sanctification, the Reformers were following in the line of the thirteenth-century theologian and philosopher Duns Scotus (ca. 1266–1308).[2] Commenting on the parallels between Duns Scotus and the Reformers, Anthony Lane observes,

> While it is true that no writer prior to the Reformation makes a formal and consistent distinction between justification and sanctification, it is not true that the distinction was never made. One example will suffice. Duns Scotus made a distinction between the "infusion

of grace [which] is a *real* change in man" and the remission of sins, which is "an ideal change within the divine mind and not within man himself."[3]

Lane continues:

> It is true that the medievals defined the word justification so as to include a real change in the sinner. While that precludes them from using Protestant terminology, it does not of itself prevent them from making the Protestant distinction using other words, as Scotus appears to have done. Again, the fact that for the medievals it is not possible for the sinner to be reckoned righteous without also being made righteous proves nothing since the Protestant doctrine also affirms the same.[4]

John M. Rist agrees, noting that Luther's understanding of justification included a "separation of ethics from salvation [that is, sanctification from justification] towards which Scotus and others had pointed the road."[5]

Second, Galler cites other examples of similar distinctions made during the medieval period.[6] For example, Thomas Aquinas viewed justification as consisting of four distinct yet causally linked steps, and Galler draws a parallel between him and the Reformers:

> While the Reformers might differ [from Thomas] on the precise steps or the sequence of the steps, their "notional distinction" between justification and sanctification by way of a causal relationship, rooted in medieval philosophy, is clearly similar to distinctions in the process of justification being made centuries before their time.[7]

Galler also points to the medieval notion of "double righteousness," noting its similarity to the Reformers' understanding of the difference between justification and sanctification. He explains that there is "medieval evidence both of *iustitia infusa* (infused righteousness) or *iustitia inhaerens* (inherent righteousness), which provides the basis for justification (its 'formal cause'), and of *iustitia acquisita* (acquired righteousness), which is subsequently established."[8] The Reformers similarly distinguished between an imputed righteousness of justification and the imparted righteousness of sanctification.[9]

Third, Galler contends that the doctrinal controversies of the sixteenth century necessitated a higher level of precision on the part of the Reformers. It is, therefore, understandable that the Reformers, in the face of such controversy, formalized a distinction that had previously been left undefined. Galler's point is that the Reformers were *refining* sound doctrine, not *inventing* new theology. To those who might accuse them of doctrinal innovation, he asks, "If controversy could force terminological precision at the end of the patristic period [during Augustine's battle against Pelagianism], why are controversy-forced refinements in terminology at the end of the medieval period questioned?"[10] While the Reformers may have articulated the doctrine of justification in a more precise way, they were not the first to posit notional distinctions between justification and sanctification.[11]

It is unfair, therefore, to accuse the Reformers of doctrinal innovation for maintaining a formal distinction between justification and sanctification, even while asserting that the two are inseparable. As Galler explains, in insisting that justification and sanctification are inseparable graces, the Reformers preserved a line of continuity with pre-Reformation theologians, even though the Reformers articulated a notional distinction between them.[12]

Finally, and more fundamentally, Lane notes that a distinction between justification (the believer's position) and sanctification (the believer's practice) can be observed by simply looking at the piety of the medieval period. He writes:

> It is true that theology prior to the Reformation made no systematic distinction between justification and sanctification. But this does not mean that the distinction was unknown . . . [since] it can be said that anyone who believes in the forgiveness of sins has made the distinction, at least implicitly. If my sins are forgiven it means that there is a difference between what I am (guilty) and how God views me (forgiven). The Protestant distinction between justification and sanctification is simply the formal development of this implicit distinction.[13]

That kind of practical distinction can be seen in the writings of Bernard of Clairvaux. Like Luther, who taught that believers are simultaneously sinful yet righteous, Bernard declared believers to be "holy sinners" who are "enslaved and free at the same time."[14] Four centuries after Bernard, the Reformers would build on that kind of sentiment, by distinguishing between the *positional righteousness* of justification and the *progressive holiness* of sanctification.

THE IMPUTED RIGHTEOUSNESS OF CHRIST

While some claim that no one in prior church history anticipated the doctrine of imputed righteousness, the reality is that glimpses of it can be found in the writings of post-Augustinian theologians.

Among Eastern writers, Theodoret of Cyrus articulates salvation in terms of the great exchange that took place on the cross. Commenting on 2 Corinthians 5:21, he writes, "[Christ] was called what we are ['sin'] in order to call us to be what he is ['the righteousness of God']."[15] In his commentary on Romans, he points to the sufficiency of Christ for salvation: "The Lord Christ is both God and the mercy seat, both the priest and the lamb, and he performed the work of our salvation by his blood, demanding only faith from us."[16] Consequently, the righteous sacrifice of Christ is more than enough to save those for whom He died.[17]

In the medieval West, Anselm of Canterbury anticipates the concept of imputation by describing salvation from sin in terms of a debt that only Christ can pay on the believer's behalf.[18] Anselm is explicit that sinners cannot satisfy what they owe by their own merits. As he declares, "Neither can I, by any merits of mine, obtain all things by which I may return to You and be acceptable in Your sight. For what can be due to my merits save the punishment of eternal death?"[19] If sinners are to be accepted in God's sight, it will not be on account of their merits. The debt of sin can only be repaid through the righteous working of another. Though the Son of God owed nothing, He became a man so that He "might pay this [debt of sin] for others who did not have the wherewithal to pay what they owed. For the life of that Man is more precious than everything which is not God, and surpasses every debt which sinners owe in satisfaction."[20] Notice that Anselm looks to Christ, whose life "surpasses every debt which sinners owe," as the only one who can satisfy God's justice.[21]

Anselm eloquently expresses this truth in a prayer:

> I have set before You my Advocate, Your beloved Son; . . . I have placed [Him] between You and me as a Mediator. I have sent Him up to You, I say, as an Intercessor through whom I trust for pardon. I have sent up in words, the Word, whom I have said to have been sent for my deeds; and I have paid to You the death of Your most holy offspring, which I believe to have been endured for me.[22]

Consequently, the sinner "who of himself merited punishment, by the Creator of the world merits pardon."[23] Thus sinners can plead with God to forgive their sins on account of the perfect obedience of Christ:

> O great Creator of the light, now forgive my faults, for the immeasurable toils' sake of Your beloved Son. Lord, I beseech You, let my impiety be forgiven because of His Piety; my obstinacy because of His meekness; my violence because of His gentleness! Now let His humility win back my pride; His patience, my impatience; His kindness, my hardness; His obedience, my disobedience; His calmness, my disquiet; His pleasantness, my bitterness; His sweetness, my anger; His love, my cruelty.[24]

Again, such language parallels Luther's "great exchange." The imperfection of the sinner is forgiven and covered by the perfect righteousness of the Savior.

Recognizing that salvation is entirely a work of God's grace, since we are "justified by [His] mercy,"[25] Anselm responds with words of praise to Christ for His redemptive work. He declares, "We adore You, O most precious price of our redemption; Atoning Victim, who by the mere wondrous sweetness of Your savor have inclined Your Father, who dwells in the heavens, to look down upon our humility, and alone have placated Him towards us."[26] It is only because of the sweet savor of the work of Christ that a holy God can look upon sinners with pleasure instead of wrath.

A powerful passage entitled "Exhortation to a Dying Man, Greatly Alarmed on Account of His Sins,"[27] which was historically credited to Anselm, clearly states that salvation depends solely on the merits of Christ. Using a question and answer method, this work seeks to console those who are about to die. It reads:

> Question; Do you confess that you have lived so wickedly, that eternal punishment is due to your own merits?
>
> Answer; I confess it.
>
> Qu. Do you repent of this?
>
> An. I do repent.
>
> Qu. Do you have the willingness to amend your life, if you had time?
>
> An. I have.

> Qu. Do you believe that the Lord Jesus Christ died for you?
>
> An. I believe it.
>
> Qu. Do you thank Him [for His passion and death]?
>
> An. I do thank Him.
>
> Qu. Do you believe that you cannot be saved except by His Death?
>
> An. I believe it.
>
> Come then, while life remains in you, in His death alone place your whole trust; in nothing else place any trust; to His death commit yourself wholly; with this alone cover yourself wholly; in this enwrap yourself wholly. And if the Lord your God wishes to judge you, say, "Lord, between Your judgment and me I present the death of our Lord Jesus Christ; in no other way can I contend with You." And if He says that you are a sinner; say, "Lord, I interpose the death of our Lord Jesus Christ between my sins and You." If He says that you have deserved condemnation; say, "Lord, I set the death of our Lord Jesus Christ between my evil deserts and You; and His merits I offer for those which I ought to have, but have not." If He says that He is angry with you; say, "Lord I set the death of our Lord Jesus Christ between Your wrath and me." And when you have completed this, say again, "Lord, I set the death of our Lord Jesus Christ between You and me."[28]

This list of poignant questions, written for members of the clergy, is followed by a set of questions written for lay-people in the church. That list culminates with the all-important question, "Do you hope and believe, that not by your own merits, but by the merits of the passion of Jesus Christ, you may attain to everlasting salvation?" The expected answer, "I do," is followed with this instruction, "If any oppose you, and should object to you, set between him and you the merits of Christ's passion."[29]

In this way, those preparing to die are instructed to trust wholly in the merits of Christ and not in themselves. The final question to the laity is especially clear in its reliance on the perfect merits of Christ for salvation. Sinners' only hope for salvation is to be covered by the righteousness of the Lord Jesus. In response to these words from the Middle Ages, A. H. Strong concludes, "The above quotation gives us reason to believe that the New Testament doctrine of justification by faith was implicitly, if not explicitly, held by many pious souls through all the ages of papal darkness."[30]

Bernard of Clairvaux also anticipated the doctrine of Christ's imputed righteousness. Like Anselm, Bernard insists that good works are insufficient to merit salvation. He acknowledges, "All that you need to know of merits is that they cannot meet your need."[31] Bernard understands that the good works of sinful human beings are worthless in the eyes of a holy God. He asks,

> What can all our righteousness be before God? Shall it not, according to the prophet, be viewed as a filthy rag: and, if it be strictly judged, shall not all our righteousness turn out to be mere unrighteousness and deficiency? What, then, shall it be concerning sins, when not even our righteousness itself can answer for itself?

> Wherefore, vehemently exclaiming with the prophet, "Enter not into judgment with your servant, O Lord," let us with all humility, flee to mercy; which alone can save our souls.[32]

Elsewhere, he adds, "You must believe, first of all that you cannot have forgiveness of sins save through the merciful forbearance [literally, pardon] of God; secondly, that no moral achievement at all can be yours except as God's gift; lastly, that by no moral effort can you merit eternal life unless it too be freely given to you."[33] In noting the Pharisee of Luke 7:39, who thought he could be saved through his own self-righteous efforts, Bernard points out, "He did not realize that righteousness or holiness is a gift of God, not the fruit of man's effort, and that the man 'to whom the Lord imputes no iniquity' (Ps. 31:2) is not only just but blessed."[34]

If the sinner is to be found pleasing in God's sight, he must rely on the merits of another. That righteous substitute is none other than Jesus Christ,[35] who died so that He might justify those who cannot justify themselves. As Bernard explains: "For the sake of your sins He will die, for the sake of your justification He will rise, in order that you, having been justified through faith, may have peace with God."[36] It is Christ's righteous sacrifice that satisfies God's justice for believers to whom that satisfaction is imputed. Elsewhere, Bernard declares,

> For what could man, the slave of sin, fast bound by the devil, do of himself to recover that righteousness which he had formerly lost? *Therefore he who lacked righteousness had another's imputed to him.* It was man who owed the

> debt, it was man who paid it. For if one, says [the apostle Paul], died for all, then all were dead, so that, as One bore the sins of all, *the satisfaction of One is imputed to all.*[37]

Notice that Bernard explicitly states that Christ's righteousness is imputed to those who had no righteousness of their own. The satisfaction of His sacrifice is credited to those who owed an infinite debt because they were slaves to sin and spiritually dead.

Even the most humble and holy Christians must rely on the Savior's righteousness and not their own. Bernard presents the apostle Paul as one such example, noting that "the crown Paul awaits is a crown of righteousness, but of God's righteousness, not his own." He continues, "This is the righteousness Paul is relying on, the promise of God, lest, in any way despising it and seeking to establish his own, he might be failing to submit to God's righteousness."[38] Applying that same principle to his own life, Bernard clings to the righteousness of the Savior rather than to any form of self-righteousness. Thus, he can say, "O Lord, I will remember Your righteousness alone. And it is mine; that is to say, You have become my righteousness from God."[39] And elsewhere he claims that the mercy of the Lord is his merit.[40] Recognizing his own inherent unworthiness, he places his heavenly hope in the merits of Christ:

> I confess myself most unworthy of the glory of heaven, and that I can never obtain it by my own merits. But my Lord possesses it upon a double title: that of natural inheritance, by being the only begotten Son of his eternal Father; and that of purchase, he having bought it with

> his precious blood. This second title he has conferred on me; and, upon this right, I hope with an assured confidence, to obtain it through his praiseworthy passion and mercy.[41]

Bernard concludes that God judges the sinner righteous in terms of faith alone based on the merits of Christ. He prayerfully declares to God,

> As for your justice, so great is the fragrance it diffuses that you are called not only just but even justice itself, the justice that makes men just. Your power to make men just is measured by your generosity in forgiving. Therefore the man who through sorrow for sin hungers and thirsts for justice, let him trust in the One who changes the sinner into a just man, and *judged righteous in terms of faith alone,* he will have peace with God.[42]

Those words provide one of the clearest anticipations of Reformation teaching from the medieval period. Sinners who hunger and thirst for righteousness can be both forgiven and "judged righteous in terms of faith alone."

In that same context, Bernard beseeches Christ with these words,

> Your passion is the last refuge, the only remedy. When wisdom fails, when righteousness is insufficient, when the merits of sanctity succumb: it then rescues us. For who, either from his own wisdom, or from his own righteousness, or from his own holiness, shall presume upon a sufficiency to salvation? . . . If Your blood interpose not for me, I am not saved.[43]

Bernard's point is that good works are utterly insufficient to save, including the good works performed by a believer. The finished work of Christ is the only grounds by which anyone can be assured of salvation. Later, in the same sermon, Bernard asks, "Whence is true righteousness, save from the mercy of Christ? . . . They alone are righteous who, from His mercy, have obtained the pardon of their sins."[44] Refusing to rely on his own righteousness, Bernard looks for that which is bestowed by divine mercy and grace on account of the work of Christ.

Commenting on these citations from a lengthy passage in Bernard's *Sermon* 22 on the Song of Solomon, Franz Posset notes the close connection with Luther: "This passage makes clear that the sixteenth-century Reformer's axiom 'faith alone' was not at all unique to him. Bernard and Luther shared this decisive conviction. This justification is imputed by God, declared Bernard, using the notion of imputation which Luther favored so much."[45] Though it was not always expressed with the precision or consistency of the sixteenth-century Reformers,[46] Bernard's articulation of Christ's imputed righteousness provides a clear anticipation of the doctrine taught by Luther and his fellow Protestants. Bernard's statements regarding the imputation of Christ's merit take on added significance in light of their influence in the thinking and writing of the Reformers.[47] Both Luther and Calvin frequently cited Bernard favorably.[48] As Gerald Bray observes, "It is instructive to remember that both Luther and John Calvin were deeply influenced by, and felt very close to, Bernard of Clairvaux."[49] Specifically, with regard to the doctrine of Christ's imputed righteousness, the Reformers viewed Bernard as a theological predecessor and ally.[50]

The medieval era, covering roughly a millennium of church history from shortly after the death of Augustine to the dawn of the Reformation, is admittedly vast. Nonetheless, in certain cases, anticipations of the Reformation doctrine of justification can be found.[51] In light of the evidence, it follows that the claims made by some—that there are no medieval anticipations of the Reformation doctrine of *sola fide*—are simply not accurate. Commenting on Luther's commitment to Scripture alone, grace alone, faith alone, and Christ alone, Franz Posset writes,

> These axioms should not be claimed as Luther's inventions, however, as has sometimes been insinuated in post-reformation and post-tridentine histories of the Church. They are grounded largely in the bernardine (and augustinian) monastic legacy which Luther retrieved and which he processed in his own way. . . . Although the doctrine of forensic justification had often been identified as the chief and distinct axiom of reformation teaching on salvation, we [have] noticed that Bernard occasionally sounds like [the] sixteenth-century reformers in this regard.[52]

He continues, "Luther's reliance on Scripture alone, grace alone, faith alone, and Christ alone referred back to axioms in the Middle Ages which were always valid."[53] In other words, neither Luther nor his fellow Reformers were the first in history to articulate the core principles of Protestant soteriology.

CHAPTER ELEVEN

COMING FULL CIRCLE

At the beginning of this book, we set out to determine whether the Reformation understanding of justification by faith alone was a sixteenth-century invention. The answer, as we've seen from our survey of church history, is conclusively no. From the homilies and commentaries of the church fathers to the writings and prayers of medieval church leaders, examples abound of authors who used the language of "faith alone" to describe salvation. Additionally, we've detected clear instances of a forensic understanding of justification, a distinction between justification and sanctification, and the teaching that Christ's righteousness is imputed to believers. And all of this coming from long before Luther and other leading Reformers.

The Reformers were convinced that the doctrine of justification by faith alone stands at the heart of the gospel. They understood its vital importance, which is why they took such a bold stand on this issue. They defended their position, first and foremost, by appealing to Scripture. Their commitment to biblical authority undergirded their commitment to gospel purity, the latter being built on the authoritative foundation of the former. Yet they also looked to church history for secondary affirmation of their views. Though they recognized that theologians from earlier periods of church history sometimes spoke about justification in ways that lacked consistent clarity, the Reformers nonetheless maintained that anticipations of *sola fide* could be found throughout pre-Reformation history—especially in the patristic age.[1]

We found that the Reformers were right to look to the patristic era for support. Many of the church fathers spoke about salvation in general, and justification in particular, in ways that parallel later Reformation teachings. We also discovered that Augustine—whose teaching on justification is strongly debated—may indeed be seen as a theological forefather of the Reformers. To be sure, Augustine introduced confusion into the study of justification through his interpretation of the word *iustificare,* which he took to mean "to make righteous" rather than "to declare righteous." Yet he also identifies aspects of justification that parallel closely the teachings of the Reformers—and more importantly, reflected what the Reformers saw in Scripture. That is why the Reformers appealed to him more than any other figure in post–New Testament history. Recognizing and appreciating those areas of continuity treats Augustine in a more balanced way and better fits the Reformers' attitude and indebtedness toward him.

We also found anticipations of the distinctive characteristics of *sola fide* in various post-Augustinian writers. In our survey of the eleven centuries between Augustine and the

Reformers, two Christian leaders stood out more than any other: Anselm of Canterbury and Bernard of Clairvaux. Along with Anselm's satisfaction theory of the atonement, we considered his devotional works, such as his *Meditations* and *Prayers*, in which he personalized and expanded on his understanding of salvation. We focused on times when he spoke about salvation using forensic language and places where he anticipated the "great exchange" of the gospel—in which the guilt of the sinner is transferred to Christ while the perfect merit of Christ is credited to the sinner. Of all of the medievals, however, Bernard is arguably the most notable example of a writer who anticipated Reformation teaching. Bernard used the language of justification by faith alone, and also taught the imputation of Christ's righteousness to the believer. The Reformers were highly influenced by Bernard's writings and held him in high regard, even if they did not accept everything he wrote.

Based on the totality of our historical survey, it simply cannot be maintained that the Reformation understanding of justification was a theological innovation never before anticipated in church history.[2] In keeping with the perspective of the Reformers, contemporary evangelicals can take solace in knowing that the doctrine of justification *sola fide* is anchored in the teaching of God's Word. Protestant evangelical theology rightly defines the gospel in terms of justification by grace alone through faith alone in Christ alone, because that is what Scripture teaches. For that reason, our primary defense of the gospel should be a biblical one. Yet as this study has demonstrated, it is also appropriate for evangelicals to appeal to church history for the sake of secondary affirmation. Clear anticipations of justification by faith alone can be found throughout the pre-Reformation period, both in the patristic era and in the Middle Ages. Consequently, evangelicals today can be greatly encouraged to know that the gospel they cherish is not a sixteenth-century invention. The truth of *sola fide* is authoritatively established in the Word of God and it is also affirmed throughout church history.

APPENDIX

VOICES FROM HISTORY

What follows are 100 selected quotes from church history highlighting salvation by grace alone and the truth that believers are justified solely through faith in Christ, apart from works.

JESUS CHRIST (CA. AD 30)

> Two men went up into the temple to pray, one a Pharisee and the other a tax collector. The Pharisee stood and was praying this to himself: "God, I thank You that I am not like other people: swindlers, unjust, adulterers, or even like this tax collector. I fast twice a week; I pay tithes of all that I get." But the tax collector, standing some distance away, was even unwilling to lift up his eyes to heaven, but was beating his breast, saying, "God, be merciful to me, the sinner!" I tell you, this man went to his house justified rather than the other; for everyone who exalts himself will be humbled, but he who humbles himself will be exalted." (Luke 18:10–14; cf. Luke 23:39–43)

As Moses lifted up the serpent in the wilderness, even so must the Son of Man be lifted up; so that whoever believes will in Him have eternal life. For God so loved the world, that He gave His only begotten Son, that whoever believes in Him shall not perish, but have eternal life. (John 3:14–16)

THE APOSTLE PETER (D. CA. 65)

Brothers, you know that in the early days God made a choice among you, that by my mouth the Gentiles would hear the word of the gospel and believe. And God, who knows the heart, testified to them giving them the Holy Spirit, just as He also did to us; and He made no distinction between us and them, cleansing their hearts by faith. Now therefore why do you put God to the test by placing upon the neck of the disciples a yoke which neither our fathers nor we have been able to bear? But we believe that we are saved through the grace of the Lord Jesus, in the same way as they also are. (Acts 15:7–11)

THE APOSTLE PAUL (D. CA. 67)

Believe in the Lord Jesus, and you will be saved, you and your household. (Acts 16:31)

Therefore let it be known to you, brethren, that through this Man [Jesus] is preached to you the forgiveness of sins; and by Him everyone who believes is justified from all things from which you could not be justified by the law of Moses. (Acts 13:38–39 NKJV)

But now apart from the Law the righteousness of God has been manifested, being witnessed by the Law and the Prophets, even the righteousness of God through faith in Jesus Christ for all those who believe; for there is no distinction; for all have sinned and fall short of the glory of God, being justified as a gift by His grace through the redemption which is in Christ Jesus; whom God displayed publicly as a propitiation in His blood through faith. This was to demonstrate His righteousness, because in the forbearance of God He passed over the sins previously committed; for the demonstration, I say, of His righteousness at the present time, so that He would be just and the justifier of the one who has faith in Jesus. . . . For we maintain that a man is justified by faith apart from works of the Law. (Rom. 3:21–28)

Now to the one who works, his wage is not credited as a favor, but as what is due. But to the one who does not work, but believes in Him who justifies the ungodly, his faith is credited as righteousness. (Rom. 4:4–5)

Therefore, having been justified by faith, we have peace with God through our Lord Jesus Christ, through whom also we have obtained our introduction by faith into this grace in which we stand; and we exult in hope of the glory of God. (Rom. 5:1–2)

But if it is by grace, it is no longer on the basis of works, otherwise grace is no longer grace. (Rom. 11:6)

Even so Abraham "believed God, and it was reckoned to him as righteousness." Therefore, be sure that it is those who are of faith who are sons of Abraham. The Scripture, foreseeing that God would justify the Gentiles by faith, preached the gospel beforehand to Abraham, saying, "All the nations will be blessed in you." So then those who are of faith are blessed with Abraham, the believer. (Galatians 3:6–9)

For by grace you have been saved through faith; and that not of yourselves, it is the gift of God; not as a result of works, so that no one may boast. (Ephesians 2:8–9)

More than that, I count all things to be loss in view of the surpassing value of knowing Christ Jesus my Lord, for whom I have suffered the loss of all things, and count them but rubbish so that I may gain Christ, and may be found in Him, not having a righteousness of my own derived from the Law, but that which is through faith in Christ, the righteousness which comes from God on the basis of faith, that I may know Him and the power of His resurrection and the fellowship of his sufferings, being conformed to His death; in order that I may attain to the resurrection from the dead. (Philippians 3:8–11)

But when the kindness of God our Savior and His love for mankind appeared, He saved us, not on the basis of deeds which we have done in righteousness, but according to His mercy, by the washing of regeneration and renewing by the Holy Spirit, whom He poured out upon us richly through Jesus Christ our Savior, so that being justified by His grace we would be made heirs according to the hope of eternal life. (Titus 3:4–7)

THE APOSTLE JOHN (D. CA. 100)

These have been written so that you may believe that Jesus is the Christ, the Son of God; and that believing you may have life in His name. (John 20:31)

CLEMENT OF ROME (D. CA. 100)

And so we, having being called through his will in Christ Jesus, are not justified through ourselves or through our own wisdom or understanding or piety, or works that we have done in holiness of heart, but through faith, by which the Almighty God has justified all who have existed from the beginning; to whom be the glory for ever and ever. Amen.[1]

POLYCARP (CA. 69–160)

Though you have not seen him, you believe in him with an inexpressible and glorious joy (which many desire to experience), knowing that by grace you have been saved, not because of works, but by the will of God through Jesus Christ.[2]

EPISTLE TO DIOGNETUS (SECOND CENTURY)

He gave His own Son as a ransom for us, the holy One for transgressors, the blameless One for the wicked, the righteous One for the unrighteous, the incorruptible One for the corruptible, the immortal One for them that are mortal. For what other thing was capable of covering our sins than His righteousness? By what other one was it possible that we, the wicked and ungodly, could be justified, than by the only Son of God? O sweet exchange! O unsearchable operation! O benefits surpassing all expectation! That the wickedness of many should be hid in a single righteous One, and that the righteousness of One should justify many transgressors![3]

IRENAEUS OF LYONS (CA. 130–202)

The Lord, therefore, was not unknown to Abraham, whose day he desired to see; nor, again, was the Lord's Father, for he had learned from the Word of the Lord, and believed Him; wherefore it was accounted to him by the Lord for righteousness. For faith towards God justifies a man.[4]

ORIGEN (CA. 182–254)

He [Paul] is saying that the justification of faith alone suffices, so that the one who only believes is justified even if he has not accomplished a single work.[5]

Who has been justified by faith alone without works of the law? Thus in my opinion that thief [who] was crucified with Christ should suffice for a suitable example. He called out to him from the cross, "Lord Jesus, remember me when you come into your kingdom!" In the Gospels, nothing else is recorded about his good works, but for the sake of this faith alone Jesus said to him, "Truly I say to you, today you will be with me in paradise."[6]

God is just, and therefore he could not justify the unjust. Therefore he required the intervention of a propitiator, so that by having faith in him those who could not be justified by their own works might be justified."[7]

MARIUS VICTORINUS (CA. 290–364)

Therefore righteousness is not from the law; that is, justification and salvation come not from the law but from faith, as is promised.[8]

The fact that you Ephesians are saved is not something that comes from yourselves. It is the gift of God. It is not from your works, but it is God's grace and God's gift, not from anything you have deserved.[9]

Only faith [*sola fides*] in Christ is salvation for us.[10]

God prefigured and foretold that man would be justified from faith. Therefore, just as it was reckoned as righteousness to Abraham because he had faith, so we too, if we have faith in Christ and every mystery of his, will be sons of Abraham. Our whole life will be accounted as righteous.[11]

A man is not justified by the works of the law but through faith and the faith of Jesus Christ. . . . It is faith alone that gives justification and sanctification."[12]

HILARY OF POITIERS (CA. 300–368)

Wages cannot be considered as a gift, because they are due to work, but God has given free grace to all men by the justification of faith.[13]

It disturbed the scribes that sin was forgiven by a man (for they considered that Jesus Christ was only a man) and that sin was forgiven by Him whereas the Law was not able to absolve it, since faith alone justifies.[14]

Because faith alone justifies . . . publicans and prostitutes will be first in the kingdom of heaven.[15]

God bestows his pardon for all our faults according to his mercy [literally, by his own gift] rather than our merit.[16]

BASIL OF CAESAREA (CA. 329–379)

This is perfect and pure boasting in God, when one is not proud on account of his own righteousness but knows that he is indeed unworthy of the true righteousness and is justified solely by faith in Christ. And Paul boasts that he despises his own righteousness, seeking that righteousness that is on account of Christ, which is the righteousness of God by faith.[17]

AMBROSE (337–397)

It is not because of your efforts, but because of the grace of Christ. "By grace you are saved," says the apostle. Therefore, it is not a matter of arrogance, but faith; to preach what you have received is not pride, but devotion.[18]

Perhaps it is that we are not justified by works, but by faith, because the weakness of the flesh is a hindrance to works, but the brightness of faith puts the error that is in man's deeds in the shadow and merits for him the forgiveness of his sins.[19]

We are not justified by the works of the law. Thus, I do not have the wherewithal to enable me to glory in my own works, I do not have the wherewithal to boast of myself, and so I will glory in Christ. I will not glory because I have been redeemed. I will not glory because I am free from sins, but because sins have been forgiven me. I will not glory because I am profitable or because anyone is profitable to me, but because Christ is an advocate in my behalf with the Father, because the blood of Christ has been poured out in my behalf.[20]

AMBROSIASTER (FOURTH CENTURY)

For the mercy of God had been given for this reason, that the law should cease, as I have often said, because God, taking pity on our weaknesses, decreed that the human race would be saved by faith alone, along with the natural law.[21]

They are justified freely because, while doing nothing or providing any repayment, they are justified by faith alone as a gift of God.[22]

God gave what he promised in order to be revealed as righteous. For he had promised that he would justify those who believe in Christ. He says in Habakkuk: "The righteous one lives by faith" (Hab. 2:4), so that while he has faith in God and in Christ, he may be righteous.[23]

Paul tells those who live under the law that they have no reason to boast basing themselves on the law and claiming to be of the race of Abraham, seeing that no one is justified before God except by faith.[24]

Those are blessed of whom God has decreed that, without work or any keeping of the law, they are justified before God by faith alone.[25]

Because this has been determined by God, that he who believes in Christ will be saved without work: by faith alone freely he receives forgiveness of sins.[26]

This he says, that without the works of the law, to an impious person (that is, a Gentile) believing in Christ, his faith is imputed for righteousness, as it was to Abraham. How then can the Jews imagine that through the works of the law they are justified with Abraham's justification, when they see that Abraham was justified not from the works of the law, but by faith alone? Therefore there is no need of the law, since an impious person is justified with God through faith alone.[27]

Paul says this because the righteousness of God is revealed in the one who believes, whether Jew or Greek. He calls it "the righteousness of God" because He [God] freely justifies the ungodly by faith, without works of the law, just as he says elsewhere: "That I may be found in him, not having a righteousness of my own, based on law, but that which is through faith in Christ, the righteousness from God that depends on faith." He says that this same righteousness is revealed in the gospel when God grants faith to man, through which he may be justified.[28]

JOHN CHRYSOSTOM (CA. 347–407)

[Regarding Peter in Acts 15:8–11:] Everywhere he places the Gentiles on an equal footing. "And he made no distinction between us and them but cleansed their hearts by faith." From faith alone, he says, they obtained the same gifts. This is also meant as a lesson to those [objectors]; this is able to teach them that faith alone is necessary, and not works or circumcision.[29]

But what is the "law of faith"? It is, being saved by grace. Here he shows God's power, in that He has not only saved, but has even justified, and led them to boasting, and this too without needing works, but looking for faith only.[30]

If then He has brought us near to Himself, when we were far off, much more will He keep us now that we are near. And let me beg you to consider how He everywhere sets down these two points; His part, and our part. On His part, however, there be things varied and numerous and diverse. For He died for us, and further reconciled us, and brought us to Himself, and gave us grace unspeakable. But we brought faith only as our contribution.[31]

Would you know how good our Master is? The Publican went up full of ten thousand wickednesses, and saying only, "Be merciful unto me," went down justified.[32]

Attend to this point. He Himself who gave the Law, had decreed, before He gave it, that the heathen should be justified by faith. . . . They said that he who kept not the Law was cursed, but he proves that he who kept it was cursed, and he who kept it not, blessed. Again, they said that he who adhered to faith alone was cursed, but he shows that he who adhered to faith alone, is blessed.[33]

For by faith alone He saved us. . . . Instead of a certain manner of life, He brought in faith. For that He might not save us to no purpose, He both Himself underwent the penalty, and also required of them the faith that is by doctrines.[34]

For as people, on receiving some great good, ask themselves if it is not a dream, as not believing it; so it is with respect to the gifts of God. What then was it that was thought incredible? That those who were enemies and sinners, justified by neither the law nor works, should immediately through faith alone be advanced to the highest favor. . . . It seemed to them incredible that a person who had misspent all his former life in vain and wicked actions should afterwards be saved by his faith alone. On this account he [Paul] says, "It is a saying to be believed."[35]

[God] has justified our race not by right actions, not by toils, not by barter and exchange, but by grace alone.

Paul, too, made this clear when he said: "But now the justice of God has been made manifest apart from the Law." But the justice [or, righteousness] of God comes through faith in Jesus Christ and not through any labor and suffering.[36]

Even faith, [Paul] says, is not from us. For if the Lord had not come, if he had not called us, how should we have been able to believe? "For how," [Paul] says, "shall they believe if they have not heard?" (Rom. 10:14). So even the act of faith is not self-initiated. It is, he says, "the gift of God" (Eph. 2:8c).[37]

The patriarch Abraham himself before receiving circumcision had been declared righteous on the score of faith alone: before circumcision, the text says, "Abraham believed God, and credit for it brought him to righteousness."[38]

Now since the Jews kept turning over and over the fact, that the Patriarch, and friend of God, was the first to receive circumcision, he [Paul] wishes to show, that it was by faith that he too was justified. And this was quite a vantage ground to insist upon. For a person who had no works, to be justified by faith, was nothing unlikely. But for a person richly adorned with good deeds, not to be made just from hence, but from faith, this is the thing to cause wonder, and to set the power of faith in a strong light.[39]

To have brought humanity, more senseless than stones, to the dignity of angels simply through bare words, and faith alone, without any hard work, is indeed a rich and glorious mystery. It is just as if one were to take a dog, quite consumed with hunger and the mange, foul and loathsome to see, and not so much as able to move but lying passed out, and make him all at once into a human being and to display him upon the royal throne.[40]

Whoever has become righteous through faith will live, not just in this life but in the one to come as well. . . . This righteousness is not ours but belongs to God, and in saying this Paul hints to us that it is abundantly available and easy to obtain. For we do not get it by toil and labor but by believing. Then, since his statement does not seem credible, if the adulterer and homosexual, the grave-robber and the magician are not only to be suddenly set free from punishment but to be made righteous, and righteous with the righteousness of God, Paul backs up his assertion from the Old Testament . . . showing that both the righteous and the sinners were justified by faith even then.[41]

JEROME (347–420)

We are saved by grace rather than works, for we can give God nothing in return for what he has bestowed on us.[42]

[Paul] shows clearly that righteousness depends not on the merit of man, but on the grace of God, who accepts the faith of those who believe, without the works or the Law.[43]

Paul says this in case the secret thought should steal upon us that "if we are not saved by our own works, at least we are saved by our own faith, and so in a way our salvation is of ourselves." Thus he added the statement that faith too is not in our own will but in God's gift.[44]

AUGUSTINE OF HIPPO (354–430)

Now, having duly considered and weighed all these circumstances and testimonies, we conclude that a man is not justified by the precepts of a holy life, but by faith in Jesus Christ; in a word, not by the law of works, but by the law of faith; not by the letter, but by the spirit; not by the merits of deeds, but by free grace.[45]

[Abraham] was justified not by his own merit, as if by works, but by the grace of God through faith.[46]

[Speaking of Old Testament saints] Of whatever virtue you may declare that the ancient righteous people were possessed, nothing saved them but the belief in the Mediator who shed his blood for the remission of their sins.[47]

The people who boast imagine that they are justified by their own efforts, and therefore they glory in themselves, not in the Lord.[48]

No man can say that it is by the merit of his own works, or by the merit of his own prayers, or by the merit of his own faith, that God's grace has been conferred upon him; nor suppose that the doctrine is true which those heretics hold, that the grace of God is given us in proportion to our own merit.[49]

There is another sense in this verse, "For nothing Thou shalt save them:" with not any merits of theirs going before Thou shall save them. . . . All in them is rough, all foul, all to be detested: and though they to Thee bring nothing whereby they may be saved; "For nothing Thou shall save them," that is, with the free gift of Thy Grace.[50]

But what about the person who does no work? Think here of some godless sinner, who has no good works to show. What of him or her? What if such a person comes to believe in God who justifies the impious? . . . When someone believes in him who justifies the impious, that faith is reckoned as justice to the believer, as David too declares that person blessed whom God has accepted and endowed with righteousness, independently of any righteous actions. What righteousness is this? The righteousness of faith, preceded by no good works, but with good works as its consequence.[51]

No one merits justification by his good works, since unless he has been justified he cannot do good works. Nevertheless God justifies the Gentiles by faith.[52]

The very reason, indeed, why he [the apostle Paul] so often declares that righteousness is imputed to us, not out of our works, but our faith, whereas faith rather works through love, is that no man should think that he arrives at faith itself through the merit of his works; for it is faith which is the beginning whence good works first proceed; since (as has already been stated) whatsoever comes not from faith is sin.[53]

CYRIL OF ALEXANDRIA (CA. 376–444)

For truly the compassion from beside the Father is Christ, as he takes away the sins, dismisses the charges and justifies by faith, and recovers the lost and makes [them] stronger than death. . . . For by him and in him we have known the Father, and we have become rich in the justification by faith.[54]

For we are justified by faith, not by works of the law, as Scripture says [Gal. 2:16]. By faith in whom, then, are we justified? Is it not in him who suffered death according to the flesh for our sake? Is it not in one Lord Jesus Christ? Have we not been redeemed by proclaiming his death and confessing his resurrection?[55]

PROSPER OF AQUITAINE (390–455)

Just as there are no crimes so detestable that they can prevent the gift of grace, so too there can be no works so eminent that they are owed in condign [deserved] judgment that which is given freely. Would it not be a debasement of redemption in Christ's blood [literally, would not the redemption of Christ's blood become valueless], and would not God's mercy be made secondary to human works, if justification, which is through grace, were owed in view of preceding merits, so that it were not the gift of a Donor, but the wages of a laborer?[56]

THEODORET OF CYRRHUS (CA. 393–457)

The doer of righteousness expects a reward, but justification by faith is the gift of the God of all.[57]

The righteousness of God is not revealed to everyone but only to those with the eyes of faith. . . . Paul quoted Habakkuk for the benefit of the Jews, because he wanted to teach them not to cling to the provisions of the law but to follow [their own] prophets. For many centuries before they had predicted that one day there would be salvation by faith alone.[58]

All we bring to grace is our faith. But even in this faith, divine grace itself has become our enabler. For [Paul] adds, "And this is not of yourselves but it is a gift of God; not of works, lest anyone should boast" (Eph. 2:8–9). It is not of our own accord that we have believed, but we have come to belief after having been called; and even when we had come to believe, He did not require of us purity of life, but approving mere faith, God bestowed on us forgiveness of sins.[59]

I consider myself wretched—in fact, wretched three times over. I am guilty of all kinds of errors. Through faith alone I look for finding some mercy in the day of the Lord's appearing.[60]

The Lord Christ is both God and the mercy seat, both the priest and the lamb, and he performed the work of our salvation by his blood, demanding only faith from us.[61]

MARCUS EREMITA (FIFTH CENTURY)

The kingdom of heaven is not a reward for works, but a gift of grace prepared by the Master for his faithful servants.[62]

FULGENTIUS OF RUSPE (462–533)

The blessed Paul argues that we are saved by faith, which he declares to be not from us but a gift from God. Thus there cannot possibly be true salvation where there is no true faith, and, since this faith is divinely enabled, it is without doubt bestowed by his free generosity.[63]

ILDEFONSUS OF TOLEDO (CA. 607–667)

Behold, he [Paul] preached the beginning of faith which, when it is in Christ, is justification for the believer.[64]

God, who makes the unclean clean and removes sins, justifies the sinner apart from works.[65]

JULIAN OF TOLEDO (642–690)

[This is] the righteousness of faith, by which we are justified. This faith is that we believe in him whom we cannot see, and that, being cleansed by faith, we will eventually see him in whom we now believe.[66]

BEDE (673–735)

The apostle Paul preached that we are justified by faith without works.[67]

SYMEON THE NEW THEOLOGIAN (949–1022)

Brethren and fathers, it is good that we make God's mercy known to all and speak to those close to us of the compassion and inexpressible bounty he has shown us. For as you know I neither fasted, nor kept vigils, nor slept on bare ground, but—to borrow the Psalmists' words—"I humbled myself" and, in short, "the Lord saved me." Or to put it even more briefly, I did no more than believe and the Lord accepted me.[68]

ANSELM OF CANTERBURY (1033–1109)

Now, the mercy of God which, when we were considering the justice of God and the sin of mankind, seemed to you to be dead, we have found to be so great, and so consonant with justice, that a greater and juster mercy cannot be imagined. What, indeed, can be conceived of more merciful than that God the Father should say to a sinner condemned to eternal torments and lacking any means of redeeming himself, "Take my only-begotten Son and give him on your behalf," and that the Son himself should say, "Take me and redeem yourself." For it is something of this sort that they say when they call us and draw us towards the Christian faith.[69]

O good Lord, do not remember Your justice against Your sinner, but remember Your mercy toward Your creature. Do not remember Your anger against the culprit, but remember Your mercy toward the miserable. The truth is that my conscience merits damnation, and my repentance suffices not for satisfaction; but surely Your mercy surpasses all offense.[70]

Look, O Lord, upon the face of Your Anointed, who became obedient to You even unto death, and let not the scars of His wounds be hidden from Your eyes forever, that You may remember how great a satisfaction for our sins You have received from Him. Would, O Lord, that You would put in the balance the sins by which we have deserved Your wrath, and the sufferings which Your innocent Son endured for us! Truly, O Lord, His sufferings will appear heavier and more worthy, that through them You should pour out Your mercies upon us, than our sins, that through them You should restrain Your compassion in anger. O Lord, Holy Father, let every tongue give thanks to You for the abundance of Your love, who spared not the only Son of Your heart, but gave Him up to death for us, that we might have so great and so faithful an Advocate in heaven before You.[71]

I have set before You my Advocate, Your beloved Son; Your glorious progeny I have placed between You and me as a Mediator. I have sent Him up to You, I say, as an Intercessor through whom I trust for pardon. I have sent up in words, the Word, whom I have said to have been sent for my deeds; and I have paid to You the death of Your most holy offspring, which I believe to have been endured for me.[72]

What sin could man commit, which the Son of God, made man, could not redeem? . . . Truly, O my God, if in a just balance were weighed the iniquities of man that sins, and the grace of the Creator who redeems, not so far is the east distant from the west, or the lowest hell from the highest point of heaven, as the love of the Redeemer surpasses the wickedness of the sinner.

Now then, O great Creator of the light, now forgive my faults, for the immeasurable toils' sake of Your beloved Son. Lord, I beseech You, let my impiety be forgiven because of His Piety; my obstinacy because of His meekness; my violence because of His gentleness! Now let His humility win back my pride; His patience, my impatience; His kindness, my hardness; His obedience, my disobedience; His calmness, my disquiet; His pleasantness, my bitterness; His sweetness, my anger; His love, my cruelty.[73]

Come then, while life remains in you, in Christ's death alone place your whole trust; in nothing else place any trust; to His death commit yourself wholly; with this alone cover yourself wholly; in this enwrap yourself wholly. And if the Lord your God wishes to judge you, say, "Lord, between Your judgment and me I present the death of our Lord Jesus Christ; in no other way can I contend with You." And if He says that you are a sinner; say, "Lord, I interpose the death of our Lord

Jesus Christ between my sins and You." If He says that you have deserved condemnation; say, "Lord, I set the death of our Lord Jesus Christ between my evil deserts and You; and His merits I offer for those which I ought to have, but have not." If He says that He is angry with you; say, "Lord I set the death of our Lord Jesus Christ between Your wrath and me." And when you have completed this, say again, "Lord, I set the death of our Lord Jesus Christ between You and me."[74]

[Question] Do you hope and believe, that not by your own merits, but by the merits of the passion of Jesus Christ, you may attain to everlasting salvation? [Answer] I do.[75]

BERNARD OF CLAIRVAUX (1090–1153)

Nobody will be justified in His sight by works of the law. . . . Conscious of our deficiency, we shall cry to heaven and God will have mercy on us. And on that day we shall know that God has saved us, not by the righteous works that we ourselves have done, but according to His mercy.[76]

Grace freely justifies me and sets me free from slavery to sin.[77]

What is hidden about us in the heart of God will be revealed for us, and His Spirit testifies and persuades our spirit that we are the children of God. But He convinces us of this by calling and justifying us by grace through faith.[78]

For the sake of your sins He will die, for the sake of your justification He will rise, in order that you, having been justified through faith, may have peace with God.[79]

Therefore my beginning is solely of grace, and I have nothing which I can attribute to myself in predestination or in calling.[80]

O you alone are truly blessed, to whom the Lord has not imputed sin; for there is no one who actually does not have sin. All have sinned; and all fall short of the glory of God. Yet, who shall bring any accusation against the elect of God? To me it is sufficient, for all righteousness, only to have Him propitiated, against whom only I have sinned. Everything, which he will have decreed not to impute to me, is thus as if it had never been. Freedom from all sin is the righteousness of God; the pure indulgence [pardon] of God is the righteousness of man.[81]

What can all our righteousness be before God? Shall it not, according to the prophet, be viewed as a filthy rag: and, if it be strictly judged, shall not all our righteousness turn out to be mere unrighteousness and deficiency? What, then, shall it be concerning sins, when not even our righteousness itself can answer for itself? Wherefore, vehemently exclaiming with the prophet, "Enter not into judgment with your servant, O Lord," let us with all humility, flee to mercy, which alone can save our souls.[82]

For what could man, the slave of sin, fast bound by the devil, do of himself to recover that righteousness which he had formerly lost? Therefore he who lacked righteousness had another's imputed to him. . . . It was man who owed the debt, it was man who paid it. For if one, says [the apostle Paul], died for all, then all were dead, so that, as One bore the sins of all, the satisfaction of One is imputed to all.[83]

The mercy of the Lord is my merit.[84]

I confess myself most unworthy of the glory of heaven, and that I can never obtain it by my own merits. But my Lord possesses it upon a double title: that of natural inheritance, by being the only begotten Son of his eternal Father; and that of purchase, he having bought it with his precious blood. This second title he has conferred on me; and, upon this right, I hope with an assured confidence, to obtain it through his praiseworthy passion and mercy.[85]

As for your justice, so great is the fragrance it diffuses that you are called not only just but even justice itself, the justice that makes men righteous. Your power to make men righteous is measured by your generosity in forgiving. Therefore let the man, who through sorrow for sin hungers and thirsts for righteousness, trust in the One who changes the sinner into a righteous man, and judged righteous in terms of faith alone, he will have peace with God.[86]

In the centuries after Bernard, we begin to see the rise of "pre-Reformers" like Peter Waldo (ca. 1140–1205), John Wycliffe (ca. 1320–1384), and Jan Huss (ca. 1369–1415). These men paved the way for the sixteenth-century Reformers, like Luther and Calvin.

ABBREVIATIONS

1 Apol.	*Apologia i (First Apology)*
1 Clem.	*1 Clement*
ACCS	*Ancient Christian Commentary on Scripture*
Ad Cor. Prim.	*Commentaria in epistulam ad Corinthios primam (Commentary on 1 Corinthians)*
Admon. Mor.	*Admonitio morienti et de peccatis suis nimium formidanti (Exhortation to a Dying Man, Greatly Alarmed on Account of His Sins)*
Ad Gal.	*Commentaria in epistulam ad Galatas (Commentary on Galatians)*
Ad Rom.	*Commentaria in epistolam ad Romanos (Commentary on Romans)*
Ad Tit.	*Commentaria in epistolam ad Titum (Commentary on Titus)*
Adv. Jud.	*Adversus Judaeos (Discourses against Judaizing Christians)*
Adv. Nest.	*Adversus Nestorium (Against Nestorius)*
ANF	*Ante-Nicene Fathers*
Apol.	*Apologeticus (Apology)*
Apol. sec.	*Apologia secunda/Apologia contra Arianos (Defense against the Arians)*
ARCIC	*Anglican Roman Catholic International Commission*
Bapt.	*De baptismo (On Baptism)*

Bapt. c. Donat.	*De baptismo contra Donatistas (On Baptism against the Donatists)*
Barn.	*Epistle of Barnabas*
BSac	*Bibliotheca Sacra*
C. du. ep. Pelag.	*Contra duas epistulas Pelagianorum ad Bonifatium (Against the Two Letters of the Pelagians, to Boniface)*
C. Jul.	*Contra Julianum (Against Julian)*
Cant. Alleg.	*In Cantica canticorum allegorica expositio (Allegorical Exposition of the Song of Songs)*
Catech.	*Catecheses (Catechetical Lectures)*
Catech. illum.	*Catecheses ad illuminados (Baptismal Instructions)*
CCSL	*Corpus Christianorum Series Latina*
Civ.	*De civitate Dei (The City of God)*
CO	*Corpus Reformatorum: Ioannis Calvini Opera quae supersunt omnia*
Comm. Eph.	*Commentariorum in Epistulam ad Ephesios (Commentary on Ephesians)*
Comm. Jo.	*Commentarii in evangelium Joannis (Commentary on the Gospel of John)*
Comm. Luc.	*Commentarius in Lucam (Commentary on Luke)*
Comm. Matt.	*Commentarius in Evangelium Matthaei (Commentary on the Gospel of Matthew)*
Comm. Oseam	*Commentarius in Oseam prophetam (Commentary on the Prophet Hosea)*
Comm. Rom.	*Commentarii in Romanos (Commentary on Romans)*

Comp. Aet. Sext.	*De comprobatione aetatis sextae (The Sixth Age)*
Corrept.	*De correptione et gratia (Admonition and Grace)*
CR	*Corpus Reformatorum*
CSEL	*Corpus Scriptorum Ecclesiasticorum Latinorum*
Cur Deus hom.	*Cur Deus homo (Why God became Man)*
De Spir. Sanct.	*De Spiritu Sancto (On the Holy Spirit)*
Ded. eccl.	*Dedicatione ecclesiae (Church Dedication)*
Diab.	*De diabolo tentatore (Concerning the Power of Demons)*
Dial.	*Dialogus cum Tryphone (Dialogue with Trypho)*
Did.	*Didache*
Diogn	*Epistle to Diognetus*
Div. quaest. LXXXIII	*De diversis quaestionibus LXXXIII (Eighty-three Different Questions)*
Div. quaest. Simpl.	*De diversis quaestionibus ad Simplicianum (Various Questions to Simplician)*
ECT	*Evangelicals and Catholics Together*
Enarrat.	*Enarrationes in Psalmos (Enarrations on the Psalms)*
Enarrat. Ep. Cath.	*In Epistulas Catholicas brevis enarratio (Enarrations on the General Epistles)*

Enchir.	*Enchiridion de fide, spe, et caritate (Enchiridion on Faith, Hope, and Love)*
Ep. Eph.	*In epistolam Pauli ad Ephesios (On Paul's Epistle to the Ephesians)*
Ep. Gal.	*In epistolam Pauli ad Galatas (On Paul's Epistle to the Galatians)*
Epist.	*Epistulae (Letters)*
Exc.	*De excessu fratris sui Satyri (On the Death of His Brother Satyrus)*
Exp. Act. Apost.	*Super Acta Apostolorum exposition (Exposition of the Acts of the Apostles)*
Exp. Jac.	*Expositio super epistolas catholicas, super divi Jacobi epsitolam (Exposition of the General Epistles, on James)*
Exp. prop. Rom.	*Expositio quarumdam propositionum ex Epistola ad Romanos (Propositions on the Epistle of Romans)*
Exp. Ps.	*Expositiones in Psalmos (Expositions of the Psalms)*
Exp. Ps. 118	*Expositio Psalm CXVIII (Exposition of Psalm 118)*
Exp. Rom.	*Explanatio in epistolam ad Romanos (Explanation of Romans)*
Faust.	*Contra Faustum Manichaeum (Against Faustus the Manichaean)*
Fest. annunt. Mar.	*In festo annuntiationis beatae Mariae virginis (For the Feast of the Annunciation of Mary)*
Fest. omn. sanct.	*In festo omnium sanctorum (For the Feast of All Saints)*

Fid. op.	*De fide et operibus (Faith and Works)*
Fort.	*Ad Fortunatum (To Fortunatus: Exhortation to Martyrdom)*
Frag.	*Fragmenta (Fragments)*
Gest. Pelag.	*De gestis Pelagii (Proceedings of Pelagius)*
Grat.	*De gratia et libero arbitrio (Grace and Free Will)*
Grat. Chr.	*De gratia Christi, et de peccato originali (The Grace of Christ and Original Sin)*
Grat. et lib. arb.	*Tractatus de gratia et libero arbitrio (On Grace and Free Will)*
Haer.	*Adversus haereses (Against Heresies)*
Hom. 1 Cor.	*Homiliae in epistulam i ad Corinthios (Homilies on 1 Corinthians)*
Hom. 1 Tim.	*Homiliae in epistulam ad Timotheum (Homilies on 1 Timothy)*
Hom. 2 Cor.	*Homiliae in epistulam ii ad Corinthios (Homilies on 2 Corinthians)*
Hom. Act.	*Homiliae in Acta apostolorum (Homilies on Acts)*
Hom. bapt.	*Homilia in sanctum baptisma (Homily on Holy Baptism)*
Hom. Col.	*Homiliae in epistulam ad Colossenses (Homilies on Colossians)*
Hom. Eph.	*Homiliae in epistulam ad Ephesios (Homilies on Ephesians)*
Hom. Ezech.	*Homiliarum in Ezechielem (Homilies on Ezekiel)*
Hom. Gal.	*Homiliae in epistulam ad Galatas commentarius (Homilies on Galatians)*

Hom. Gen.	*Homiliae in Genesim (Homilies on Genesis)*
Hom. Heb.	*Homiliae in epistulam ad Hebraeos (Homilies on Hebrews)*
Hom. humil.	*Homila de humilitate (Homily on Humility)*
Hom. Jo.	*Homiliae in Joannem (Homilies on John)*
Hom. Matt.	*Homiliae in Matthaeum (Homilies on Matthew)*
Hom. Phil.	*Homiliae in epistulam ad Philippenses (Homilies on Philippians)*
Hom. Ps. CXIV	*Homilia in Psalmum CXIV (Homily on Psalm 114)*
Hom. Rom.	*Homiliae in epistulam ad Romanos (Homilies on Romans)*
Hom. Tit.	*Homiliae in epistulam ad Titum (Homilies on Titus)*
HTR	*Harvard Theological Review*
Ign. Eph.	*Ignatius's Epistle to the Ephesians*
Inc.	*De incarnatione (On the Incarnation)*
Inc. Fil.	*De incarnatione Filii Dei (On the Incarnation of the Son of God)*
Interp. 2 Cor.	*Interpretatio secundae epistolae ad Corinthios (Interpretation of 2 Corinthians)*
Interp. Eph.	*Interpretatio epistolae ad Ephesios (Interpretation of Ephesians)*
Interp. Ps.	*Interpretatio in Psalmos (Interpretations of the Psalms)*
Interp. Rom.	*Interpretatio epistolae ad Romanos (Interpretation of Romans)*

Itin. des.	*De itinere deserti (Journey through the Desert)*
J Ecclesiast Hist.	*Journal of Ecclesiastical History*
Jac.	*De Jacob et vita beata (Jacob and the Happy Life)*
JETS	*Journal of the Evangelical Theological Society*
LW	*Luther's Works: American Edition*
Marc.	*Adversus Marcionem (Against Marcion)*
Mart.	*Exhortatio ad martyrium (Exhortation to Martyrdom)*
Med. et orat.	*Meditationum et orationum (Meditations and Prayers)*
MSJ	*Master's Seminary Journal*
NAC	*New American Commentary*
NICNT	*New International Commentary on the New Testament*
Ob. Val.	*De obitu Valentianiani consolation (Consolation on the Death of Emperor Valentinian III)*
Oct Epiph.	*In octava epiphaniae*
Oper. just.	*De his qui putant se ex operibus justificari (Those Who Think They Are Justified from Works)*
Orat.	*Orationes (Orations)*
Paed.	*Paedagogus (Christ the Educator)*
Paen.	*De paenitentia (On Repentance)*
Pat.	*De bono patientiae (The Advantage of Patience)*
Pecc. merit.	*De peccatorum meritis et remissione (Guilt and Remission of Sins)*

Pelag.	*Adversus Pelagianos (Against the Pelagians)*
Perf.	*De perfectione justitiae hominis (Perfection in Human Righteousness)*
PG	*Patrologiae cursus completus: Series Graeca*
PL	*Patrologiae cursus completus: Series Latina*
PNTC	*The Pillar New Testament Commentary*
Pol. Phil.	*Polycarp's Epistle to the Philippians*
Praed.	*De praedestinatione sanctorum (The Predestination of the Saints)*
Pro Dom. 1 Nov.	*Pro Dominica 1 Novembris (For Sunday, November 1)*
Ps. XC	*In Psalmum XC, qui habitat (On the Psalm, He That Dwelleth)*
Quis div.	*Quis dives salvetur (Salvation of the Rich)*
Sacr.	*De sacramentis (The Sacraments)*
S. Bern. vit. prim.	*Sancti Bernardi vita prima (First Life of Bernard)*
SBO	*Sanctus Bernhardus Opera omnia (Works of Bernard)*
Serm.	*Sermones (Sermons)*
Serm. Cant.	*Sermones in Cantica canticorum (Sermons on the Song of Songs)*
Sim. et Ann.	*Sermo de Simeone et Anna (Sermon on Simeon and Anna)*
Spir. et litt.	*De spiritu et littera (The Spirit and the Letter)*

Symb. Apost.	*Commentarius in symbolum Apostolorum (Commentary on the Apostle's Creed)*
Tract. bapt.	*Tractatus de baptismo (Tractate on Baptism)*
Tract. Ev. Jo.	*In Evangelium Johannis tractatus (Tractates on the Gospel of John)*
Tract. Ps.	*Tractatus in Psalmos (Tractates on the Psalms)*
Trin.	*De Trinitate (On the Trinity)*
Vir. Mar.	*De virginitate perpetua sanctae Mariae (The Perpetual Virginity of Mary)*
Virginit.	*De sancta virginitate (Holy Virginity)*
Voc. Gent	*Vocatione Gentium (Call of All Nations)*
WA	*D. Martin Luthers Werke: Kritische Gesamtausgabe, Schriften*
WTJ	*Westminster Theological Journal*

NOTES

Introduction

1. Francis Beckwith originally published these comments on his blog in May 2007. That blog is no longer online. However, similar sentiments are found in Francis J. Beckwith, *Return to Rome: Confessions of an Evangelical Catholic* (Grand Rapids: Brazos Press, 2009). See also Todd Pruitt, "Beckwith Back to Rome," *The Alliance of Confessing Evangelicals* (July 30, 2007), http://www.alliancenet.org/mos/1517/beckwith-back-to-rome.
2. For a look at the early church's commitment to the doctrine of *sola Scriptura*, see Nathan Busenitz, "The Ground and Pillar of the Faith: The Witness of Pre-Reformation History to the Doctrine of *Sola Scriptura*," in *The Inerrant Word: Biblical, Historical, Theological, and Pastoral Perspectives*, ed. John MacArthur (Wheaton, IL: Crossway, 2016), 115–133. Also see, William Webster, *Holy Scripture: The Ground and Pillar of Our Faith*, vol. 2 (Battle Ground, WA: Christian Resources, 2001); James White, "Sola Scriptura and the Early Church," in *Sola Scriptura*, ed. Don Kistler (Lake Mary, FL: Reformation Trust, 2009), 17–37.

Chapter 1: An Invention or a Recovery?

1. Martin Luther, *WA* 40/3.352. Cited in Thomas Schreiner, *Faith Alone: The Doctrine of Justification* (Grand Rapids: Zondervan, 2015), 40, n. 20.
2. For a survey of the Reformers demonstrating their insistence on repentance as an essential part of saving faith, see William Webster, *The Gospel of the Reformation* (Battle Ground, WA: Christian Resources, 1997).
3. Contemporary Catholic authors who reject the doctrine of faith alone include Robert A. Sungenis, Devin Rose, Stephen K. Ray, Scott Hahn, Francis J. Beckwith, Patrick Madrid, David Currie, Peter J. Kreeft, and Ronald K. Tacelli. Historically, Roman Catholic opposition to the doctrine of *sola fide* can be traced from Jacques-Bénigne Bossuet (1627–1704) and the Counter Reformation to 19th century leaders like John Henry Newman (1801–1890). Cf. Owen Chadwick, *From Bossuet to Newman: The Idea of Doctrinal Development* (Cambridge: Cambridge University Press, 1957).
4. Dave Armstrong, *Development of Catholic Doctrine: Evolution, Revolution, or an Organic Process?* (Raleigh, NC: Lulu, 2007), 13.
5. Ibid.
6. Ibid., 42–43.

7. R. C. Sproul, *What Is Reformed Theology?* (Grand Rapids: Baker, 1997), 28.
8. Jaroslav Pelikan, *The Riddle of Roman Catholicism* (New York: Abingdon Press, 1959), 48–49. See also Joel C. Elowsky, *We Believe in the Holy Spirit* (Downers Grove, IL: InterVarsity Press, 2009), 86.
9. John Calvin, *Institutes of the Christian Religion, 1536 Edition*, trans. Ford Lewis Battles (Grand Rapids: Eerdmans, 1989), 6. See also John Calvin, "Reply to Sadoleto," in *A Reformation Debate*, ed. J. C. Olin (New York: Harper, 1966), 62.
10. Philipp Melanchthon, *CR*, vol. 2, ed. Karl Gottlieb Bretschneider (New York and London: Johnson Reprint Corp. Frankfurt am Main: Minerva, 1963), column 884.
11. Martin Chemnitz, *Examination of the Council of Trent* in *Chemnitz's Works*, 4 vols., trans. Fred Kramer (St. Louis: Concordia, 1971), 1:505–513.
12. John Owen, *Justification by Faith* (repr., Grand Rapids: Sovereign Grace, 1971).
13. Jonathan Edwards, *Justification by Faith Alone* (repr., Morgan, PA: Soli Deo Gloria, 2000).
14. George Stanley Faber, *The Primitive Doctrine of Justification*, 2nd ed. (London: Seely and Burnside, 1839).
15. James Buchanan, *The Doctrine of Justification: An Outline of Its History in the Church and of Its Exposition from Scripture* (Edinburgh, Scotland: T&T Clark, 1867; repr., Grand Rapids: Baker, 1955).
16. Ibid., 80.
17. Anthony N. S. Lane, *Justification by Faith in Catholic-Protestant Dialogue: An Evangelical Assessment* (New York: T & T Clark, 2006), 137.
18. Matthew C. Heckel, "Is R. C. Sproul Wrong about Martin Luther? An Analysis of R. C. Sproul's *Faith Alone: The Evangelical Doctrine of Justification* with Respect to Augustine, Luther, Calvin, and Catholic Luther Scholarship," *JETS* 47, no. 1 (March 2004): 93.
19. Ibid.
20. Alister E. McGrath, *Iustitia Dei: A History of the Doctrine of Justification*, 3rd ed. (Cambridge: Cambridge University Press, 2005), 217. See also Alister E. McGrath, "Forerunners of the Reformation? A Critical Examination of the Evidence for Precursors of the Reformation Doctrines of Justification," *HTR* 75, no. 2 (1982): 219–220.
21. McGrath, "Forerunners of the Reformation?" 222–23; McGrath, *Iustitia Dei*, 212–13.
22. McGrath, "Forerunners of the Reformation?" 222.
23. Ibid., 219–20. See also *Iustitia Dei*, 211, where McGrath adds that without forerunners to their views of justification, "the Reformers' claim to catholicity would be seriously prejudiced, if not totally discredited."
24. Ibid., 241–42. See also *Iustitia Dei*, 218. It should be noted that McGrath views the Reformation position on justification positively. See Alister McGrath, *An Introduction to Christianity* (Cambridge, MA: Blackwell Publishers, 1997), 153–54. Elsewhere, McGrath writes: "In many ways, the Reformation may be regarded as a rediscovery of the Pauline writings, especially of the doctrine of justification by grace through faith" (Alister E.

McGrath, *Justification by Faith* [Grand Rapids: Zondervan, 1988], 53). See also Alister E. McGrath, "What Shall We Make of Ecumenism?" in *Roman Catholicism: Evangelical Protestants Analyze What Divides and Unites Us*, ed. John Armstrong (Chicago: Moody Press, 1994), 202–203.

25. See, for example, Dave Armstrong, *Bible Conversations* (Raleigh, NC: Lulu, 2007), 151; Steven K. Ray, *Crossing the Tiber: Evangelical Protestants Discover the Historical Church* (San Francisco: Ignatius Press, 1997), 27, n. 24; Robert A. Sungenis, *Not by Faith Alone: A Biblical Study of the Catholic Doctrine of Justification* (Goleta, CA: Queenship Pub Co., 1997), xxxi.
26. Francis J. Beckwith, *Return to Rome: Confessions of an Evangelical Catholic* (Grand Rapids: Brazos Press, 2009), 84–85.
27. Ibid., 85–92. Beckwith cites a number of church fathers, including Irenaeus, Cyril of Jerusalem, Chrysostom, and Augustine, to support his claims.
28. McGrath, "Forerunners to the Reformation?" 236. In spite of this emphasis on discontinuity, McGrath can elsewhere state: "Although some polemical accounts of the reformation tend to suggest that the Reformers abandoned fifteen hundred years of Christian tradition in order to found what amounted to a new religion, this view rests upon a series of misunderstandings" (Alister E. McGrath, *ARCIC II and Justification: An Evangelical Anglican Assessment of 'Salvation and the Church'* [Oxford: Latimer House, 1987], 7; cited from Sungenis, *Not by Faith Alone*, xxxi).

Chapter 2: Regaining Biblical Clarity

1. In this chapter and throughout this book, we will limit our study of the Reformers to the leading Reformers in the Lutheran and Reformed branches of the Reformation. Specifically, we will consider the writings of Martin Luther, Philip Melanchthon, John Calvin, and Martin Chemnitz. While recognizing that there was a diversity of opinion among other sixteenth-century Reformers, we will be using the term *Reformers* to refer specifically to Luther, Melanchthon, Calvin, and Chemnitz. Their positions on justification come to represent the standard Reformation viewpoint for later Lutheran and Reformed churches.
2. "Geneva Confession of 1536," in *Reformed Confessions of the Sixteenth Century*, ed. Arthur C. Cochrane (Louisville, KY: Westminster John Knox Press, 2003), 120.
3. Martin Luther, *Contra malignum Iohannis Eccii iudicium super aliquot articulis a fratribus quibusdam ei suppositis Martini Lutheri defensio* in *WA*, 2.626. Quoted in and trans. from John W. Montgomery, *God's Inerrant Word* (Minneapolis: Bethany Fellowship, 1974), 84.
4. Martin Chemnitz, *Examination of the Council of Trent*, in *Chemnitz's Works*, 4 vols., trans. Fred Kramer (St. Louis: Concordia, 1971), 1:477.
5. John Calvin, *Institutes of the Christian Religion*, ed. John T. McNeill, trans. Ford Lewis Battles (Louisville, KY: Westminster John Knox Press, 1960), 3.11.2–3.
6. For example, see Luther, *WA* 38.206; Paul Althaus, *The Theology of Martin Luther* (Minneapolis: Fortress Press, 1966), 338.

7. Noting the importance of *sola fide*, Luther declared, "If the article of justification be once lost, then is all true doctrine lost" (Martin Luther, *A Commentary on St. Paul's Epistle to the Galatians*, trans. Erasmus Middleton, ed. John Prince Fallowes [Grand Rapids: Kregel, 1979], xvi; *WA* 40.47.28). Calvin similarly regarded it as the "main hinge upon which religion turns" (*Institutes* 3.11.1).
8. Martin Luther, "Lectures on Galatians, 1535," in *Luther's Works*, vol. 26, trans. Jaroslav Pelikan (St. Louis: Concordia, 1963), 57–58.
9. Philip Melanchthon, *Melanchthon on Christian Doctrine: Loci Communes, 1555*, trans. and ed. Clyde L. Manschreck (New York: Oxford University Press, 1965), 162.
10. Philip Melanchthon, *Commentary on Romans*, trans. Fred Kramer (St. Louis: Concordia, 1992), 25. See also Melanchthon, *Melanchthon on Christian Doctrine: Loci Communes, 1555*, 156.
11. Calvin, *Institutes*, 3.12.1.
12. Ibid.
13. Ibid., 3.11.2. See also 3.14.12.
14. It is acknowledged that not all the Reformers viewed justification in precisely the same way. See Alister E. McGrath, *Iustitia Dei: A History of the Doctrine of Justification*, 3rd ed. (Cambridge: Cambridge University Press, 2005), 234–56, for a discussion about the similarities and differences between Luther and others like Johannes von Staupitz, Andreas Karlstadt, Johann Bugenhagen, Andreas Osiander, Francesco Stancari, Huldrych Zwingli, Johannes Oecolampadius, Heinrich Bullinger, and Martin Bucer. This author is convinced that Luther and Melanchthon were in agreement on their understanding of justification. See, for example, Carl Trueman, "*Simul peccator et justus*: Martin Luther and Justification," in *Justification in Perspective*, ed. Bruce L. McCormack (Grand Rapids: Baker Academic, 2006), 91–92. And John Calvin held essentially the same understanding of justification.
15. See Calvin, *Institutes*, 3.11.2.
16. Melanchthon, *Commentary on Romans*, 25.
17. Calvin, *Institutes*, 3.11.11.
18. Chemnitz, *Examination of the Council of Trent*, in *Chemnitz's Works*, 1:470–471, 476.
19. Ibid., 1:474.
20. Ibid., 1:475.
21. Calvin, *Institutes*, 3.11.11.
22. Martin Luther, *Commentary on the Epistle to the Romans*, trans. J. Theodore Mueller (Grand Rapids: Zondervan, 1954; repr., Grand Rapids: Kregel, 1967), 97. Chemnitz, *Examination of the Council of Trent*, in *Chemnitz's Works*, 1:473, agrees, noting that both in Rom. 8:33–34 and "also in Rom. 5 justification and condemnation are repeatedly placed in opposition to each other." Chemnitz also notes Matt. 12:37 as an example of this (Ibid., 1:476).
23. John Calvin, *The Second Epistle of Paul the Apostle to the Corinthians and the Epistles to Timothy, Titus and Philemon*, trans. T. A. Smail, eds. David W. and Thomas F. Torrance (Grand Rapids: Eerdmans, 1964), 233. Calvin also mentions Matt. 11:19 and Luke 7:35, 39 in this same context.

24. John Calvin, *A Harmony of the Gospels Matthew, Mark and Luke*, 3 vols., trans. T. H. L. Parker, eds. David W. and Thomas F. Torrance (Grand Rapids: Eerdmans, 1972), 2:9–10.
25. See Chemnitz, *Examination of the Council of Trent*, in *Chemnitz's Works*, 1:487, 489.
26. Based on his study of Romans, Melanchthon, *Commentary on Romans*, 25, concludes, "Thus we know for certain that in these disputations of Paul justification signifies the remission of sins and acceptance to eternal life, as the fourth chapter of Romans testifies in a sufficiently clear manner, where it defines justification as the forgiveness of sins. Therefore when we say we are justified by faith it is the same thing as saying that we are accounted just by God on account of Christ when we believe." John Calvin, *The Epistles of Paul the Apostle to the Romans and to the Thessalonians*, trans. Ross Mackenzie, eds. David W. and Thomas F. Torrance (Grand Rapids: Eerdmans, 1959), 5, interpreted Romans through a similar lens, asserting that "the main subject of the whole Epistle . . . is that we are justified by faith."
27. Commenting on Romans 2:13, John Calvin, *The Epistles of Paul the Apostle to the Romans and to the Thessalonians*, 47, writes, "We do not deny that absolute righteousness is prescribed in the law, but since all men are convicted of offense, we assert the necessity of seeking for another righteousness. Indeed, we can prove from this passage that no one is justified by works. If only those who fulfill the law are justified by the law, it follows that no one is justified, for no one can be found who can boast of having fulfilled the law." See also Melanchthon, *Commentary on Romans*, 142–43.
28. As Melanchthon, *Commentary on Romans*, 40, explains, "The Word of God nevertheless testifies that no one satisfies the Law. It accuses men who trust in their own righteousness, and puts forward the Mediator, the Son of God. . . . The voice of the Gospel . . . commands us to approach God although we are unworthy, but are trusting in the Mediator, the Son of God."
29. Modern commentators agree with the Reformers' assessment. In the words of Douglas Moo, *The Epistle to the Romans*, The New International Commentary on the New Testament (Grand Rapids: Eerdmans, 1997), 86: "It is now generally agreed, then, that *dikaioō* in Paul means not 'make righteous' but 'declare righteous,' or 'acquit,' on the analogy of the verdict pronounced by a judge. To justify signifies, according to forensic usage, to acquit a guilty one and declare him or her righteous." See also Everett F. Harrison, "Romans," in *The Expositor's Bible Commentary*, 12 vols., ed. Frank E. Gaebelein (Grand Rapids: Zondervan, 1976), 10:42.

Chapter 3: Clothed in Christ's Righteousness

1. These definitions of "justification" and "sanctification" are from Alister E. McGrath, *Iustitia Dei: A History of the Doctrine of Justification*, 3rd ed. (Cambridge: Cambridge University Press, 2005), 213.
2. Since justification is declarative and immediate, rather than transformative and gradual, it must be differentiated from regeneration and progressive sanctification. Whereas justification consists of divine pardon and a legal declaration of righteousness, sanctification involves the Spirit's continuing

work of transforming the regenerated sinner into the image of Christ (2 Cor. 3:18). Progressive sanctification begins at the moment of regeneration—which occurs at the same time as justification—when the sinner is born again and his heart is transformed by the Holy Spirit (see John 3:3–8; Titus 3:5).

3. Martin Luther, *Commentary on Galatians*, ed. John Prince Fallowes, trans. Erasmus Middleton (Grand Rapids: Kregel, 1979), 148; *WA* 40.402.24. See also Martin Luther, "Concerning Christian Liberty," in *Luther's Primary Works*, eds. Henry Wace and C. A. Buchheim (London: Hodder & Stoughton, 1896), 275–277, 288.
4. Luther, *Commentary on Galatians*, 151–52. On Gal. 3:10.
5. Martin Luther, "Two Kinds of Righteousness," in *Martin Luther's Basic Theological Writings*, eds. Timothy F. Lull and William R. Russell (Minneapolis: Fortress, 1989), 156–58. Cited from William Webster, *The Gospel of the Reformation* (Battle Ground, WA: Christian Resources, 1997), 72–73.
6. For a discussion of Luther's emphasis on "alien righteousness" (*iustitia aliena*), see Paul ChulHong Kang, *Justification: The Imputation of Christ's Righteousness from Reformation Theology to the American Great Awakening and the Korean Revivals* (New York: Peter Lang, 2006), 65.
7. Luther, *Commentary on Galatians*, 151–52.
8. Luther, "Two Kinds of Righteousness," 157–58.
9. Luther, *Commentary on Galatians*, 222.
10. Philip Melanchthon, *Melanchthon on Christian Doctrine: Loci Communes, 1555*, trans. and ed. by Clyde L. Manschreck (New York: Oxford University Press, 1965), 163. Also see Philip Melanchthon, *Commentary on Romans*, trans. by Fred Kramer (St. Louis: Concordia, 1992), 144.
11. Melanchthon, *Melanchthon on Christian Doctrine: Loci Communes, 1555*, 171. See also 175–86; Philip Melanchthon, "Love and Hope," in *Melanchthon and Bucer* (The Library of Christian Classics Volume XIX) (Philadelphia: Westminster, 1969), 112.
12. John Calvin, *Institutes of the Christian Religion*, ed. John T. McNeill, trans. Ford Lewis Battles (Louisville, KY: Westminster John Knox Press, 1960), 3.11.14.
13. Ibid., 3.11.11.
14. Ibid., 3.11.6.
15. Ibid., 3.11.6.
16. Ibid., 3.16.1. Regarding this passage, Alistair E. McGrath, *Studies in Doctrine* (Grand Rapids: Zondervan, 1997), 395, explains, "In other words, although justification and sanctification may be *distinguished*, they cannot be *separated*."
17. See Calvin, *Institutes*, 3.14.9: "Christ lives in us in two ways. The one life consists in governing us by his Spirit, and directing all our actions; the other, in making us partakers of his righteousness; so that, while we can do nothing of ourselves, we are accepted in the sight of God. The first relates to regeneration, the second to justification by free grace."
18. John Calvin, *Commentaries on the Epistles of Paul to the Galatians and Ephesians*, trans. William Pringle (repr., Grand Rapids: Baker, 1979), 74.

19. Calvin, *Institutes*, 3.11.6. See I. John Hesselink, "Pneumatology," in *The Calvin Handbook*, ed. Herman J. Selderhuis (Grand Rapids: Eerdmans, 2009), 307, who writes, "A key verse in this connection [between justification and sanctification] is 1 Corinthians 1:30, a text Calvin returns to again and again." See also Calvin, *The First Epistle of Paul the Apostle to the Corinthians*, trans. John W. Fraser, eds. David W. and Thomas F. Torrance (Grand Rapids: Eerdmans, 1959), 46, where Calvin states that "it would be wrong, to confuse what Paul expressly separates." See also, *Examination of the Council of Trent*, in *Chemnitz's Works*, 4 vols., trans. Fred Kramer (St. Louis: Concordia, 1971),, 1:472.
20. John Calvin, *The Epistles of Paul the Apostle to the Romans and to the Thessalonians*, trans. Ross Mackenzie, eds. David W. and Thomas F. Torrance (Grand Rapids: Eerdmans, 1959), 7–8.
21. See Melanchthon, *Commentary on Romans*, 151; Calvin, *The Epistles of Paul the Apostle to the Romans and to the Thessalonians*, 136; Chemnitz, *Examination of the Council of Trent*, in *Chemnitz's Works*, 1:472.
22. Melanchthon, *Commentary on Romans*, 160.
23. See Luther's Lectures on Romans, *WA* 56.269–73.
24. As Luther, *Commentary on Galatians*, 166–67, explained, "And this is a singular consolation for all Christians, so to clothe Christ with our sins, and to wrap Him in my sins, thy sins, and the sins of the whole world, and so to behold Him bearing all our iniquities."
25. Luther, *Commentary on Galatians*, 172. I have updated the English for clarity.
26. Martin Luther, *Commentary on the Epistle to the Romans*, trans. J. Theodore Mueller (Grand Rapids: Zondervan, 1954; repr., Grand Rapids: Kregel, 1967), 96–97.
27. See Luther, *Commentary on the Epistle to the Romans*, xix. Commenting on Gal. 3:27, Luther articulates the benefits of being clothed in the imputed righteousness of Christ: "To be appareled with Christ according to the gospel, is not to be appareled with the law, nor with works, but with an incomparable gift; that is to say, with remission of sins, righteousness, peace, consolation, joy of spirit, salvation, life, and Christ Himself" (Luther, *Commentary on Galatians*, 222).
28. Melanchthon, *On Christian Doctrine: Loci Communes, 1555*, 156. See also 169.
29. Ibid., 162. It might be noted that Melanchthon linked this righteousness with Christ's active obedience here on earth. See 167–68.
30. Calvin, *Institutes*, 3.11.23.
31. Ibid., 3.14.12. For similar statements from Chemnitz, see *Examination of the Council of Trent* in *Chemnitz's Works*, 1:501.
32. Chemnitz, *Examination of the Council of Trent*, in *Chemnitz's Works*, 1:502.
33. For Acts 13:38–39, see Calvin, *Institutes*, 3.11.3. Regarding Rom. 3:21–4:5, see Melanchthon, *On Christian Doctrine: Loci Communes, 1555*, 156; Calvin, *Institutes*, 3.11.4; Chemnitz, *Examination of the Council of Trent*, in *Chemnitz's Works*, 4.17–18. For Rom. 5:18–19, see Luther, *Commentary on*

the Epistle to the Romans, 97; Calvin, *Institutes*, 3.11.23; Chemnitz, *Examination of the Council of Trent*, in *Chemnitz's Works*, 1.7.6. Concerning Rom. 10:4, see Melanchthon, *Commentary on Romans*, 195; Calvin, *The Epistle of Paul the Apostle to the Romans and to the Thessalonians*, 221–22. For 1 Cor. 1:30, see Calvin, *The First Epistle of Paul the Apostle to the Corinthians*, 46; Chemnitz, *Examination of the Council of Trent*, in *Chemnitz's Works*, 1.3.15.

34. Chemnitz, *Examination of the Council of Trent*, in *Chemnitz's Works*, 1:502.
35. John Calvin, *The Second Epistle of Paul the Apostle to the Corinthians and the Epistles to Timothy, Titus and Philemon*, trans. T. A. Small (Grand Rapids: Eerdmans, 1959), 81–82.
36. Calvin, *Institutes*, 3.11.4.
37. In addition to pointing to Phil. 3:7–9, Calvin, *Institutes*, 3.11.11, also highlights Rom. 7:24, where Paul states that he did not rely on his own righteousness.
38. John Calvin, *The Epistles of Paul The Apostle to the Galatians, Ephesians, Philippians and Colossians* [Calvin's Commentaries], trans. T. H. L. Parker, eds. David W. and Thomas F. Torrance (Grand Rapids: Eerdmans, 1959), 275. See also Chemnitz, *Examination of the Council of Trent*, in *Chemnitz's Works*, 1:486. Chemnitz continues by quoting Phil. 3:9–10.
39. To these passages teaching the imputation of Christ's righteousness, Chemnitz, *Examination of the Council of Trent*, in *Chemnitz's Works*, 1:502–504, adds Isa. 53:5–6, 11; Jer. 23:6; Matt. 20:28; Rom. 5:9; 8:3–4, 32; Gal. 3:1, 27; 4:4–5; 1 Tim. 2:6.
40. See John M. Headley, *Luther's View of Church History* (New Haven, CT: Yale University Press, 1963), 143–61; Manfred Schulze, "Martin Luther and the Church Fathers," in *The Reception of the Church Fathers in the West: From the Carolingians to the Maurists*, 2 vols., ed. Irena Backus (Leiden, Netherlands: E. J. Brill, 1997), 2:612; James R. Payton, *Getting the Reformation Wrong: Correcting Some Misunderstandings* (Downers Grove, IL: InterVarsity, 2010), 139–40; Mark Ellingsen, "Augustinian Origins of the Reformation Reconsidered," *Scottish Journal of Theology* 64, no. 1 (February 2011): 13–28. Though Luther is critical of Augustine at times, he never fully rejects him (see Ellingsen, "Augustinian Origins," 21).
41. See Timothy J. Wengert, "The Biblical Commentaries of Philip Melanchthon," in *Philip Melanchthon: Theologian in Classroom, Confession, and Controversy*, eds. Irene Dingel, Robert Kolb, Nicole Kuropka, and Timothy J. Wengert (Bristol, CT: Vandenhoeck & Ruprecht, 2012), 45; Peter Fraenkel, *Testimonia Patrum: The Function of Patristic Argument in the Theology of Philip Melanchthon* (Geneva: Librairie E. Droz, 1961); E. P. Meijering, *Melanchthon and Patristic Thought: The Doctrines of Christ and Grace, the Trinity and the Creation* (Leiden, Netherlands: E. J. Brill, 1983), 19–108; Sachiko Kusukawa, "Melanchthon," in *The Cambridge Companion to Reformation Theology*, eds. David Bagchi and David C. Steinmetz (New York: Cambridge, 2004), 62–63.
42. See Douglas H. Shantz, "Vermigli on Tradition and the Fathers," in *Peter Martyr Vermigli and the European Reformations: Semper Reformanda*, ed. Frank A. James III (Leiden, Netherlands: E. J. Brill, 2004), 135, who observes that Melanchthon "noted the errors of the Fathers including Origen's

misuse of Paul, Tertullian's condemnation of second marriages, Cyprian's call for rebaptism of heretics, and Gregory's approval of the sacrament of the dead."

43. Melanchthon, *Commentary on Romans*, 34.
44. Melanchthon, *On Christian Doctrine: Loci Communes, 1555*, 68–69. This same perspective is reflected in the Augsburg Confession, of which Melanchthon was the chief writer: "Since this teaching is grounded clearly on the Holy Scriptures and is not contrary or opposed to that of the universal Christian church, or even the Roman church (in so far as the latter's teaching is reflected in the writings of the Fathers), we think that our opponents cannot disagree with us in the articles set forth above" (Article XXI of *The Augsburg Confession*, cited from *The Book of Concord*, trans. Theodore Gerhardt Tappert [Minneapolis: Fortress Press, 1959], 47).
45. A number of studies have been done on Calvin's use of the church fathers, including Anthony N. S. Lane, *John Calvin: Student of the Church Fathers* (Edinburgh, Scotland: Bloomsbury T&T Clark, 1991), and Johannes van Oort, "John Calvin and the Church Fathers," in *The Reception of the Church Fathers in the West: From the Carolingians to the Maurists*, ed. Irena Backus (Leiden, Netherlands: E. J. Brill, 1997), 661–700. See also Irena Backus, "Calvin and the Greek Fathers," in *Continuity and Change: The Harvest of Late-Medieval and Reformation History*, eds. Robert J. Bast and Andrew C. Gow (Leiden, Netherlands: E. J. Brill, 2000), 253–78; Anthony N. S. Lane, "The Sources of Calvin's Citations in His Genesis Commentary," in *Interpreting the Bible: Historical and Theological Studies in Honour of David F. Wright*, ed. A. N. S. Lane (Leicester, England: InterVarsity Press, 1997), 47–96.
46. Lane, *Student of the Church Fathers*, 41, n. 198.
47. Ibid., 41, n. 197, n. 198; 42, n. 209; 81.
48. See Calvin, *Institutes*, 3.11.22, 3.12.3, where he cites both Augustine and Bernard. See also Barbara Pinkin, "Calvin's Reception of Paul," in *A Companion to Paul in the Reformation*, ed. R. Ward Holder (Leiden, Netherlands: E. J. Brill, 2009), 271–72.
49. In the preface to his *Institutes*, Calvin emphasized this point in his dedicatory letter to Francis I, the king of France.
50. Chemnitz recognized that many of the Latin fathers, following Augustine's interpretation of the Latin word *iustificare*, defined justification as including regeneration and sanctification. In spite of that misunderstanding of the term, Chemnitz argues that they still represent the biblical teaching on justification. Thus, he writes, "Although the fathers usually follow the analogy of the Latin composition in the word justify, they are nevertheless often compelled by the evidence of Pauline argumentation to acknowledge this proper and genuine meaning which we have shown" (*Examination of the Council of Trent*, in *Chemnitz's Works*, 1:475).
51. Ibid., 1:505.
52. Ibid., 1:505–13.
53. Ibid., 1:512–13.
54. McGrath, *Iustitia Dei*, 211.

Chapter 4: Saved by Grace

1. Thomas Oden, *The Justification Reader* (Grand Rapids: Eerdmans, 2002), 49. As Oden explains earlier in his work, "It is a familiar assumption of many modern Protestant laity and clergy that the classical writers of the first millennium knew little or nothing of justification by grace through faith as understood by Paul, Luther, Calvin, and the Reformation. This is a distorted assumption shared ironically by both modern liberal Protestants and modern evangelical Protestants" (10). He adds, "There is strong central affirmation of the Pauline doctrine of justification in the patristic writers, which later became the defining doctrine of the Reformation" (24).
2. D. H. Williams, "Justification by Faith: A Patristic Doctrine," *J Ecclesiast Hist.* 57, no. 4 (October 2006): 649. Williams adds, "Theological utilization of the principle of justification by faith has its roots among patristic writers, as the Reformers themselves found when they sought precedents for their teaching" (650).
3. This chapter is not arguing for a patristic consensus on the doctrine of justification by faith, since some patristic works like the *Shepherd of Hermas* seem to make salvation contingent on good works. Nonetheless, there are clear instances in which leading church fathers speak about justification in a way that parallels the teachings of the sixteenth-century Reformers. But even these church fathers are not always consistent with themselves. As Joel C. Elowsky, ed., *We Believe in the Holy Spirit* (Downers Grove, IL: IVP Academic, 2009), 85, acknowledges, "It is clear that the Fathers use the word *justify* in a number of senses and not always consistently—which is not so much a critique as a reflection of the fact that they were not writing treatises on this particular doctrine."
4. Clement of Rome, *1 Clem.* 32.4. Trans. from Michael W. Holmes, *The Apostolic Fathers* (Grand Rapids: Baker Academic, 2007), 87. Though not highlighted in this chapter, there is also evidence for justification through faith alone in the writings of second-century theologian Ignatius of Antioch (see Thomas Schreiner, *Faith Alone: The Doctrine of Justification* [Grand Rapids: Zondervan, 2015], 27–28).
5. Jordan Cooper, *The Righteousness of One: An Evaluation of Early Patristic Soteriology in Light of the New Perspective on Paul* (Eugene, OR: Wipf and Stock, 2013), 77. See also Brian John Arnold, "Justification One Hundred Years after Paul," Ph.D. dissertation (Louisville, KY: The Southern Baptist Seminary, 2013), 54–55.
6. Origen, *Comm. Rom.* 3.9, *PG* 14.952, quoted in and trans. from Thomas P. Scheck, "Origen's Interpretation of Romans," in *A Companion to St. Paul in the Middle Ages*, ed. Steven R. Cartright (Leiden, Netherlands: E. J. Brill, 2012), 33.
7. Origen, *Comm. Rom.*, 3.9. *PG* 14.952–53, quoted in and trans. from Elowsky, *We Believe in the Holy Spirit*, 99.
8. Scheck, "Origen's Interpretation of Romans," 34.
9. Hilary, *Comm. Matt.* 20.7. *PL* 9.1030. Trans. from Hilary of Poitiers, *Commentary on Matthew*, The Fathers of the Church, trans. D. H. Williams (Washington, D.C.: The Catholic University of America Press, 2012), 212.

10. Ibid., 8.6. *PL* 9.961, quoted in and trans. from D. H. Williams, "Justification by Faith," 658.
11. Ibid., 21.15. *PL* 9.1041, quoted in and trans. from D. H. Williams, "Justification by Faith," 660. Hilary also states, "God bestows his pardon for all our faults according to his mercy [literally, by his own gift] rather than our merit" (Hillary, Ibid., 18.10. *PL* 9.1022. Trans. from Hilary of Poitiers, *Commentary on Matthew*, 199).
12. Williams, "Justification by Faith," 657.
13. Marius Victorinus, *Ep. Gal.* 2 (on Gal. 3:21). *PL* 8.1172, quoted in and trans. from Mark J. Edwards, *Galatians, Ephesians, Philippians*, ACCS (Downers Grove, IL: InterVaristy Press, 1999), 48.
14. Marius Victorinus, *Ep. Eph.* 1 (on Eph. 2:7). *PL* 8.1255. See Oden, *The Justification Reader*, 48.
15. Ibid., 1 (on Eph. 2.9). *PL* 8.1256. Trans. from Oden, *The Justification Reader*, 48.
16. Victorinus, *Ep. Eph.*, 1 (on Eph. 2:15). *PL* 8.1258. Trans. from Joseph A. Fitzmyer, *Romans: A New Translation with Introduction and Commentary by Joseph A. Fitzmyer*, The Anchor Bible, vol. 33 (New York: Doubleday, 1993), 361.
17. Robert Eno, *Recherches augustiniennes* (Paris: Institut des Études Augustiniennes, 1984), 19.6.
18. Ian Christopher Levy, Philip D. W. Krey, and Thomas Ryan, *The Letter to the Romans*, The Bible in Medieval Tradition (Grand Rapids: Eerdmans, 2013), 9.
19. Ambrose, *Sacr.* 5.4.19. *PL* 16.450. See Oden, *The Justification Reader*, 108.
20. Ambrose, *Jac.* 2.2.9. *PL* 14.618. Trans. adapted from *The Fathers of the Church*, 127 vols. (Washington, D.C.: The Catholic University of America Press, 1972), 65:150–51.
21. See Leif Grane, ed., *The Augsburg Confession: A Commentary* (Minneapolis: Fortress Press, 1959); Jonathan R. Huggins, *Living Justification: A Historical-Theological Study of the Reformed Doctrine of Justification in the Writings of John Calvin, Jonathan Edwards, and N. T. Wright* (Eugene, OR: Wipf and Stock, 2013), 25.
22. "Ambrosiaster" is the name given to an anonymous, fourth-century Bible commentator whose writings were mistakenly credited to Ambrose. See D. G. Hunter, "Ambrosiaster," in *Dictionary of Major Biblical Interpreters*, ed. Donald K. McKim (Downers Grove, IL: InterVarsity Press, 2007), 123–26.
23. Ambrosiaster, *Ad Rom.*, on Rom. 1:11. *PL* 17.53, quoted in and trans. from Gerald Bray, *Romans*, ACCS (Downers Grove, IL: InterVarsity, 1998), 23.
24. Ibid., on Rom. 3:24. *PL* 17.79, trans. from Elowsky, *We Believe in the Holy Spirit*, 98.
25. Ibid., on Rom. 3:27. *PL* 17.80, trans. from Bray, *Romans*, ACCS, 103. Also see his comments on verse 26.
26. Ibid., on Rom. 4:6. *PL* 17.83, trans. from Bray, *Romans*, ACCS, 113. In his commentary on 1 Cor. 1:4, Ambrosiaster similarly writes, "Because this has been determined by God, that he who believes in Christ will be saved without work: by faith alone freely he receives forgiveness of sins" (Ambrosiaster, *Ad Cor. Prim.*, on 1 Cor. 1:4. *PL* 17.185).

27. Gerald Bray, "Ambrosiaster," in *Reading Romans through the Centuries: From the Early Church to Karl Barth*, eds. Jeffrey P. Greenman and Timothy Larsen (Grand Rapids: Brazos, 2005), 25–26.
28. See Christopher A. Hall, "John Chrysostom," in *Reading Romans through the Centuries: From the Early Church to Karl Barth*, eds. Jeffrey P. Greenman and Timothy Larsen (Grand Rapids: Brazos, 2005), 45–47.
29. John Chrysostom, *Hom. Act.* 32. *PG* 60.235, quoted in and trans. from Francis Martin, ed., *Acts*, ACCS (Downers Grove, IL: InterVarsity 2006), 183.
30. Ibid., 36. *PG* 60.259. Trans. from *NPNF*, First Series, 11.225.
31. John Chrysostom, *Hom. Rom.* 7 (on Rom. 3:27). *PG* 60.446. Trans. from *NPNF*, First Series, 11.379. Elsewhere, he states, "Would you know how good our Master is? The Publican went up full of ten thousand wickednesses, and saying only, 'Be merciful unto me,' went down justified" (*Hom. 1 Cor.* 8 [on 1 Cor. 3:1–3]. *PG* 61.73. Trans. from *NPNF*, First Series, 12.47).
32. Ibid., 9 (on Rom. 5:2). *PG* 60.468. Trans. from *NPNF*, First Series, 11.396.
33. John Chrysostom, *Hom. Rom.* 7. *PG* 60.443. Trans. from Bray, *Romans*, ACCS, 100. Elsewhere, Chrysostom writes, "For this is the only gift that we brought in to God, believing Him in what He promised shall come, and it was by this way alone we were saved. . . . What then saved thee? It was your hoping in God alone, and trusting to Him about His promises and gifts, and you needed to bring in nothing besides that" (See *Hom. Rom.* 14 [on Rom. 8:24]. *PG* 60.532. Trans. from *NPNF*, First Series, 11.446. English rendered clearer.)
34. John Chrysostom, *Hom. Eph.* (on Eph. 2:8). *PG* 62.33. Trans. adapted from Oden, *The Justification Reader*, 44.
35. John Chrysostom, *Hom. Gal.* (on Gal. 3:8). *PG* 61.651. Trans. from *NPNF*, First Series, 13.26.
36. Ibid. (on Gal. 3:12). *PG* 61.652. Trans. from *NPNF*, First Series, 13:26.
37. John Chrysostom, *Hom. Eph.* 5 (on Eph. 2:13–15). *PG* 62.39–40. Trans. adapted from *NPNF*, First Series, 13.72.
38. John Chrysostom, *Adv. Jud.* 7.3. *PG* 48.919.
39. John Chrysostom, *Hom. 1 Tim.* (on 1 Tim.) 1:15–16. *PG* 62.520–21. Trans. from Elowsky, *We Believe in the Holy Spirit*, 98. See also John Chrysostom, *Hom. Tit.* 5 (on Titus 3:4–6). *PG* 62.692.
40. Ibid.
41. See R. Ward Holder, "Calvin's Hermeneutic and Tradition: An Augustinian Reception of Romans 7," in *Reformation Readings of Romans*, eds. Kathy Ehrensperger and R. Ward Holder (Edinburgh, Scotland: T&T Clark, 2008), 101–102.
42. In spite of appeals to Jerome by Protestants like George Stanley Faber, some scholars deny that Jerome truly was an advocate of justification by faith alone. Along those lines, Jordan Cooper, *The Righteousness of One: An Evaluation of Early Patristic Soteriology in Light of the New Perspective on Paul* (Eugene, OR: Wipf & Stock, 2013), 30, writes, "Faber begins his work with the presupposition that there is a unanimous consensus among the fathers.

This forces him to defend the thesis that fathers such as Jerome and Clement of Alexandria taught Protestant distinctives, even though a casual reading of these sources would prove otherwise." See also his remarks on p. 35.

43. Jerome, *Comm. Eph.* 1.2.1. *PL* 26.46, 8. quoted in and trans. from Oden, *The Justification Reader*, 48.
44. Jerome, *Adv. Pelag.* 2.7. *PL* 23.568, quoted in and trans. from Oden, *The Justification Reader*, 112.
45. Ibid., 1.13. *PL* 23.527. Trans. from Elowsky, *We Believe in the Holy Spirit*, 91.
46. Jerome, *Comm. Eph.* 1.2.8–9. *PL* 26:460.
47. Justin, *Dial.* 92. *PG* 6.696. Trans. from *ANF*, 1.245. For more on Justin's view of justification, see Schriener, *Faith Alone*, 30–31.
48. Irenaeus, *Haer.* 4.5.5. *PG* 7.986. Trans. from *ANF*, 1.467.
49. Ibid., 4.21.1. *PG* 7.1043–44. Trans. from *ANF*, 1.492.
50. Ibid., 5.32.2. *PG* 7.1211. Trans. from *ANF*, 1.561.
51. John Chrysostom, *Hom. Gal.* (on Gal. 3:6). *PG* 61.650.
52. John Chrysostom, *Hom. Gen.* 27.3. *PG* 53.243. Trans. from Robert C. Hill, *St. John Chrysostom: Homilies on Genesis 1–17*, Fathers of the Church (Washington, D.C.: The Catholic University of America Press, 1990), 74.167.
53. John Chrysostom, *Hom. Rom.* 8 (on Rom. 4:1–2). *PG* 60.454. Trans. from *NPNF*, First Series, 11.385.
54. As Nick Needham, "Justification in the Early Church Fathers," in *Justification in Perspective*, ed. Bruce L. McCormack (Grand Rapids: Baker Academic, 2006), 38, observes, "There is a strong strand of patristic teaching that ascribes initial justification to faith—either to faith in an unqualified way, or to faith in contrast with works, or even specifically to 'faith alone.'"
55. Admittedly, the church fathers were fighting different theological battles than those faced by the Reformers. Justification was not at the center of controversy like it would be in the sixteenth century. Consequently, early Christian writers did not spend as much time addressing it as later theologians would. Nonetheless, numerous examples can be produced in which the church fathers anticipate the Reformation understanding of *sola fide*.

Chapter 5: Justification—A Divine Declaration

1. Nick Needham, "Justification in the Early Church Fathers," in *Justification in Perspective*, ed. Bruce L. McCormack (Grand Rapids: Baker Academic, 2006), 25–53, identifies examples and helpful categories for evaluating the patristic understanding of justification. This chapter and parts of the next are indebted to and attempt to build on Needham's pioneering work.
2. Needham, "Justification in the Early Church Fathers," 36.
3. Ibid., 29.
4. Joel C. Elowsky, ed., *We Believe in the Holy Spirit* (Downers Grove, IL: IVP Academic, 2009), 86.
5. Also, the fathers sometimes apply the language of justification to God. Since He cannot be made righteous in a progressive sense, the fathers seemingly viewed such language as a manifest declaration of His righteousness. See

Clement, *1 Clem.* 16.12; Justin, *1 Apol.* 51; *Dial.* 13; Ambrose, *Exp. Luc.* 6.2. Cf. Needham, "Justification in the Early Church Fathers," 28, n. 8.

6. John Chrysostom, *Hom. Rom.* 6 (on Rom. 3:4). *PG* 60.438. Trans. from Elowsky, *We Believe in the Holy Spirit*, 91.
7. Needham, "Justification in the Early Church Fathers," 26.
8. John Chrysostom, *Hom. Rom.* 15 (on Rom. 8:34). Trans. adapted from Elowsky, *We Believe in the Holy Spirit*, 93.
9. John Chrysostom, *Exp. Ps.* Psalm 142.3 [143]. *PG* 55.450. Trans. from Robert C. Hill, *St. John Chrysostom: Commentary on the Psalms*, 2 vols. (Brookline, MA: Holy Cross Orthodox Press, 1998), 2:309.
10. John Chrysostom, *Hom. Rom.* 7 (on Rom. 3:27). *PG* 60.445. Trans. adapted from *NPNF*, First Series, 11.378–79.
11. John Chrysostom, *Hom. 1 Tim.* 4 (on 1 Tim. 1:16). *PG* 62.522. Trans. from Elowsky, *We Believe in the Holy Spirit*, 105–106.
12. John Chrysostom, *Hom. 2 Cor.* 11.6. Trans. from *NPNF*, First Series, 12.335.
13. Hilary of Poitiers, *Trin.* 10.65. *PL* 10.393. Trans. from *NPNF*, Second Series, 9.200. See also, Origen, *Comm. Rom.* 3.1. *PG* 14.923.
14. Needham, "Justification in the Early Church Fathers," 30.
15. Ambrose, *Paen.* 2.7.53. *PL* 16.510. Trans. from *NPNF*, Second Series, 10.352. Cf. Needham, "Justification in the Early Church Fathers," 31.
16. Rufinus, *Symb. Apost.* 40. *PL* 21.377. Trans. adapted from Elowsky, *We Believe in the Holy Spirit*, 93–94.
17. Brian J. Arnold demonstrates that a forensic understanding of justification was also present in the hymnology of the early church, specifically in *The Odes of Solomon* (see Brian John Arnold, "Justification One Hundred Years after Paul," Ph.D. dissertation [Louisville, KY: The Southern Baptist Seminary, 2013], 196). See also Thomas Schreiner, *Faith Alone: The Doctrine of Justification* (Grand Rapids: Zondervan, 2015), 29–30.
18. Needham, "Justification in the Early Church Fathers," 29.
19. Origen, *Comm. Rom.* 5.2. *PG* 14.1021–22. Trans. from Gerald Bray, *Romans*, ACCS (Downers Grove, IL: InterVarsity, 1998), 138. Emphasis added.
20. Methodius, *Sim. et Ann.* 8. *PG* 18.368. See also Athanasius, *First Letter to the Monks*, Letter 52.3. Also, Athanasius, *To the Bishops of Egypt* 19. Emphasis added. Cf. Needham, "Justification in the Early Church Fathers," 29.
21. Gregory of Nazianzus, *Orat.* 38.4. *PG* 36.316. Emphasis added.
22. Ambrose, *Exc.* 2.6. *PL* 16.1317. Trans. from Needham, "Justification in the Early Church Fathers," 30. Elsewhere, Ambrose similarly states, "But the flesh of Christ condemned sin, which He felt not at His birth, and crucified by His death, so that in our flesh there might be justification through grace, in which before there had been pollution by guilt" (Ambrose, *On Repentance* 1.3.13. *PL* 16.470).
23. Ambrosiaster, *Ad Rom.* (on Rom. 5:16). *PL* 17.97. Trans. from Bray, *Romans*, ACCS, 145. Emphasis added.
24. John Chrysostom, *Hom. Gal.* (on Gal. 2:17). *PG* 61.643. Trans. from *NPNF*, First Series, 13.20. Emphasis added. English updated for clarity.

Cf. Needham, "Justification in the Church Fathers," 29–30, n. 17. A similar distinction is found in the early fifth century commentary of Pseudo-Constantius, *The Holy Letter of St. Paul to the Romans*, cited in Bray, *Romans*, ACCS, 142.

25. Marius Victorinus, *Ep. Gal.* 1 (on Gal. 2:15–16). *PL* 8.1164. Trans. from Hugh George Anderson, T. Austin Murphy, and Joseph A. Burgess, *Justification by Faith: Lutherans and Catholics in Dialogue VII* (Minneapolis: Augsburg Publishing House, 1985), 114. Cf. Needham, "Justification in the Early Church Fathers," 28, n. 9.
26. Ambrosiaster, *Ad Cor. Prim.* (on 1 Cor. 1:30–31). *PL* 17.191–92. Trans. from Gerald Bray, *1–2 Corinthians*, ACCS (Downers Grove, IL: InterVarsity Press, 2012), 18. Here, Ambrosiaster's focus seems to be on an application of justification rather than a definition of it. Those who have been justified worship the true God.
27. John Chrysostom, *Hom. 2 Cor.* 17.1. *PG* 61.518. See also *Hom. Jo.* 28.1; *Hom. 2 Cor.* 12.1. Needham, "Justification in the Early Church Fathers," 28–29, n. 9, observes, "When Chrysostom wants to speak of sanctification with the *dik-* word group, he seems to use the verb *poieō* ('to do' or 'to make') with *dikaios* ('righteous'), rather than *dikaioō* ('to justify'). See, e.g., *Homilies on Matthew* 3.6, where he says that humility makes sinners righteous, and *Homilies on Matthew* 16.3 and *Homilies on Romans* 7, on 3:31, where he says that the original purpose of the law was to make people righteous." It might also be noted that Chrysostom, like many of the church fathers, taught that regeneration was concurrent with water baptism. The fact that he distinguished justification from water baptism provides further evidence that he did not equate justification with regeneration. See Chrysostom, *Hom. 2 Cor.* 2.8. *PG* 61.401.
28. Polycarp, *Pol. Phil.* 1.2–3. Trans. from Michael W. Holmes, ed., *The Apostolic Fathers* (Grand Rapids: Baker Academic, 2007), 281.
29. Ignatius, *Ign. Eph.* 14. Trans. from Holmes, *The Apostolic Fathers*, 195.
30. Origen, *Comm. Rom.* 4.1. *PG* 14.965. Trans. from Elowsky, *We Believe in the Holy Spirit*, 130.
31. Cyprian, *Pat.* 10. *PL* 4.628–29.
32. Ambrosiaster, *Ad Tit.* (on Titus 3:4–7). *PL* 17.502–3. Quoted from Ambrosiaster, *Commentaries on Galatians–Philemon*, trans. and ed. Gerald Bray (Downers Grove, IL: InterVarsity Press, 2009), 159.
33. See Hilary of Poitiers, *Comm. Matt.* 6.4.
34. Justin Martyr, *1 Apol.* 16. *PG* 6.353. Trans. from *ANF*, 1.168.
35. Didymus, *Enarrat. ep. cath.* (on James 2:26). *PG* 39.1752. Trans. from Thomas C. Oden, *The Good Works Reader* (Grand Rapids: Eerdmans, 2007), 337.
36. John Chrysostom, *Hom. Rom.* 18 (on Rom. 11:6). *PG* 60.579. Trans. from *NPNF*, First Series, 11:483. See also John Chrysostom, *Homilies on Ephesians* 4.2.9.
37. Origen, *Comm. Rom.* 3.9. *PG* 14.953. Trans. from Elowsky, *We Believe in the Holy Spirit*, 100.

38. Ibid., 4.7. *PG* 14.986. Trans. from Bray, *Romans*, ACCS, 120. See also Origen, *Comm. Jo.* 19.152.
39. Ambrosiaster, *Ad Rom.* (on Rom. 2:7). *PL* 17.66. Trans. from Bray, *Romans*, ACCS, 59. Though outside the scope of the present study, it would seem that at least for some of the church fathers, the use of "merit" terminology largely corresponds to later Protestant teaching regarding heavenly rewards. Conversely, when "merit" is seen as some form of "just deserts" or "works-righteousness" that earns salvation it is often condemned by the church fathers. See Nick Needham, "Justification in the Early Church Fathers," 52–53. Needham cites the following patristic passages in this regard: Origen, *On First Principles* 2.3.3. See also 3.1.12; Hilary of Poitiers, *Tractate on Psalm 51* (*PL* 9.322); Marius Victorinus, *Epistle to the Ephesians* 1.2.7; 1.3.7–8; Jerome, *Dialogue against the Pelagians* 1.16; 2.7, 25, 29.
40. Ambrosiaster, *Ad Gal.* 5:6. *PL* 17.366. Trans. from Robert B. Eno, "Some Patristic Views on the Relationship of Faith and Works in Justification," in *Justification by Faith: Lutherans and Catholics in Dialogue VII*, 116.
41. Apparent inconsistencies in Chrysostom's articulation of justification by faith alone arise from the fact that, as a preacher, he sometimes emphasized different truths to fit the needs of his audience. See David Rylaarsdam, *John Chrysostom on Divine Pedagogy: The Coherence of His Theology and Preaching* (New York: Oxford University Press, 2014), 149–50.
42. John Chrysostom, *Hom. Jo.* 10 (on John 1:13). *PG* 59.76–77. See also John Chrysostom, *Hom. Phil.* 5; John Chrysostom, *Hom. Heb.* 7.1.
43. John Chrysostom, *Hom. Gen.* 2.5. *PG* 53.31. Trans. from Bray, *James, 1–2 Peter, 1–3 John, Jude*, ACCS, 34.
44. See John Chrysostom, *Hom. Gen.* 47.18; *Hom. Matt.* 47.3; 69.2; *Hom. Jo.* 10.3; 54.1; *Hom. Rom.* 5 (on Rom. 2:7); *Hom. Gal.* (on Gal. 5:6); *Hom. Eph.* 1 (on Eph. 1:4); 4 (on Eph. 2:8–10); *Hom. Phil.* 11. William J. Byron, *One Faith, Many Faithful* (Mahwah, NJ: Paulist Press, 1995), 148, summarizes Chrysostom's perspective: "For St. John Chrysostom, faith must be made manifest in the way one lives (*Ad populum Antiochenum* V, 5–6 [*PG* 49, 77]: *In Matthaeum*, Homilia LXIV, 4 [*PG* 58, 164]). It is not only a matter of wisdom or vision or hearing. Justification is by faith alone (*In epistolam ad Romanos*, Homilia VIII, 2 (*PG* 60, 456–57); it is a gift, a grace (*In Joannem*, Homilia LI on Jn 7, 37–44 [*PG* 59, 285]). At the same time, faith without works is dead (*In Matthaeum*, Homlia XXIV, 1 [*PG* 57, 321–22]; *In epistolam ad Ephesios*, Homilia IV, 3 [*PG* 62, 34–35])."
45. John Chrysostom, *Hom. Jo.* 46.4 (on John 6:52). *PG* 59.262.
46. Needham, "Justification in the Early Church Fathers," 43. See Needham's helpful discussion of the salvific efficacy attributed to works of penance in patristic literature (44–46). Needham concludes his survey by noting, "One wonders if the real intent of this strand of patristic teaching was to affirm that faith must *continually* appropriate God's undeserved mercy and that such appropriation takes place in faith's actions—in living faith, not fruitless faith" (Ibid., 45–46; emphasis original).
47. See, for example, Philip Melanchthon, "Love and Hope," in *Melanchthon and Bucer*, ed. Wilhelm Pauck, The Library of Christian Classics (Philadelphia: Westminster, 1969), 111–19; John Chrysostom, *Diab.* 2.

48. In the face of heresies (like Marcionism), which disregarded good works as unimportant, the early church fathers often emphasized the moral responsibility inherent in the Christian life. Moreover, after the conversion of the Roman Empire to Christianity (in the fourth century), nominal forms of Christianity became commonplace. Thus, the focus of preaching and writing naturally tended to emphasize the *fruit* of good works rather than the *foundation* of faith.
49. Justin Martyr, *Dial.* 47. *PG* 6.577, 580. Trans. from *ANF*, 1.218–19. See also Cyprian, *Treatise* 5, An Address to Demetrianus, 25.
50. On this point, see Anthony N. S. Lane, *Justification by Faith in Catholic-Protestant Dialogue: An Evangelical Assessment* (New York: T & T Clark, 2006), 39.
51. Needham, "Justification in the Early Church Fathers," 28. Needham later notes that Clement of Alexandria was an exception to this rule (Ibid., 37).

Chapter 6: The Great Exchange

1. Origen, *Comm. Rom.* 3.6. *PG* 14.940–41. Trans. from Joel C. Elowsky, ed., *We Believe in the Holy Spirit* (Downers Grove, IL: IVP Academic, 2009), 91.
2. John Chrysostom, *Hom. 1 Tim.* 4 (on 1 Tim. 1:15). *PG* 62.521. Trans. from *NPNF*, First Series, 13.420.
3. Basil of Caesarea, *Hom. Ps. CXIV*, 5. *PG* 29.492. Trans. from Elowsky, *We Believe in the Holy Spirit*, 99.
4. Ambrose, *Exp. Ps. 118*, 42. *PL* 15.1496–97. Trans. from Nick Needham, *Daily Readings from the Early Church Fathers* (Ross-shire, Scotland: Christian Focus, 2017), reading for October 21st. See also Jerome, *Pelag.* 1.13.
5. Needham, "Justification in the Church Fathers," 34, lists a number of places in which the church fathers taught penal substitution, including: Irenaeus, *Haer.* 5.17.2; Origen, *Comm. Jo.* (*PG* 14:160); Cyprian, *Pat.* 6–7; Eusebius (*PG* 22:726–27); Athanasius, *Inc.* 6–7, 25; *Apol. sec.* 1.60; 2.7; 2.47; 2.55; 2.67; 2.69; 3.33; Hilary of Poitiers, *Trin.* 10.47–48; Cyril of Jerusalem, *Catech.* 13.2, 13.33; Gregory of Nazianzus, *Orat.* 30.5; 30.20; 38.1; 40.45; *Epist.* 101; Chrysostom, *Hom. Gal.* (on 1:19, 3:13–14); *Hom. Col.* 6 (on 2:14); *Hom. 1 Tim.* 7 (on 2:6); *Hom. Heb.* 17.4. See also Steve Jeffery, Michael Ovey, and Andrew Sach, *Pierced for Our Transgressions: Recovering the Glory of Penal Substitution* (Wheaton, IL: Crossway, 2007), 161–85.
6. Polycarp, *Pol. Phil.* 8.1. Trans. from Michael W. Holmes, ed., *The Apostolic Fathers* (Grand Rapids: Baker Academic, 2007), 289–91.
7. Irenaeus, *Haer.* 5.17.3. *PG* 7.1170. Trans. from *ANF*, 1.545. See also Justin Martyr, *Dial.* 95; Clement of Alexandria, *Quis div.* 39. Cf. Needham, "Justification in the Early Church," 32.
8. Origen, *Comm. Rom.* 3.8. *PG* 14.946. Trans. from Thomas C. Oden, *The Justification Reader* (Grand Rapids: Eerdmans, 2002), 63.
9. Cyprian, *Pat.* 6. *PL* 4.626. Trans. from *ANF*, 5:485.
10. Athanasius, *Inc.* 9.1–2. *PG* 25.112. Trans. from Athanasius, *On the Incarnation* (New York: St. Vladimir's Seminary Press, 1993), 35. See also Athanasius, *Apol. sec.* 2.69.

11. Gregory of Nazianzus, *Orat.* 30.5. *PG* 36.108–109. Trans. from *NPNF*, Second Series, 7.311. As Chrysostom explained, "That one man should be punished on account of another does not seem reasonable, but that one man should be saved on account of another is both more suitable and more reasonable. So if it is true that the former happened, much more should the latter have happened as well!" (John Chrysostom, *Hom. Rom.* 10 (on Rom. 5:15). *PG* 60.475–76. Trans. from *NPNF*, First Series, 11.402.
12. Ambrose, *Jac.* 1.6.21. *PL* 14.607. Trans. from Michael P. McHugh, *St. Ambrose: Seven Exegetical Works* (Washington, D.C.: Catholic University of America, 1972), 133.
13. Chrysostom speaks of the countless benefits that are received at the moment of salvation in *Hom. Rom.* 9 and *Hom. Rom.* 14. See also also, *Hom. Col.* 5. Among these benefits was the gift of divine righteousness.
14. Tertullian, *Marc.* 5.3. *PL* 2.507. Trans. from *ANF*, 4:35. Cf. Needham, "Justification in the Early Church," 33, n. 27.
15. Marius Victorinus, *Ep. Gal.* 1 (on Gal. 3.7). *PL* 8.1169. Trans. adapted from Mark J. Edwards, *Galatians, Ephesians, Philippians*, ACCS (Downers Grove, IL: InterVarsity Press, 1999), 37.
16. Ambrosiaster, *Ad Rom.* (on Rom. 4:5). *PL* 17:82–83. Trans. from Bray, *Romans*, ACCS, 112.
17. Ibid. (on Rom. 1:17). *PL* 17.56. Trans. from Bray, *Romans*, ACCS, 31.
18. Ibid. (on Rom. 3:22). *PL* 17.79. Trans. adapted from Bray, *Romans*, ACCS, 99–100.
19. John Chrysostom, *Hom. Rom.* 7. *PG* 60.444. Trans. from Elowsky, *We Believe in the Holy Spirit*, 94.
20. John Chrysostom, *Hom. Phil.* 11. *PG* 62.265. Trans. adapted from *NPNF*, First Series, 13.235.
21. John Chrysostom, *Hom. Rom.* 2. *PG* 60.409. Trans. from Bray, *Romans*, ACCS, 30.
22. *Diogn.* 9.2–5. Trans. from Oden, *The Justification Reader*, 65. Justin Martyr similarly speaks of "those out of all the nations who are pious and righteous through the faith of Christ" (Justin Martyr, *Dial.* 52). *PG* 6.592.
23. Michael A. G. Haykin, *Rediscovering the Church Fathers: Who They Were and How They Shaped the Church* (Wheaton, IL: Crossway, 2011), 19.
24. Jordan Cooper, *The Righteousness of One: An Evaluation of Early Patristic Soteriology in Light of the New Perspective on Paul* (Eugene, OR: Wipf & Stock, 2013), 94–95. See also Brian J. Arnold, who writes, "Chapter 9 of the *Epistle to Diognetus* resonates with the twin Pauline doctrines of penal substitution and forensic justification" (Brian John Arnold, "Justification One Hundred Years after Paul," Ph.D. dissertation [Louisville, KY: The Southern Baptist Seminary, 2013], 135).
25. Ibid.
26. Basil, *Hom. humil.* 20.3. *PG* 31.529. Trans. from Elowsky, *We Believe in the Holy Spirit*, 98. See also Cyril of Jerusalem (ca. 313–386), who contrasts a righteousness that might be accumulated over a lifetime of good works with the righteousness received instantly through faith in Christ. He writes, "Oh the great loving-kindness of God! For the righteous were many years in pleasing Him: but what they succeeded in gaining by many years of

well-pleasing, this Jesus now bestows on you in a single hour. For if you shall believe that Jesus Christ is Lord, and that God raised Him from the dead, you shall be saved." Cyril of Jerusalem, *Catech.* 5.10. *PG* 33.517. Also see, Jerome, *Tract. Ps.* 66 (on Psalm 88 [89]) in which Jerome explains that the believer's entrance into heaven is made possible specifically through the righteousness of the second Adam, namely Christ (cf. Jerome, *The Homilies of Saint Jerome*, vol. 2 [Homilies 60–96], trans. Marie L. Ewald [Washington, D.C.: Catholic University of America Press, 1966], 68).

27. Michael Haykin, *Rediscovering the Church Fathers*, 114. See also David F. Wright, "Basil the Great in the Protestant Reformers," in *Studia Patristica* 17:3, ed. Elizabeth A. Livingston (Oxford: Pergamon, 1982), 1153.
28. John Chrysostom, *Hom. Rom.* 9. (on Rom. 4:25). *PG* 60.467. Trans. from *NPNF*, First Series, 11.395.
29. Ibid., 10. (on Rom. 5:16). *PG* 60.476. Trans. from *NPNF*, First Series, 11.403.
30. John Chrysostom, *Hom. 2 Cor.* 11.6. *PG* 61.478–79. Trans. adapted from Elowsky, *We Believe in the Holy Spirit*, 103.
31. John Chrysostom, *Hom. Rom.* 10 (on Rom. 5:17). *PG* 60.476–77. Trans. adapted from *NPNF*, First Series, 11.403.
32. Ibid. A few sentences later, Chrysostom reminds his readers that through Christ "they may be justified."
33. John Chrysostom, *Hom. Jo.* 46.4. *PG* 59.262. Emphasis added.
34. John Chrysostom, *Catech. illum.* 4.12. Trans. from Gerald Bray, *1–2 Corinthians*, ACCS (Downers Grove, IL: InterVarsity Press, 2012), 247.
35. See Elowsky, *We Believe in the Holy Spirit*, 87–88.
36. Cooper, *The Righteousness of One*, 135.
37. D. H. Williams, "Justification by Faith: A Patristic Doctrine," *J Ecclesiast Hist.* 57, no. 4 (October 2006): 666.

Chapter 7: A Forerunner to the Reformers?

1. For example, see Steven J. Lawson, *Pillars of Grace* (Orlando, FL: Reformation Trust, 2011), 216; R. C. Sproul, "Augustine and Pelagius," *Tabletalk* (June 1996): 11; John Piper, *The Legacy of Sovereign Joy* (Wheaton, IL: Crossway, 2006), 24. Piper writes, "Under Christ, Augustine's influence on Luther and Calvin was second only to the influence of the apostle Paul. . . . The great German and the great Frenchman drank from the great African, and God gave the life of the Reformation."
2. Alister E. McGrath, *Reformation Thought: An Introduction* (Oxford: Blackwell, 1993), 103.
3. This is not intended to be an exhaustive list, but rather one drawn primarily from McGrath's summary of Augustine's soteriology in Alister E. McGrath, *Iustitia Dei: A History of the Doctrine of Justification*, 3rd ed. (Cambridge: Cambridge University Press, 2005), 40–41. For other aspects of continuity between Augustine and the Reformers, such as the Law-Gospel dialectic and the tension between reason and faith, see Mark Ellingsen, "Augustinian Origins of the Reformation Reconsidered," *Scottish Journal of Theology* 64, no. 1 (February 2011): 25–26.

4. See McGrath, *Iustitia Dei*, 40. It might be noted, however, that in Augustine's view, not every person who is regenerated (baptized) will ultimately be saved. Only those who persevere to the end can be regarded as elect. See Augustine, *Treatise on Rebuke and Grace*, 42; McGrath, *Iustitia Dei*, 45; Lawson, *Pillars of Grace*, 243–45.
5. Augustine, *Praed.* 17.34. *PL* 44.985. Trans. from *The Works of Saint Augustine*, ed. John E. Rotelle, trans. Roland J. Teske (Hyde Park, NY: New City Press, 1999), 177–78. See also Augustine, *Praed.* 38; *Persev.* 53; *Tract. Ev. Jo.* 7.14.
6. Ibid., 17.34. *PL* 44.986. Trans. from John A. Mourant and William J. Collinge, *Saint Augustine: Four Anti-Pelagian Writings* (Washington, D.C.: The Catholic University of America Press, 1992), 260. See also Lawson, *Pillars of Grace*, 237–40.
7. Lawson, *Pillars of Grace*, 234–36.
8. Augustine, *Enchir.* 30. *PL* 40.246–47.
9. McGrath, *Iustitia Dei*, 43.
10. Ibid., 49–50.
11. Alister E. McGrath, "Forerunners of the Reformation? A Critical Examination of the Evidence for Precursors of the Reformation Doctrines of Justification," *HTR* 75, no. 2 (1982): 232. See also Bruce Demarest, *The Cross and Salvation* (Wheaton, IL: Crossway, 1997), 402–403; Ellingsen, "Augustinian Origins of the Reformation Reconsidered," 27.
12. See McGrath, *Iustitia Dei*, 44. Norman L. Geisler and Ralph E. MacKenzie, *Roman Catholics and Evangelicals* (Grand Rapids: Baker Academic, 1995), 98, note that: "Luther and Augustine both believed that *iustitia Dei* (righteousness of God) is a righteousness that is a gift from God to us, rather than the righteousness that God possesses in his own Person." See also McGrath, "Forerunners to the Reformation?" 230.
13. See Augustine, *Epist.* 186.3.10. *PL* 33.819. *CSEL* 57.52–53. Also see Augustine, *Enarrat. Ps.* 32.1.4.
14. See McGrath, *Iustitia Dei*, 42.
15. Augustine, *Epistle* 194.3.7. *PL* 33.877. Trans. from David F. Wright, "Justification in Augustine," in *Justification in Perspective*, ed. Bruce L. McCormack (Grand Rapids: Baker Academic, 2006), 65.
16. Augustine, *Epist.* 214.4. *PL* 33.970. Trans. from *NPNF*, First Series, 5:438. Elsewhere in his letters, Augustine writes: "The people who boast imagine that they are justified by their own efforts, and therefore they glory in themselves, not in the Lord" (Augustine, *Epist.* 214.3. *PL* 33.969–70. Trans. from Gerald Bray, *1–2 Corinthians*, ACCS [Downers Grove, IL: InterVarsity Press, 2012], 39). Cf. Augustine *Epist.* 215.1. *PL* 33.971. Also see Augustine, *Letters 204–270*, Fathers of the Church, trans. Wilfrid Parsons (Washington , D.C.: The Catholic University of America Press, 1981), 60.
17. Augustine, *Spir. et litt.* 6 (9). *PL* 44.205. Trans. from *NPNF*, First Series, 5:86.
18. Ibid., 13 (22). *PL* 44.214–15. Trans. from *NPNF*, First Series, 5:93.
19. See also Augustine, *Grat. Chr.* 27 (26). *PL* 44.374. Trans. from *NPNF*, First Series, 5:227, where he states that we "must not suppose that any merits

of our own preceded our reception of the gift. For what merits could we possibly have had at the time when we loved not God?"

20. Augustine, *Grat. Chr.* 34 (31). *PL* 44.377. Trans. from *NPNF*, First Series, 5:230.
21. Augustine, *C. du. ep. Pelag.* 1.21.39. *PL* 44.569. Trans. from Joel C. Elowsky, ed., *We Believe in the Holy Spirit* (Downers Grove, IL: IVP Academic, 2009), 96.
22. Augustine, *Exp. prop. Rom.* 20. *PL* 35.2066. Trans. from Thomas C. Oden, *The Justification Reader* (Grand Rapids: Eerdmans, 2002), 145.
23. Augustine, *Enarrat. Ps.* 22.3 [23.3]. *PL* 36.182. Trans. from *NPNF*, First Series, 8:60. English updated for readability.
24. Ibid., 55.12 [56.11]. *PL* 36.655. Trans. from *NPNF*, First Series, 8:222. English updated for readability.
25. Ibid., 70.2.2 [71.19]. *PL* 36.822. Trans. from *NPNF*, First Series, 8:322. See also Augustine, *Expositions on the Psalms* 68.10. English updated for readability.
26. Ibid., 85.2 [86.2]. *PL* 37.1082. Trans. from *NPNF*, First Series, 8:410.
27. Augustine's *Enchiridion* reiterates this point, emphasizing that the human race cannot "be restored through the merit of their own works." Augustine, *Enchir.* 30. *PL* 40.246. Trans. from *NPNF*, First Series, 3:247. The sinner on whom God has set His redeeming love has "no room to glory in any merit of his own, but only in the riches of divine grace." Ibid., *Enchir.* 98. *PL* 40.277–78. Trans. from *NPNF*, First Series, 3:268. Those to whom God shows mercy "are freed from misery not on account of any merit of their own, but solely through the pity of God." Ibid., *Enchir.* 112. *PL* 40.284. Trans. from *NPNF*, First Series, 3:273.
28. Paul ChulHong Kang, *Justification: The Imputation of Christ's Righteousness from Reformation Theology to the American Great Awakening and the Korean Revivals* (New York: Peter Lang, 2006), observes that "Augustine discards human meritorious works in salvation. Human beings, he argues, are justified by faith through God's grace alone. By grace alone (*sola gratia*), God crowns them not with human merits, but with his gifts; that is, human beings are crowned with God's righteousness by his grace alone" (34).
29. For example, McGrath readily acknowledges Augustine's emphasis on God's grace in salvation. Yet he contends it is an insufficient basis on which to claim Augustine as a "forerunner" to the Reformation understanding of justification by faith. According to McGrath, Augustine's insistence on salvation *sola gratia* ("by grace alone") does not necessarily mean that he also taught justification *sola fide* ("through faith alone"). Thus, it is argued that only by applying more specific criteria can one legitimately consider Augustine to be a forerunner to the Reformation doctrine of justification by faith alone. (McGrath, "Forerunners to the Reformation?" 223, 228.)
30. Ibid., 223.
31. Ibid.
32. Ibid.
33. McGrath, *Iustitia Dei*, 46.
34. McGrath, "Forerunners to the Reformation?" 235.

35. McGrath credits Melanchthon for breaking with Augustine by introducing the concept of forensic righteousness. See McGrath, *Reformation Thought*, 108; McGrath, "Forerunners of the Reformation?" 229; McGrath, *Iustitia Dei*, 47.
36. See Demarest, *The Cross and Salvation*, 351, who writes, "Since Augustine concisely represented the *ordo salutis* as predestination, calling, justification, and glorification, he viewed justification broadly as the entire movement of salvation from regeneration through sanctification."
37. See Donald K. McKim, *Theological Turning Points* (Louisville, KY: Westminster John Knox, 1988), 88, who writes, "The term *justification* for Augustine refers to the process by which one becomes righteous, as the Holy Spirit sheds the spirit of love in one's heart. . . . Justification occurs at baptism and continues through life as an internal growth of righteousness in the believer." McGrath, "Forerunners to the Reformation?" 230, similarly concludes, "Justification is not understood by Augustine in a highly forensic manner, but as a process with perfection as its goal."
38. McGrath, *Iustitia Dei*, 47. On this point, Gerald Bray, *God Has Spoken: A History of Christian Theology* (Wheaton, IL: Crossway, 2014), 513, adds: "To describe the reception of God's righteousness by sinful human beings, Augustine chose the word *iustificare* and its derivatives, and this usage passed into the Western tradition. He himself believed that the word meant 'to make righteous,' since it was composed of the two Latin words *iustum* ('righteous') and *facere* ('make'), but it was not clear what that entailed. To the extent that it was a translation of the Greek verb *dikaioun* it meant 'pass judgment on'—usually taken in the negative sense but in this case understood positively, as 'acquit' rather than 'condemn'—but Augustine also used *iustificare* to convey the idea of 'transforming someone into a righteous person,' which *dikaioun* does not (and cannot) mean. This is important, because it was this additional implication that was to cause trouble and misunderstanding later on."
39. Augustine, *Tract. Ev. Jo.* 3.9 (on John 1:15–18). *PL* 35.1400. Trans. from *NPNF*, First Series, 7:21. See Gregg R. Allison, *Historical Theology* (Grand Rapids: Zondervan, 2011), 501. See also Augustine, *On the Spirit and the Letter* 1.10.16.
40. Augustine, *Epist.* 214.4. *PL* 33.970. Trans. from *NPNF*, First Series, 5:438. English updated for clarity.
41. Augustine, *Serm.* 169.11.13. *PL* 38.923.
42. Augustine, *Spir. et litt.* 26.45. PL 44.228. Trans. from Elowsky, *We Believe in the Holy Spirit*, 130. See also *NPNF*, First Series, 5:102. Cf. McGrath, *Iustitia Dei*, 47.
43. See Thomas R. Schreiner, *40 Questions about Christians and Biblical Law* (Grand Rapids: Kregel, 2010), 120, who writes: "The evidence supporting a declarative or forensic meaning for the verb justify in Paul is significant. The Augustinian view that justify means to make righteous is not supported by the use of the verb in the Pauline writings."
44. See McGrath, *Iustitia Dei*, 43, 49. Also see Geisler and MacKenzie, *Roman Catholics and Evangelicals*, 98.
45. McGrath, *Iustitia Dei*, 43, 47.

46. Along these lines, McGrath, *Iustita Dei*, 43–44, says of Augustine, "Eternal life is indeed the reward for merit—but merit is itself a gift from God, so that the whole process must be seen as having its origin in the divine liberality, rather than in human works."
47. McGrath, "Forerunners to the Reformation?" 231; McGrath, *Iustitia Dei*, 48.
48. McGrath, *Iustitia Dei*, 48–49; McGrath, *Reformation Thought*, 106; McGrath, "Forerunners to the Reformation?," 231–32.
49. McGrath, *Reformation Thought*, 96; Geisler and MacKenzie, *Roman Catholics and Evangelicals*, 99.
50. McGrath, *Reformation Thought*, 96.
51. McGrath, *Iustitia Dei*, 45.
52. Ibid., 46.
53. According to McGrath, "Forerunners to the Reformation?" 241, "The doctrines of justification associated with the Lutheran and Reformed Confessions may be concluded to constitute genuine theological nova. The creative genius of Protestantism lies at least in part in its new understanding of the nature of justification, which has such profound consequences for Protestant spirituality."
54. McGrath, "Forerunners to the Reformation?" 239.

Chapter 8: The Doctor of Grace

1. Alister E. McGrath, "Forerunners of the Reformation? A Critical Examination of the Evidence for Precursors of the Reformation Doctrines of Justification," *HTR* 75, no. 2 (1982): 235, says of the differences between Augustine and the Reformers (regarding their views on justification): "There can be no question of any basic continuity between them."
2. Parts of this chapter are indebted to the work of Mark Ellingsen ("Augustinian Origins of the Reformation Reconsidered," *Scottish Journal of Theology* 64, no. 1 [February 2011]: 13–28) and David F. Wright ("Justification in Augustine," in *Justification in Perspective*, ed. Bruce L. McCormack [Grand Rapids: Baker Academic, 2006], 55–72).
3. As Norman L. Geisler and Ralph E. MacKenzie, *Roman Catholics and Evangelicals* (Grand Rapids: Baker Academic, 1995), 99, explain, "In spite of significant differences in their systems, Luther and Augustine were united in their belief that man is spiritually destitute and, apart from God's grace, is incapable of producing any semblance of spiritual merit. Luther was, indeed (at least concerning the basic tenets of justification), a spiritual son of the bishop of Hippo."
4. As Wright, "Justification in Augustine," 55, explains, "Augustine never addressed the topic of justification in a precise and focused way in any of his works and certainly never devoted a treatise or a sermon or a letter; and barely even a whole chapter or section of one of these, to it. So a good case could be made for holding that Augustine did not have a doctrine of justification." Later, Wright adds, "Since Augustine hardly ever, and never extensively, addressed the question of the different meanings of *justifico* in a systematic manner, we are looking at some of the dispersed evidence for

his use of it apparently in some other sense than 'make righteous'" (59). This helps explain why later interpreters of Augustine have not agreed about his teachings on justification. As one scholar observes, "Augustine's view of justification is broad and unclear in whole. In this respect, it is evident that 'Augustine's view of justification' has been dependent upon the interpretations of his theological descendants." (Hyun-Jin Cho, *Jonathan Edwards on Justification* [Lanham, MD: University Press of America, 2012], 18. See also Wright, "Justification in Augustine," 56, who states, "I know of no place in his corpus where he directly addresses the meaning of *justifico* as a question to be resolved.")

5. Ellingsen, "Augustinian Origins of the Reformation Reconsidered," 15.
6. See Ellingsen, "Augustinian Origins of the Reformation Reconsidered," 25, for example: "To some extent the critics and Catholic interpreters of Augustine are correct. He said a lot of characteristically Roman Catholic things, relying on images that are not in line with Luther's later thinking. But when addressing certain heresies (especially in the anti-Pelagian writings) or when just expositing the logic of faith, many of Luther's characteristic Reformation themes are identifiable in the Augustinian corpus."
7. Augustine, *Enarrat. Ps.*, 31.7. *PL* 36.263. Trans. from John E. Rotelle, *Expositions of the Psalms 1–32* (Hyde Park, NY: New City Press, 2000), 11.370.
8. Augustine, *Spir. et litt.* 1.26.45. *PL* 44.228. Trans. from *NPNF*, First Series, 5.102. See Mark Ellingsen, *The Richness of Augustine* (Louisville, KY: Westminster John Knox Press, 2005), 84.
9. Augustine, *Pecc. merit.* 1.14 (18). *PL* 44.119. Trans. from *NPNF*, First Series, 5.21–22. See also ibid., 1.27.43; 2.32.52 (*NPNF* 5.31–32, 65); *Spir. et litt.* 18.31 (*NPNF*, First Series, 5.96); *C. du. ep. Pelag.* 3.5.14 (*NPNF*, First Series, 5:408–9). See also Ellingsen, "Augustinian Origins of the Reformation Reconsidered," 27.
10. Ibid., 1.12 (15). *PL* 44.117. Trans. from *NPNF*, First Series, 5:20.
11. Augustine, *Epist.* 157.3.14. *PL* 33.680. Trans. from Gerald Bray, *1–2 Corinthians*, ACCS (Downers Grove, IL: InterVarsity Press, 2012), 156. Augustine contrasts justification with condemnation a number of times throughout this same letter. See also Augustine, *The Merits and Remission of Sins and Infant Baptism* 1.13.18, where Augustine cites Romans 5:18.
12. See Wright, "Justification in Augustine," 56, who states, "There is evidence that Augustine was aware of a declarative sense of *justifico* ('I justify')."
13. See Bradley G. Green, "Augustine," in *Shapers of Christian Orthodoxy: Engaging with Early and Medieval Theologians*, ed. Bradley G. Green (Downers Grove, IL: InterVarsity Press, 2010), 259.
14. Such runs contrary to McGrath's claim that "there is *no hint* in Augustine of any notion of justification purely in terms of 'reputing as righteous' or 'treating as righteous'" (Alister E. McGrath, *Iustitia Dei: A History of the Doctrine of Justification*, 3rd ed. [Cambridge: Cambridge University Press, 2005], 47; emphasis mine).
15. Wright, "Justification in Augustine," 57–58. I am indebted to Wright's research for the examples included in this section.
16. Augustine, *Grat.* 6 (13). *PL* 44.889–90. Trans. from *NPNF*, First Series, 5:449.

17. Augustine, *Div. quaest. Simpl.* 1.2.3. *PL* 40.113. Trans. adapted from John H. S. Burleigh, *Augustine: Earlier Writings*, The Library of Christian Classics (Philadelphia: The Westminster Press, 1953). Certain parts follow the rendering of Wright, "Justification in Augustine," 57–58.
18. Ibid., 1.2.5. *PL* 40.114. Trans. from Burleigh, *Augustine: Earlier Writings*, 389.
19. Ibid., 1.2.18. *PL* 40.123. Trans. from Burleigh, *Augustine: Earlier Writings*, 400. Later in that same context, Augustine poses the rhetorical question, "Who can live righteously and do good works unless he has been justified by faith?" Ibid., 1.2.21. *PL* 40.126–27. Trans. from Burleigh, *Augustine: Earlier Writings*, 405.
20. Augustine, *Enarrat. Ps.* 110.3 [111.3]. *PL* 37.1464. *NPNF*, First Series, 8:545. Also see, Augustine, *Letters* 194.3.6. *PL* 33:876.
21. Augustine, *Serm.* 158.6.6; 7.7. *PL* 38:865–66.
22. Wright, "Justification in Augustine," 71.
23. John Gerstner, *Jonathan Edwards: A Mini-Theology* (Wheaton, IL: Tyndale House, 1987), 70. See also N. R. Needham, *2000 Years of Christ's Power: Part Three: Renaissance and Reformation* (London: Grace Publications Trust, 2004), 86, n. 26.
24. Along these lines, James Buchanan, *The Doctrine of Justification: An Outline of Its History in the Church and of Its Exposition from Scripture* (1867; repr., London: Banner of Truth, 1961), 90, asserts that "Augustine, in common with all the Latin Fathers, used the term *merits*, not to denote legal, or moral desert, properly so called, but to signify, either simply a means of obtaining some blessing, or, at the most, an action that is rewardable, not 'of debt, but of grace.'"
25. R. C. Sproul, *Now That's a Good Question* (Carol Stream, IL: Tyndale House, 2011), 287–88. See also R. C. Sproul, *Faith Alone: The Evangelical Doctrine of Justification* (Grand Rapids: Baker Books, 1995), 148, where Sproul writes, "Augustine spoke of 'God's crowning his own gifts.' The Reformers understood this to mean that, though God distributes rewards according to our works, it remains a gracious distribution and is based on no merit inhering in them."
26. Augustine, *Epist.* 194.5.19. *PL* 33.880. See also Augustine, *Grat.* 6 (15). *PL* 44.890–91.
27. Augustine, *Corrept.* 13.41. *PL* 44.942.
28. Augustine, *Enchir.* 99. *PL* 40.278. Trans. from *NPNF*, First Series, 3:269. See also Augustine, *Tract. Ev. Jo.* 3.9 (*PL* 35.1400).
29. Augustine, *Faust.* 33.1. *PL* 42.511, quoted in Joel C. Elowsky, ed., *We Believe in the Holy Spirit* (Downers Grove, IL: IVP Academic, 2009), 99.
30. Augustine, *Grat.* 9.21. *PL* 44.893. It might be noted that, according to Augustine, the level of heavenly reward for each believer will differ according to one's good works. See *Virginit.* 26. *PL* 40.410; *On Grace and Free Will* 10, 14.
31. Augustine, *Enchir.* 68. *PL* 40.264. Trans. from *NPNF*, First Series, 3:259 (emphasis mine).
32. Ibid.

33. Augustine, *Gest. Pelag.* 14.34. *PL* 44.341. See also Augustine, *De Trinitate* (*On the Trinity*) 13.12.17–15.19 where Augustine speaks of the righteousness of Christ as being that which sufficiently paid the debt owed by sinners.
34. Augustine, *Spir. et litt.* 9.15. *PL* 44.209. Trans. from Gerald Bray, *Romans*, ACCS (Downers Grove, IL: InterVarsity, 1998), 99. See also *NPNF*, First Series, 5:89. See Ellingsen, "Augustinian Origins of the Reformation Reconsidered," 16–17.
35. Augustine, *Spir. et litt.*, 18.31. *PL* 44.220. Trans. from *NPNF* 5.96.
36. Augustine, *Tract. Ev. Jo.* 26.1. *PL* 35.1606–1607. Trans. from Elowsky, *We Believe in the Holy Spirit*, 102. See also *NPNF*, First Series, 7:168.
37. Augustine, *Enchir.*, 41; *NPNF* 3:251.
38. Augustine, *Perf.* 1.27; *NPNF* 5.168; *Tract. Ev. Jo.* 26.6.1; *NPNF* 7.168; *Spir. et litt.* 16.45; *NPNF* 5.102. See Ellingsen, "Augustinian Origins of the Reformation Reconsidered," 27, who states, "Such comments, as well as remarks referring to our 'being clothed' in righteousness of God, 'bestowing righteousness' on the faithful, seem to imply the passivity of faith and the righteousness that saves—language characteristic of Luther" (citing, Augustine, *Praed.* 19.39; *NPNF* 5.517).
39. Ellingsen, "Augustinian Origins of the Reformation Reconsidered," 27.
40. M. Eugene Osterhaven, *The Faith of the Church* (Grand Rapids: Eerdmans, 1982), 104.
41. McGrath, *Iustitia Dei*, 46.
42. For example, see Augustine, *Enchir.* 117. *PL* 40.286–87. See *NPNF*, First Series, 3:274–75. Cf. Wright, "Justification in Augustine," 69.
43. Thus, Augustine writes, "It can be said that God's commandments pertain to faith alone, if it is not a dead [faith], but rather understood as that live faith, which works through love" (*Fid. op.* 22.40. *CSEL* 41.84–85. Trans. from Joseph A. Fitzmyer, *Romans: A New Translation with Introduction and Commentary by Joseph A. Fitzmyer*, The Anchor Bible, vol. 33 [New York: Doubleday, 1993], 361).
44. A number of Augustinian scholars have responded critically to those who would make this kind of assertion. For example, see Jairzinho Lopes Pereira, *Augustine of Hippo and Martin Luther on Original Sin and Justification of the Sinner* (Bristol, CT: Vandenhoeck & Ruprecht, 2013), 236. Also see, Wright, "Justification in Augustine," 66.
45. Wright, "Justification in Augustine," 66. On that same page, Wright continues, "So we must forcefully insist . . . that Galatians 5:6 stands preeminently for the genuineness of faith, which is God's gift toward justification. This is nearly always the context in which this Pauline clause is cited."
46. For example, see Augustine, *Serm.* 53.10.10–11. *PL* 38.368–369. Trans. from Francis, *Acts*, ACCS, 183–84. See also Augustine, *Grat.* 7.18. *PL* 44:892.
47. Augustine, *Tract. Ev. Jo.* 29.6. *PL* 35.1631. Trans. from Wright, "Justification in Augustine," 67–68.
48. Augustine, *Serm.* 144.2.2. *PL* 38:788. Trans. from Wright, "Justification in Augustine," 68.

49. See Wright, "Justification in Augustine," 66: "Since he [Augustine] is extremely careful to clarify that justification is received *sine operibus, sine ullis praecedentibus meritis* ("without works, without any preceding merits") he seems consequently careful to avoid linking justification to works that must ensue in the justified. Hence the necessity of these works of holiness essentially attests the reality, the authenticity, of faith in the justified.... Thus Augustine unmistakably preserved the distinction between faith as the free grace-gift of God and the fruitful life of good works to which it must give rise.... So often one feels that his meaning would be well conveyed by the use of "alone"—faith alone without works—but the phrase *sola fide* does not occur in his corpus in this sense. It is generally deployed with a pejorative meaning, of those who perversely relied on 'faith alone' while refusing to abandon their vices and pursue good works."
50. Augustine, *Enarrat. Ps.* 31.3–4. *PL* 36.259. Trans from Elowsky, *We Believe in the Holy Spirit*, 128–29.
51. Ibid. He writes, "I have nothing but praise for the superstructure of action, but I see the foundation of faith: I admire the good work as a fruit, but I recognize that it springs from the root of faith."
52. Augustine, *Spir. et litt.* 36.65. *PL* 44:245. Trans. from Wright, "Justification in Augustine," 62–63.
53. Augustine, *Exp. prop. Rom.* 21. *PL* 35.2066. Trans. from Bray, *Romans*, ACCS, 112. See also *Augustine on Romans*, Society of Biblical Literature Text and Translations, trans. Paula Fredriksen Landes (Chico, CA: Scholars Press, 1982), 8.
54. See Ellingsen, "Augustinian Origins of the Reformation Reconsidered," 16–25.
55. Wright, "Justification in Augustine," 71. See also p. 70.
56. Ellingsen, "Augustinian Origins of the Reformation Reconsidered," 28.
57. Contra McGrath, Ellingsen writes, "Luther offers a new reading of Augustine in his medieval interpretative context (in the late Middle Ages the Augustinian Order was especially focused on Augustine's anti-Pelagian writings). But to claim that the Reformer's insights are just a matter of his creativity and biblical insight, not rooted in what Augustine actually wrote, shows a faulty reading of the richness of Augustine" (Ibid., 27–28).
58. As Calvin explains, "For that matter, Augustine's view, or at any rate his manner of stating it, we must not entirely accept. For even though he admirably deprives man of all credit for righteousness and transfers it to God's grace, he still subsumes grace under sanctification, by which we are reborn in newness of life through the Spirit" (John Calvin, *Institutes of the Christian Religion*, ed. John T. McNeill, trans. Ford Lewis Battles [Louisville, KY: Westminster John Knox Press, 1960], 3.11.15.). See also Anthony N. S. Lane, *John Calvin: Student of the Church Fathers* (Edinburgh, Scotland: T&T Clark, 1999), 99.
59. Luther, for example, could be critical of Augustine. Yet, he generally held the church father in high regard. See Ellingsen, "Augustinian Origins of the Reformation Reconsidered," 16–25.
60. Augustine, *Letters*, 148.15.

Chapter 9: Pardoned from Sin

1. Although McGrath limits his survey to Western theologians, the Reformers sought support for their views from both Eastern and Western traditions. Consequently, this study includes both Eastern theologians (like Cyril and Theodoret) and Western theologians (like Anselm and Bernard).
2. Cyril of Alexandria, *Adv. Nest.* 3.2. *PG* 76.132. Trans. from Norman Russell, *Cyril of Alexandria* (New York: Routledge, 2000), 165.
3. Cyril of Alexandria, *Comm. Oseam* 65. *PG* 71.168. Trans. from Albert Ferreiro, ed., *The Twelve Prophets*, ACCS: Old Testament (Downers Grove, IL: InterVarsity Press, 2003), 29. Elsewhere, Cyril writes, "We have acquired the forgiveness of our former sins and have been justified freely by the mercy and grace of Christ" (Cyril of Alexandria, *Exp. Rom.*, on Rom. 3:27. *PG* 74.780. Trans. from Thomas C. Oden, *The Justification Reader* [Grand Rapids: Eerdmans, 2002], 108. See also Cyril of Alexandria, *Comm. Luc.* 47 [on Luke 9:2]. *PG* 72.641).
4. Theodoret, *Interp. Rom.* (on Rom. 4:4). *PG* 82.88. Trans. from Gerald Bray, *Romans*, ACCS (Downers Grove, IL: InterVarsity, 1998), 108.
5. Ibid. (on Rom. 1:17). *PG* 82.57, 60. Trans. from Bray, *Romans*, ACCS, 31.
6. Theodoret, *Interp. Eph.* (on Eph. 2:8–9). *PG* 82.521. Trans. from Oden, *The Justification Reader*, 44. In this same commentary, Theodoret says of Christ, "He Himself has paid our debt. Then Paul explains more plainly how great the gift is: 'You are saved by grace.' For it is not because of the excellence of our lives that we have been called, but because of the love of our Savior" (on Eph. 2:4–5. *PG* 82.520. Trans. from Oden, *The Justification Reader*, 113).
7. Theodoret, *Epist.* 83. *PG* 83.1269. Trans. from Joel C. Elowsky, ed., *We Believe in the Holy Spirit* (Downers Grove, IL: IVP Academic, 2009), 99.
8. As Oden, *The Justification Reader*, 44, concludes, "Key textual evidences from Origen, John Chrysostom, and Theodoret of Cyrrhus show that leading eastern patristic writers anticipated standard classic Reformation teaching on justification." See also Robert Letham, *Through Western Eyes: Eastern Orthodoxy: A Reformed Perspective* (Ross-shire, U.K.: Mentor, 2010), 251.
9. Marcus Eremita, *Oper. just.* 2. *PG* 65.929. Trans. from *The Philokalia*, compiled by St. Nikodimus of the Holy Mountain and St. Makarios of Corinth, 4 vols, ed. by G. E. H. Palmer, Philip Sherrard, and Kallistos Ware (London: Faber and Faber, 1990), 1:125. Marcus also explains that mere intellectual knowledge is useless by itself, since faith without works is dead: "He who relies on theoretical knowledge alone is not yet a faithful servant: a faithful servant is one who expresses his faith in Christ through obedience to His commandments" (1:5; *PG* 65.932).
10. See Letham, *Through Western Eyes*, 251.
11. Marcus Eremita, *Oper. just.* 17 [18]. *PG* 65.932. Trans. from *The Philokalia*, 1:126. Half a millennium later, Symeon the New Theologian (949–1022) reflects a similar perspective when he confesses his own salvation to be by grace through faith apart from works: "I neither fasted, nor kept vigils, nor slept on bare ground, but—to borrow the Psalmist's words—'I humbled myself' and, in short, 'the Lord saved me.' Or to put it even more briefly, I did no more than believe and the Lord accepted me" (Symeon the New

Theologian, *Catechesis* 22, "On Faith." *PG* 120.693. Trans. from *The Philokalia*, 4:16; Letham, *Through Western Eyes*, 250–51).

12. As Gregg R. Allison, *Historical Theology* (Grand Rapids: Zondervan, 2011), 504, explains, "The influence of Augustine was most clearly seen in the medieval period in the writings of the Augustinians, church leaders who echoed and defended his theology."
13. Prosper of Aquitaine, *Voc. Gent.* 1.24. *PL* 51.679. Trans. from Elowsky, *We Believe in the Holy Spirit*, 97.
14. Ibid., 1.17. *PL* 51.669. Trans. adapted from Oden, *The Justification Reader*, 46.
15. Fulgentius, *Inc. Fil.* 1. *PL* 65.573. Trans. from Oden, *The Justification Reader*, 48.
16. Ildefonsus of Toledo, *Itin. des.* 89. *PL* 96.190. Trans. adapted from Allison, *Historical Theology*, 504.
17. Ildefonsus, *Vir. Mar.*, incipit. *PL* 96.54. Trans. from Allison, *Historical Theology*, 504. Reflecting on the contributions of theologians like Ildefonsus, Gregg Allison concludes that some of the "medieval Augustinians emphasized that grace was received by faith alone." Allison, *Historical Theology*, 504.
18. Bede (673–735), *Exp. Jac.* (on James 2:20). *PL* 93.22. Trans. from Gerald Bray, *James, 1–2 Peter, 1–3 John, Jude*, ACCS (Downers Grove, IL: InterVarsity Press, 2000), 31. See also Bede, *Cant. Alleg.* 1. *PL* 91.1071; *Exp. Act. Apost.* 15.9. *PL* 92.976.
19. Ibid. In this context, Bede explains how Paul's teaching corresponds to the words of James, that faith without works is dead (see James 2:26). Bede warns against those who think they can profess faith in Christ while living evil lives.
20. Commenting on Bernard, Luther exclaimed, "In his sermons Bernard is superior to all teachers, even to Augustine himself, because he preaches Christ so excellently" (quoted in Philip Schaff and David S. Schaff, *History of the Christian Church*, 8 vols. [repr., Peabody, MA: Hendrickson Publishers, 2002], 5:351).
21. Bernard of Clairvaux, *Serm. Cant.* 50.2. *PL* 183.1021. Trans. from *Honey and Salt: Selected Spiritual Writings of Saint Bernard of Clairvaux*, ed. John F. Thornton and Susan B. Varenne (New York: Random House, 2007), 170. Elsewhere, Bernard writes, "What is hidden about us in the heart of God will be revealed for us, and His Spirit testifies and persuades our spirit that we are the children of God. But He convinces us of this by calling and justifying us by grace through faith" (Bernard of Clairvaux, *Ded. eccl.* 5, 7. *PL* 183.533. Trans. from Else Marie Wiberg Pedersen, "The Significance of the *Sola Fide* and the *Sola Gratia* in the Theologies of Bernard of Clairvaux (1090–1153) and Martin Luther (1483–1546)," http://web.augsburg.edu/~mcguire/EMWPedersen_Bernard_Luther.pdf).
22. Bernard of Clairvaux, *Pro Dom. 1 Nov.* 4. *PL* 183.353. Trans. from W. Stanford Reid, "Bernard of Clairvaux in the Thought of John Calvin," *WTJ* 41, no. 1 (1979): 142.

23. Bernard of Clairvaux, *Serm. Cant.*, 67.10. *PL* 183.1107. Trans. from J. S. Whale, *The Protestant Tradition* (New York: Cambridge University Press, 1959), 45. See also Bernard, *Grat. et lib. arb.* 14.47. *PL* 182.1026.
24. N. R. Needham, *2000 Years of Christ's Power, Part Three* (London: Grace Publications, 2004), 86, n. 26. See also Steven J. Lawson, *Pillars of Grace* (Orlando, FL: Reformation Trust, 2011), 325.
25. Joseph A. Fitzmyer notes that Thomas Aquinas also used the phrase *sola fide* in his commentaries on Romans (4.1), Galatians (2.4), and 1 Timothy (1.3) (Joseph A. Fitzmyer, *Romans: A New Translation with Introduction and Commentary* by Joseph A. Fitzmyer, The Anchor Bible, vol. 33 [New York: Doubleday, 1993], 360–61). However, Robert L. Reymond, "Dr. John H. Gerstner on Thomas Aquinas as a Protestant," *WTJ* 59, no. 1 (Spring 1997): 113–21, has convincingly demonstrated that Thomas did not understand justification in a way that anticipated later Reformation teaching.
26. Cassiodorus uses the phrase *sola fide* in his commentary on Romans 4:5. See Charles P. Carlson Jr., *Justification in Earlier Medieval Theology* (The Hauge, Netherlands: Martinus Nijhoff, 1975), 27. For Cassiodorus's commentary on Romans, see *PL* 68:415–686.
27. Lanfranc uses the phrase *sola fide* in his commentary on Romans 3:27. See Carlson, *Justification in Earlier Medieval Theology*, 43. For Lanfanc's commentary on Paul's epistles, see *PL* 150:101–406.
28. Bruno explains that *sola fide* is sufficient for justification in his discussion of Romans 4. See Carlson, *Justification in Earlier Medieval Theology*, 46. Carlson also notes the influence of Chrysostom on Bruno's exegesis (45). For Bruno's exposition of Paul's epistles, see *PL* 153:11–566.
29. Robert uses the phrase *sola fide* in his commentary on Romans 4:4. See Carlson, *Justification in Earlier Medieval Theology*, 54. For Robert's commentary on Paul's epistles, see R. M. Martin, ed., *Oeuvres de Robert de Melun*, tome II: *Questiones theologice de epistolis Pauli, Spicilegium Sacrum Lovaniense* 18 (Louvain, 1938).
30. Nonetheless, as Carlson, *Justification in Earlier Medieval Theology*, 68, explains, "The impression remains that the term 'justification' had relatively minor significance for these interpreters; it occurs in a sense which is technically little more than a synonym for remission of sins."
31. As Fitzmyer notes, the language of "faith alone" can be found in the writings of Origen (*Commentary on Romans*, 3; *PG* 14.952); Hilary (*Commentary on Matthew* 8:6; *PL* 9.961); Basil (*Sermon on Humility*, 20.3; *PG* 31.529); Marius Victorinus (*Commentary on Galatians*, 2.15–16); Ambrosiaster (*Commentary on Romans* 3.24; *CSEL* 81.1.119); John Chrysostom (*Homilies on Titus* 3.3; *PG* 62.679); Augustine (*De fide et operibus* 22.40; *CSEL* 41.84–85); Cyril of Alexandria (*On the Gospel of John*, 10.15.7; *PG* 74.368); Theodoret (*Affectionum curatio* 7; *PG* 93.100); Bernard, (*Sermon on the Song of Solomon* 22.8; *PL* 183.881); Theophylact (*Exposition on Galatians*, 3.12–13; *PG* 124.988); and Thomas Aquinas, *Exposition in 1 Timothy* 1.3) (Fitzmyer, *Romans*, 360–61).
32. After surveying medieval commentaries on Romans, Carlson, *Justification in Earlier Medieval Theology*, 40, writes, "The medieval concept of justifica-

tion is always basically forensic, but given only a theological, and not legal, interpretation." Carlson sees Hatto of Vercelli (ca. 885–961) as a leading example of a medieval commentator who articulated a forensic understanding of justification.

33. Gregory the Great, *Hom. Ezech.* 1.7.24. *PL* 76.853. Trans. from Elowsky, *We Believe in the Holy Spirit*, 91.
34. Bernard of Clairvaux, *Serm. Cant.* 23.15. *PL* 183.892. Trans. from George Stanley Faber, *The Primitive Doctrine of Justification Investigated*, 2nd ed. (London: Seely and Burnside, 1839), 157. English updated for clarity.
35. Alister E. McGrath, *Iustitia Dei: A History of the Doctrine of Justification*, 3rd ed. (Cambridge: Cambridge University Press), 81, notes the historic significance of Anselm's perspective: "Anselm's soteriology is dominated by the understanding of justice as moral rectitude, and it marks a decisive turning point in the medieval discussion of the 'righteousness of God.'" See also Michael J. Vlach, "Penal Substitution in Church History," *MSJ* 20, no. 2 (Fall 2009): 202.
36. Anselm of Canterbury, *Cur Deus hom.* 1.11. *PL* 158.376–77. Trans. from Janet Fairweather, in *Anselm of Canterbury: The Major Works*, eds. Brian Davies and G. R. Evans (Oxford: Oxford University Press, 1998), 283. Hereafter, *Anselm: Major Works*.
37. Anselm writes, "Consider it, then, an absolute certainty, that God cannot remit a sin unpunished, without recompense, that is, without the voluntary paying off of a debt, and that a sinner cannot, without this, attain to a state of blessedness, not even the state which was his before he sinned" (Ibid., 1.19. *PL* 158.391. Trans. from *Anselm: Major Works*, 302).
38. Ibid., 1.24. *PL* 158.397. Trans. from *Anselm: Major Works*, 310. And again, "A man who is a sinner is in no way capable of doing this, for one sinner cannot make another sinner righteous" (Ibid., 1.23. *PL* 158.396. Trans. from *Anselm: Major Works*, 309). Significantly, Anselm uses the term *justificare* here, so that the phrase should be literally translated: "A sinner can in no way justify another sinner."
39. McGrath, *Iustitia Dei*, 80. See also Anselm, *Cur Deus hom.* 2.18.
40. McGrath provides a fuller overview of Anselm's position in *Iustitia Dei*, 75–82.
41. Anselm of Canterbury, *Cur Deus hom.* 2.19. *PL* 158.426.
42. Ibid., 2.21. *PL* 158.430. Trans. from *Anselm: Major Works*, 354.
43. Ibid., 1.24. *PL* 158.399. Trans. from *Anselm: Major Works*, 313.
44. Robert E. Van Voorst, *Readings in Christianity*, 3rd ed. (Stamford, CT: Wadsworth, Cengage Learning, 2015), 147, writes that "Anselm advanced a judicial or 'forensic' theory of the atonement: only one who is both divine and human can, by being punished, 'make satisfaction' (atone) for human sin." See also Peter Harrison, *The Bible, Protestantism, and the Rise of Natural Science* (New York: Cambridge University Press, 2001), 36; Timothy J. Gorringe, "Atonement," in *The Blackwell Companion to Political Theology*, eds. Peter Scott and William T. Cavanaugh (Malden, MA: John Wiley & Sons, 2008), 369, asserts that "Anselm effectively marries sacrificial and forensic imagery" in his theory of the atonement; William Henry Lazareth, *Luther*,

the Bible, and Social Ethics (Minneapolis: Augsburg Fortress, 2001), 187; D. Stephen Long, "Justification and Atonement," in *The Cambridge Companion to Evangelical Theology*, eds. Timothy Larsen and Daniel J. Treier (New York: Cambridge University Press, 2007), 82.

45. David Brown, "Anselm on Atonement," in *The Cambridge Companion to Anselm*, eds. Brian Davies and Brian Leftow (New York: Cambridge University Press, 2004), 292–93, suggests that Anselm "is not as far distant from justification by faith as Protestant commentators so commonly assume." See also Norman L. Geisler and Ralph E. MacKenzie, *Roman Catholics and Evangelicals* (Grand Rapids: Baker Academic, 1995), 91; Marit Trelstad, "Putting the Cross in Context: Atonement through Covenant," in *Transformative Lutheran Theologies*, ed. Mary J. Streufert (Minneapolis: Fortress Press, 2010), 111; Darren C. Marks, *Bringing Theology to Life: Key Doctrines for Christian Faith and Mission* (Downers Grove, IL: InterVarsity Press, 2009), 70, who writes, "The magisterial Protestants such as Martin Luther and John Calvin (1509–1564) viewed salvation as forensic justification.... Forensic justification relies heavily on Anselm of Canterbury's influential book *Why the God-Man?* (*Cur Deus hom*)."
46. John W. De Gruchy, *Reconciliation: Restoring Justice* (Minneapolis: Augsburg Fortress, 2002), 60. See also Donald MacLeod, *Christ Crucified: Understanding the Atonement* (Downers Grove, IL: InterVarsity Press, 2014), 175–76; Michael M. Winter, *The Atonement* (Collegeville, MN: The Liturgical Press, 1995), 63.
47. Jaroslav Pelikan, *The Christian Tradition: A History of the Development of Doctrine: Vol. 4: Reformation of Church and Dogma (1300 – 1700)* (Chicago: University of Chicago Press, 1985), 161–62. Pelikan, however, points out, "In Luther, and even in these later Lutherans, the repetition of this vocabulary did not necessarily imply an acceptance of Anselm's entire schema."
48. F. W. Dillistone, *The Christian Understanding of Atonement* (Philadelphia: Westminster Press, 1968), 195–96.
49. Anselm, *Cur Deus hom.* 2.16. *PL* 158.417–418. Trans. from *Anselm: Major Works*, 338–39. Though Anselm goes on in this context to speak of post-conversion acts of penitence, the point remains that he is depicting Christ's work of redemption here within a forensic framework in which a king pardons his enemies on the basis of the work of a substitute. In his subsequent explanation, Anselm calls this a "parable" about Christ bringing redemption to mankind.
50. Another link between the Reformers and their medieval precursors has been proposed by scholars like Stephen Strehle, who observes that Melanchthon's concept of forensic justification was derived from Erasmus's translation of Romans 4:3, in which Erasmus rendered the Greek verb *logizomai* with the Latin *imputo* ("to impute") rather than the Vulgate's *reputo* ("to repute"). See Stephen Strehle, *The Catholic Roots of the Protestant Gospel: Encounter Between the Middle Ages and the Gospel* (Leiden, Netherlands: E. J. Brill, 1995), 67–68; Paul O'Callaghan, *Fides Christi: The Justification Debate* (Dublin: Four Courts Press, 1997), 49.

51. As G. R. Evans, *Anselm* (New York: Continuum Books, 2001), x, has pointed out, Anselm's theology cannot be fully appreciated without seeing it applied personally in his devotional writings.
52. Anselm, *Med. et orat.*, Oratio 2. *PL* 158.859. Trans. from Anselm, *Meditations and Prayers to the Holy Trinity and Our Lord Jesus Christ*, trans. E. B. Pusey (Oxford: John Henry Parker, 1856), 181. Hereafter, *Meditations and Prayers*. English updated for clarity.
53. Ibid.
54. Ibid., Meditatio 2. *PL* 158.724–25. *Meditations and Prayers*, 29–30. English updated for clarity.
55. Ibid.
56. Ibid. Trans. from *Meditations and Prayers*, 108. English updated for clarity. While it is true that Anselm emphasizes the necessity of repentance and the importance of good works in the lives of believers, his ultimate hope is not in his own works but in God's grace. Of his works, he declares, "My conscience merits damnation, and my repentance suffices not for satisfaction; but surely Your mercy surpasses all offense" (Meditatio 3. *PL* 158.729. Trans. adapted *from Meditations and Prayers*, 36.)
57. Ibid., Oratio 2. *PL* 158.861. Trans. from *Meditations and Prayers*, 183–84. English updated for clarity.
58. Ibid., Meditatio 12. *PL* 158.772. Trans. from *Meditations and Prayers*, 110. English updated for clarity.
59. See, for example, John Calvin, *Institutes of the Christian Religion*, ed. John T. McNeill, trans. Ford Lewis Battles (Louisville, KY: Westminster John Knox Press, 1960), 2.17.4; 2.17.5. As Roger E. Olson, *The Mosaic of Christian Belief: Twenty Centuries of Unity and Diversity* (Downers Grove, IL: InterVarsity Press, 2002), 260, explains, "The basic structure of Calvin's and the Reformed theologians' model is similar to Anselm's. Calvin even referred to Christ's payment of a debt owed by humanity to God." See also Ray S. Anderson, *The Soul of Ministry* (Louisville, KY: Westminster John Knox Press, 1997), 237; Dirk J. Smit, *Essays on Being Reformed: Collected Essays 3* (Stellenbosch, South Africa: SUN MeDIA, 2009), 93; Brown, "Anselm on Atonement," 296.

Chapter 10: Reckoned as Righteous

1. Jayson Scott Galler, "Logic and Argumentation in *The Book of Concord*" (Austin, TX: University of Texas, 2007), https://repositories.lib.utexas.edu/bitstream/handle/2152/3474/gallerd16268.pdf, 356–72.
2. Ibid., 359–60; see also 402. Galler contends, "The distinction between justification and sanctification [made by the Reformers] may well then be understood as an example of the kind of formal distinction made by John Duns Scotus (and perhaps to a lesser extent by William Ockham)" (373).
3. Anthony N. S. Lane, *Justification by Faith in Catholic-Protestant Dialogue: An Evangelical Assessment* (New York: T & T Clark, 2006), 139–40.
4. Ibid.
5. John M. Rist, *Augustine Deformed* (New York: Cambridge University Press, 2014), 182. See also Gerald Bray, *God Has Spoken: A History of Christian*

Theology (Wheaton, IL: Crossway, 2014), 519–20. Stephen Strehle, *The Catholic Roots of the Protestant Gospel: Encounter Between the Middle Ages and the Gospel* (Leiden, Netherlands: E. J. Brill, 1995), 69, similarly identifies commonality between the Reformers and the Nominalists by asserting that "both separate the forgiveness of sin from an infused state of grace or what God does in us." See also Paul Ricoeur, *The Just* (Chicago: University of Chicago Press, 2000), 15.

6. Galler, "Logic and Argumentation in *The Book of Concord*," 360.
7. Ibid., 360–61.
8. Ibid., 371.
9. Ibid.
10. Ibid.
11. Ibid., 401.
12. Ibid., 372–73.
13. Tony Lane, "Ten Theses on Justification and Sanctification," in *Mission and Meaning: Essays Presented to Peter Cotterell*, eds. Antony Billington, Tony Lane, and Max Turner (Carlisle, England: Paternoster Press, 1995), 197. Lane goes on to show that theologians like Duns Scotus and Bernard of Clairvaux understood such a distinction.
14. Bernard of Clairvaux, *Serm. Cant.* 3.2, *PL* 183.794; 81.9, *PL* 183.1175. See Franz Posset, *Pater Bernhardus: Martin Luther and Bernard of Clairvaux* (Kalamazoo, MI: Cistercian Publications, 1999), 203. Similarly, Bernard distinguishes between the flower of faith and the fruit of good works. He writes, "If however, you want to attribute both of these, the flowers and the fruit, to the one person according to their moral sense, understand the flower as faith, the fruit as action. Nor do I think that this will seem wrong to you, if, just as the flower by necessity precedes the fruit, so faith ought to come before good works" (*Serm. Cant.* 51.2; *PL* 183.1025. Trans. from Posset, *Pater Bernhardus*, 190–91).
15. Theodoret, *Interp. 2 Cor.* (on 2 Cor. 5:21). *PG* 82.412. Trans. from Gerald Bray, *1–2 Corinthians*, ACCS (Downers Grove, IL: InterVarsity Press, 2012), 249.
16. Theodoret, *Interp. Rom.* (on Rom. 3:25). *PG* 82.84–85. Trans. from Bray, *Romans*, ACCS, 102.
17. Theodoret, *Interp. Ps.* 21.2 (on Psalm 22:1). *PG* 80:1012. Trans. from Robert C. Hill, *Theodoret of Cyrus: Commentary on the Psalms, 1–72*, The Fathers of the Church, vol. 101 (Washington, D.C.: The Catholic University of America Press, 2000), 146–47. See also "Imputation of Righteousness in Church History," Alpha & Omega Ministries (Nov. 20, 2012): http://www.aomin.org/aoblog/index.php/2012/11/20/imputation-of-righteousness-in-church-history-as-discussed-on-the-dividing-line-today/. Also Oecumenius, *Commentary on 1 Peter* (on 1 Pet. 3:18). *PG* 119.556; Gerald Bray, *James, 1–2 Peter, 1–3 John, Jude*, ACCS (Downers Grove, IL: InterVarsity Press, 2000), 107.
18. As Thomas C. Oden, *The Justification Reader* (Grand Rapids: Eerdmans, 2002), 92, explains, "This is what is meant by imputation: One's debit balance may be charged to another. Or someone's plus balance may be credited

to another. By imputation a debit or credit is applied to one's own account due to an action of another."

19. Anselm of Canterbury, *Med. et orat.*, Meditatio 7. *PL* 158.744. Trans. from *Meditations and Prayers*, 61–62. English updated for clarity.
20. Ibid., Meditatio 11. *PL* 158.765. Trans. from *Meditations and Prayers*, 97–98. English updated for clarity.
21. Elsewhere, Anselm uses the illustration of a balance, noting that if the weight of his sins were put on one side of the scales, the only thing heavy enough to tip the balance would be the finished work of Christ. As Anselm exclaims, "Truly, O Lord, His sufferings will appear heavier and more worthy, that through them You should pour out Your mercies upon us, than our sins, that through them You should restrain Your compassion in anger," Meditatio 9. *PL* 158.757. Trans. from *Meditations and Prayers*, 83–84. English updated for clarity.
22. Ibid., Oratio 2. *PL* 158.863. Trans. from *Meditations and Prayers*, 186. English updated for clarity.
23. Ibid. *PL* 158.864. Trans. from *Meditations and Prayers*, 187.
24. Ibid. *PL* 158.865. Trans. from *Meditations and Prayers*, 187–88. English updated for clarity.
25. Ibid., Oratio 6. *PL* 158.874–875. Trans. from *Meditations and Prayers*, 205. English updated for clarity.
26. Ibid., Meditatio 9. *PL* 158.749. Trans. from *Meditations and Prayers*, 70–71. English updated for clarity.
27. John Piper, *Brothers, We Are Not Professionals* (Nashville: Broadman & Holman, 2002), 19, cites this passage to assert, "The Great Scholastic theologian, Anselm (1033–1109), was probably also an exponent of justification by faith alone." Commenting on this passage, Jonathan R. Huggins, *Living Justification* (Eugene, OR: Wipf & Stock, 2013), 28, writes: "Notice the idea of Christ's merits being applied to the sinner as a basis for their acceptance. And this merit seems to be equated with what Jesus did in his death. Christ's death is the event that turns away God's wrath [and] allows one's sins to be forgiven. This touches surely upon atonement theology, but relatedly, speaks to justification as involving the merits of Christ being applied to believers. We are not quite presented with a full doctrine of the 'imputation of Christ's active obedience/righteousness' as the basis of justification. But there is evidence for some development in that direction."
28. Anselm of Canterbury, *Admon. mor. PL* 158:686–687. Trans. from *Meditations and Prayers*, 275–77. English updated for clarity. Some scholars have suggested that this work is anonymous and incorrectly credited to Anselm. Even if that is the case, the work still stands as an important medieval witness to the need for sinners to rest fully in the merits of Christ for salvation.
29. Ibid. Trans. from *Meditations and Prayers*, 275–77. English updated for clarity.
30. A. H. Strong, *Systematic Theology* (Old Tappan, NJ: Fleming H. Revell, 1907), 849. See also John Gerstner, *Jonathan Edwards: A Mini Theology* (Wheaton, IL: Tyndale House, 1987), 71–72.

31. Bernard of Clairvaux, *Serm. Cant.* 68.6. *PL* 183.1111. Trans. from Whale, *The Protestant Tradition*, 46.
32. Bernard of Clairvaux, *Fest. omn. sanct.* 1.11. *PL* 183.459. Trans. from George Stanley Faber, *The Primitive Doctrine of Justification Investigated*, 2nd ed. (London: Seely and Burnside, 1839), 185.
33. Bernard of Clairvaux, *Fest. annunt. Mar.* 1.1. *PL* 183.383. Trans. from Whale, *The Protestant Tradition*, 45–46.
34. Ibid., 22.9. *PL* 183.882. Trans. from Posset, *Pater Bernhardus*, 186.
35. As Bernard declares, "Concerning Righteousness itself shall be our joy, when Christ our life shall appear, and when we shall appear with Him in glory. For He is the person, of God the Father, who was made unto us Righteousness" (Bernard of Clairvaux, *Oct. epiph.* 5. *PL* 183.154. Trans. from Faber, *The Primitive Doctrine of Justification Investigated*, 184).
36. Bernard of Clairvaux, *Serm. Cant.* 2.8. *PL* 183.793. Trans. adapted from Pedersen, "The Significance of the *Sola Fide* and the *Sola Gratia* in the Theologies of Bernard of Clairvaux (1090–1153) and Martin Luther (1483–1546)," http://web.augsburg.edu/~mcguire/EMWPedersen_Bernard_Luther.pdf, 11.
37. Bernard of Clairvaux, *Epist.* 190.6. *PL* 182.1065. Trans. from John Mabillon, ed., *Life and Works of Saint Bernard, Abbot of Clairvaux*, trans. Samuel J. Eales (London: John Hodges, 1889), 2.580–581 (emphaasis mine).
38. Bernard of Clairvaux, *Grat. et lib. arb.* 14.51. *PL* 182.1029.
39. Bernard of Clairvaux, *Serm. Cant.* 61.5. *PL* 183.1073. See also Pedersen, "The Significance of the *Sola Fide* and the *Sola Gratia* in the Theologies of Bernard of Clairvaux (1090–1153) and Martin Luther (1483–1546)," 11.
40. Ibid. *PL* 183.1073. Trans. from Whale, *The Protestant Tradition*, 46.
41. St. Bernard as recorded by William of St. Thierry, *S. Bern. vit. prim.* 1.12. *PL* 185.258. Trans. from Alban Butler, *The Lives of the Fathers, Martyrs, and Other Principal Saints*, vol. 8 (Dublin: James Duffy, 1845), 231. English updated for clarity. See also N. R. Needham, *2000 Years of Christ's Power, Part Three* (London: Grace Publications, 2004), 90.
42. Bernard of Clairvaux, *Serm. Cant.* 22.8. *PL* 183.881. Trans. from Posset, *Pater Bernhardus*, 186. Emphasis added.
43. Ibid., 22.8. *PL* 183.882. Trans. from Faber, *The Primitive Doctrine of Justification Investigated*, 187. English updated for clarity.
44. Ibid., 22.11. *PL* 183.884. Trans. from Faber, *The Primitive Doctrine of Justification Investigated*, 187. English updated for clarity.
45. Posset, *Pater Bernhardus*, 186. Posset demonstrates that Luther had access to these Bernadine quotes (ibid., 188), and with regard to justification by faith, "Luther always considered Bernard to be the true witness to the gospel and his 'father' in the faith" (ibid., 189). Elsewhere, Franz Posset, *The Real Luther* (St. Louis: Concordia, 2011), 127, asserts that "the historical Luther's doctrine of justification is identical with the one of Saint Bernard." As Luther himself stated, "I regard [Bernard] as the most pious of all monks, and prefer him to all others. . . . He is the only one worthy of the name 'Father Bernard' and of being studied diligently. . . . St. Bernard was a man so lofty in spirit that I almost venture to set him above all other celebrated

teachers both ancient and modern" (Martin Luther, *Sermon on the Gospel of John*, 33, in Martin Luther, *Luther's Works*, vol. 22–24, ed. Jaroslav Pelikan [St. Louis: Concordia, 1957], 22.388).

46. See Whale, *The Protestant Tradition*, 45. Also see Thomas M. Lindsay, *A History of the Reformation*, 2 vols. (Charles Scribner's, 1906; repr., Eugene, OR: Wipf and Stock, 1999), 2.443, n. 1. See also Albrecht Ritschl, *A Critical History of the Christian Doctrine of Justification and Reconciliation*, trans. John S. Black (Edinburgh, Scotland: Edmonston and Douglas, 1872), 95–101.
47. Admittedly, the Reformers did not agree with everything they found in Bernard. See Michael Casey, "Foreword," 7–13, in Posset, *Pater Bernhardus*, 12; Anthony N. S. Lane, *John Calvin: Student of the Church Fathers* (Edinburgh, Scotland: Bloomsbury T&T Clark, 1991), 100–101. In acknowledging such areas of disagreement, Lane notes, "Bernard lived before the sixteenth-century controversies, and so it is wrong to expect him to have given consistent answers to questions that had not yet been raised. But there is a strand of his teaching which clearly prefigures the distinctive features of the protestant doctrine [of justification]" (A. N. S. Lane, "Bernard of Clairvaux: A Forerunner of John Calvin," in *Bernhardus Magister*, ed. John R. Sommerfeldt [Kalamazoo, MI: Cistercian Publications, 1992], 543).
48. Mark A. Noll and Carolyn Nystrom, *Is the Reformation Over? An Evangelical Assessment of Contemporary Roman Catholicism* (Grand Rapids: Baker Academic, 2008), 51. See also Whale, *The Protestant Tradition*, 46; Kirk R. MacGregor, *A Central European Synthesis of Radical and Magisterial Reform* (Lanham, MD: University Press of America, 2006), 18, adds, "Calvin's use of Bernard, on the whole, is remarkably positive, with forty-three ringing endorsements regarding the latter's perceived doctrinal faithfulness to Scripture out of forty-seven total citations."
49. Bray, *God Has Spoken*, 508, n. 236. See also Adriaan H. Bredero, *Bernard of Clairvaux: Between Cult and History* (Grand Rapids: Eerdmans, 1971), 174–75.
50. On this point, Anthony Lane, *Justification by Faith in Catholic-Protestant Dialogue*, 140, asks, "What about acceptance on the basis of Christ's righteousness being reckoned or imputed to our account? Here again the Protestant doctrine is not totally without precedent. Bernard can urge his readers to put their trust in God's mercy rather than their own merits. In particular he can speak of the imputing to us of Christ's righteousness." See also Lane, *John Calvin: Student of the Church Fathers*, 87–150; Lane, "Bernard of Clairvaux: A Forerunner of John Calvin," 533–545; A. N. S. Lane, *Calvin and Bernard of Clairvaux* (Princeton, NJ: Princeton Theological Seminary, 1996); W. Stanford Reid, "Bernard of Clairvaux in the Thought of John Calvin," *WTJ* 41, no. 1 (1979): 127–45; Dennis E. Tamburello, *Union with Christ: John Calvin and the Mysticism of St. Bernard* (Louisville, KY: John Knox Press, 1994), 14.
51. In this regard, Lane, *Justification by Faith in Catholic-Protestant Dialogue*, 138, writes, "What about the three distinctives of the Reformation position as listed by Alister McGrath? First, the definition of justification. It is clear that the normal definition during the patristic and medieval periods

referred primarily to inner renewal by the Holy Spirit, but the Protestant definition is occasionally found as an exception."

52. Posset, *Pater Bernhardus*, 381, 384. See also Franz Posset, "*Divus Bernhardus*: Saint Bernard as Spiritual and Theological Mentor of the Reformer Martin Luther," in *Bernardus Magister*, ed. John R. Sommerfeldt (Spencer, MA: Cistercian Publications, 1992), 517–532.
53. Ibid., 394. Posset is specifically responding to the opinions of Berndt Hamm. However, his comments would similarly apply to McGrath's thesis regarding the Reformers' doctrine of *sola fide*.

Chapter 11: Coming Full Circle

1. See Chemnitz, *Examination of the Council of Trent*, in *Chemnitz's Works*, 4 vols., trans., Fred Kramer (St. Louis: Concordia, 1971), 1:505.
2. As Anthony Lane articulates: "Alister McGrath lists three characteristic features of the Protestant understanding of the nature of justification. The first two of these are the definition of justification as involving a change of status before God rather than a change of state and, following from this, the deliberate and systematic distinction between justification and sanctification. He also claims that no theologian before the Reformation made such a systematic distinction. Does it matter if this is so? Is it not a purely antiquarian issue, of no present relevance? No. If a particular doctrine was unknown before the Reformation, one would have to conclude either that it was not true or that it was not in fact an important doctrine or that the church has been seriously in error for most of its existence. This last option would accord with the tendency in some Protestant circles to treat church history as if it began in 1517 with Luther nailing up the *Ninety-five Theses*. But is it really plausible to suggest that the church almost immediately after its birth went into hibernation for over 1400 years? Fortunately, we are not required to choose between these alternatives" (Tony Lane, "Ten Theses on Justification and Sanctification," in *Mission and Meaning: Essays Presented to Peter Cotterell*, eds. Antony Billington, Tony Lane, and Max Turner (Carlisle, England: Paternoster Press, 1995), 196–97. Lane continues by noting McGrath's failure to account for the writings of Bernard of Clairvaux and Duns Scotus.

Appendix: Voices from History

1. Clement of Rome, *1 Clem.* 32.4. Trans. from Michael W. Holmes, ed., *The Apostolic Fathers* (Grand Rapids: Baker Academic, 2007), 87.
2. Polycarp, *Pol. Phil.* 1.2–3. Trans. from Holmes, *The Apostolic Fathers*, 281.
3. *Diogn.* 9.2–5. Trans. from Thomas C. Oden, *The Justification Reader* (Grand Rapids: Eerdmans, 2002), 65.
4. Irenaeus, *Haer.* 4.5.5. *PG* 7.986. Trans. from *ANF*, 1.467.
5. Origen, *Comm. Rom.* 3.9. *PG* 14.952. Trans. from Thomas P. Scheck, "Origen's Interpretation of Romans," in *A Companion to St. Paul in the Middle Ages*, ed. Steven R. Cartright (Leiden, Netherlands: E. J. Brill, 2012), 33.
6. Ibid., 3.9. *PG* 14.952–53. Trans. from Joel C. Elowsky, ed., *We Believe in the Holy Spirit* (Downers Grove, IL: IVP Academic, 2009), 99.

7. Origen, *Comm. Rom.* 3.8. *PG* 14.946. Trans. from Oden, *The Justification Reader*, 63.
8. Marius Victorinus, *Ep. Gal.* 2 (on Gal. 3:21). *PL* 8.1172. Trans. from Mark J. Edwards, *Galatians, Ephesians, Philippians*, ACCS (Downers Grove, IL: InterVarsity Press, 1999), 48.
9. Ibid., 1 (on Eph. 2.9). *PL* 8.1256. Trans. from Oden, *The Justification Reader*, 48.
10. Ibid., 1 (on Eph. 2:15). *PL* 8.1258. Trans. from Joseph A. Fitzmyer, *Romans: A New Translation with Introduction and Commentary by Joseph A. Fitzmyer*, The Anchor Bible, vol. 33 (New York: Doubleday, 1993), 361.
11. Marius Victorinus, *Ep. Gal.* 1 (on Gal. 3.7). *PL* 8.1169. Trans. adapted from Edwards, *Galatians, Ephesians, Philippians*, ACCS, 37.
12. Marius Victorinus, *Ep. Gal.* 1 (on Gal. 2:15–16). *PL* 8.1164. Trans. from Hugh George Anderson, T. Austin Murphy, and Joseph A. Burgess, *Justification by Faith: Lutherans and Catholics in Dialogue VII* (Minneapolis: Augsburg Publishing House, 1985), 114.
13. Hilary, *Comm. Matt.* 20.7. *PL* 9.1030. Trans. from Hilary of Poitiers, *Commentary on Matthew*, The Fathers of the Church, trans. D. H. Williams (Washington, D.C.: The Catholic University of America Press, 2012), 212.
14. Ibid., 8.6. *PL* 9.961. Trans. from D. H. Williams, "Justification by Faith: A Patristic Doctrine," *J Ecclesiast Hist.* 57, no. 4 (October 2006): 658.
15. Ibid., 21.15. *PL* 9.1041. Trans. from Williams, "Justification by Faith," 660.
16. Ibid., 18.10. *PL* 9.1022. Trans. from Hilary of Poitiers, *Commentary on Matthew*, 199.
17. Basil, *Hom. humil.* 20.3. *PG* 31.529. Trans. from Elowsky, *We Believe in the Holy Spirit*, 98.
18. Ambrose, *Sacr.* 5.4.19. *PL* 16.450. See Oden, *The Justification Reader*, 108.
19. Ambrose, *Jac.* 2.2.9. *PL* 14.618. Trans. adapted from *The Fathers of the Church* (Washington, D.C.: The Catholic University of America Press, 1972), 65:150–51.
20. Ambrose, *Jac.* 1.6.21. *PL* 14.607. Trans. from Michael P. McHugh, *St Ambrose: Seven Exegetical Works* (Washington, D.C.: Catholic University of America, 1972), 133.
21. Ambrosiaster, *Ad Rom.* (on Rom. 1:11). *PL* 17.53. Trans. adapted from Gerald Bray, *Romans*, ACCS (Downers Grove, IL: InterVarsity, 1998), 23.
22. Ibid. (on Rom. 3:24). *PL* 17.79. Trans. from Elowsky, *We Believe in the Holy Spirit*, 98.
23. Ibid. (on Rom. 3:26). *PL* 17.80. Trans. adapted from Oden, *The Justification Reader*, 63. See also Williams, "Justification by Faith," 662–63.
24. Ibid. (on Rom. 3:27). *PL* 17.80. Trans. from Bray, *Romans*, ACCS, 103.
25. Ibid. (on Rom. 4:6). *PL* 17.83. Trans. from Bray, *Romans*, ACCS, 113.
26. Ambrosiaster, *Ad Cor. Prim.* (on 1 Cor. 1:4). *PL* 17.185.
27. Ambrosiaster, *Ad Rom.* (on Rom. 4:5). *PL* 17:82–83. Trans. from Bray, *Romans*, ACCS, 112.
28. Ibid. (on Rom. 1:17). *PL* 17.56. Trans. from Bray, *Romans*, ACCS, 31.
29. John Chrysostom, *Hom. Act.* 32. *PG* 60.235. Trans. from Francis Martin, ed., *Acts*, ACCS (Downers Grove, IL: InterVarsity, 2006), 183.

30. John Chrysostom, *Hom. Rom.* 7 (on Rom. 3:27). *PG* 60.446. Trans. from *NPNF*, First Series, 11.379.
31. Ibid., 9 (on Rom. 5:2). *PG* 60.468. Trans. from *NPNF*, First Series, 11.396. English updated slightly.
32. John Chrysostom, *Hom. 1 Cor.* 8 (on 1 Cor. 3:1–3). *PG* 61.73. Trans. from *NPNF*, First Series, 12.47.
33. John Chrysostom, *Hom. Gal.* (on Gal. 3:8). *PG* 61.651. Trans. from *NPNF*, First Series, 13.26.
34. John Chrysostom, *Hom. Eph.* 5 (on Eph. 2:13–15). *PG* 62.39–40. Trans. adapted from *NPNF*, First Series, 13.72.
35. John Chrysostom, *Hom. 1 Tim.* (on 1 Tim. 1:15–16). *PG* 62.520–21. Trans. from Elowsky, *We Believe in the Holy Spirit*, 98.
36. John Chrysostom, *Adv. Jud.* 7.3. *PG* 48.919.
37. John Chrysostom, *Hom. Eph.* (on Eph. 2:8). *PG* 62.33. Trans. from Oden, *The Justification Reader*, 44.
38. John Chrysostom, *Hom. Gen.* 27.3. *PG* 53.243. Trans. from Robert C. Hill, *St. John Chrysostom: Homilies on Genesis 1–17*, Fathers of the Church (Washington, D.C.: The Catholic University of America Press, 1990), 74.167.
39. John Chrysostom, *Hom. Rom.* 8 (on Rom. 4:1–2). *PG* 60.454. Trans. from *NPNF*, First Series, 11.385.
40. John Chrysostom, *Hom. Col.* 5 (on Col. 1:26–28). *PG* 62.332. Trans. from Elowsky, *We Believe in the Holy Spirit*, 98. See also *NPNF*, First Series, 13.280.
41. John Chrysostom, *Hom. Rom.* 2. *PG* 60.409. Trans. from Bray, *Romans*, ACCS, 30.
42. Jerome, *Comm. Eph.* 1.2.1. *PL* 26.468. Trans. from Oden, *The Justification Reader*, 48.
43. Jerome, *Adv. Pelag.* 2.7. *PL* 23.568. Trans. from Oden, *The Justification Reader*, 112.
44. Jerome, *Comm. Eph.* 1.2.8–9. *PL* 26:460. Trans. from Edwards, *Galatians, Ephesians, Philippians*, ACCS, 133.
45. Ibid., 13 (22). *PL* 44.214–15. Trans. from *NPNF*, First Series, 5:93.
46. Augustine, *Exp. prop. Rom.* 20. *PL* 35.2066. Trans. from Oden, *The Justification Reader*, 145.
47. Augustine, *C. du. ep. Pelag.* 1.21.39. *PL* 44.569. Trans. from Elowsky, *We Believe in the Holy Spirit*, 96.
48. Augustine, *Epist.* 214.3. *PL* 33.969–70. Trans. from Gerald Bray, *1–2 Corinthians*, ACCS (Downers Grove, IL: InterVarsity Press, 2012), 39. See also Augustine, *Letters 204–270*, Fathers of the Church, trans. Wilfrid Parsons (Washington, D.C.: The Catholic University of America Press, 1981), 60.
49. Augustine, *Epist.* 214.4. *PL* 33.970. Trans. from *NPNF*, First Series, 5:438.
50. Augustine, *Enarrat. Ps.*, 55.12 [56.11]. *PL* 36.655. Trans. from *NPNF*, First Series, 8:222.
51. Augustine, *Enarrat. Ps.*, 31.7. *PL* 36.263. Trans. from John E. Rotelle, *Expositions of the Psalms 1–32* (Hyde Park, NY: New City Press, 2000), 11.370.

52. Ibid., 1.2.5. *PL* 40.114. Trans. from John H. S. Burleigh, *Augustine: Earlier Writings*, The Library of Christian Classics (Philadelphia: The Westminster Press, 1953), 389.
53. Augustine, *Gest. Pelag.* 14.34. *PL* 44.341.
54. Cyril of Alexandria, *Comm. Oseam* 65. *PG* 71.168. Trans. from Albert Ferreiro, ed., *The Twelve Prophets*, ACCS: Old Testament (Downers Grove, IL: InterVarsity Press, 2003), 29.
55. Cyril of Alexandria, *Adv. Nest.* 3.2. *PG* 76.132. Trans. from Norman Russell, *Cyril of Alexandria* (New York: Routledge, 2000), 165.
56. Ibid., 1.17. *PL* 51.669. Trans. from Oden, *The Justification Reader*, 46.
57. Theodoret, *Interp. Rom.* (on Rom. 4:4). *PG* 82.88. Trans. from Bray, *Romans*, ACCS, 108.
58. Ibid. (on Rom. 1:17). *PG* 82.57, 60. Trans. from Bray, *Romans*, ACCS, 31.
59. Theodoret, *Interp. Eph.* (on Eph. 2:8–9). *PG* 82.521. Trans. from Oden, *The Justification Reader*, 44.
60. Theodoret, *Epist.* 83. *PG* 83.1269. Trans. from Elowsky, *We Believe in the Holy Spirit*, 99.
61. Theodoret, *Interp. Rom.* (on Rom. 3:25). *PG* 82.84–85. Trans. from Bray, *Romans*, ACCS, 102.
62. Marcus Eremita, *Oper. just.* 2. *PG* 65.929. Trans. from *The Philokalia*, compiled by St. Nikodimus of the Holy Mountain and St. Makarios of Corinth, 4 vols., eds. G. E. H. Palmer, Philip Sherrard, and Kallistos Ware (London: Faber and Faber, 1990), 1:125.
63. Fulgentius, *Inc. Fil.* 1. *PL* 65.573. Trans. from Oden, *The Justification Reader*, 48.
64. Ildefonsus of Toledo, *Itin. des.* 89. *PL* 96.190. Trans. adapted from Gregg R. Allison, *Historical Theology* (Grand Rapids: Zondervan, 2011), 504.
65. Ildefonsus, *Vir. Mar.*, incipit. *PL* 96.54. Trans. from Allison, *Historical Theology*, 504.
66. Julian of Toledo, *Comp. Aet. Sext.* 2.14. *PL* 96.569. Trans. from Allison, *Historical Theology*, 504.
67. Bede (673–735), *Exp. Jac.* (on James 2:20). *PL* 93.22. Trans. from Gerald Bray, *James, 1–2 Peter, 1–3 John, Jude*, ACCS (Downers Grove, IL: InterVarsity Press, 2000), 31.
68. Symeon the New Theologian, *Catechesis* 22. "On Faith." *PG* 120.693. Trans. from *The Philokalia*, 4:16.
69. Anselm, *Cur Deus hom.*, 2.21. *PL* 158.430. Trans. from *Anselm: Major Works*, 354.
70. Ibid., Meditatio 3. *PL* 158.729. Trans. from *Meditations and Prayers*, 36. English updated for clarity.
71. Ibid., Meditatio 9. *PL* 158.757. Trans. from *Meditations and Prayers*, 83–84. English updated for clarity.
72. Ibid., Oratio 2. *PL* 158.863. Trans. from *Meditations and Prayers*, 186. English updated for clarity.
73. Ibid. *PL* 158.865. Trans. from *Meditations and Prayers*, 187–88. English updated for clarity.

74. Anselm of Canterbury, *Admon. mor. PL* 158:686–687. Trans. from *Meditations and Prayers*, 275–77. English updated for clarity.
75. Ibid.
76. Bernard of Clairvaux, *Serm. Cant.* 50.2. *PL* 183.1021. Trans. from *Honey and Salt: Selected Spiritual Writings of Saint Bernard of Clairvaux*, eds. John F. Thornton and Susan B. Varenne (New York: Random House, 2007), 170.
77. Ibid., 67.10. *PL* 183.1107. Trans. from J. S. Whale, *The Protestant Tradition* (New York: Cambridge University Press, 1959), 45.
78. Bernard of Clairvaux, *Ded. eccl.* 5, 7. *PL* 183.533. Trans. from Else Marie Wiberg Pedersen, "The Significance of the *Sola Fide* and the *Sola Gratia* in the Theologies of Bernard of Clairvaux (1090–1153) and Martin Luther (1483–1546)," http://web.augsburg.edu/~mcguire/EMWPedersen_Bernard_Luther.pdf.
79. Bernard of Clairvaux, *Serm. Cant.* 2.8. *PL* 183.793. Trans. adapted from Pedersen, "The Significance of the *Sola Fide* and the *Sola Gratia* in the Theologies of Bernard of Clairvaux (1090–1153) and Martin Luther (1483–1546)," 11.
80. Bernard of Clairvaux, *Pro Dom. 1 Nov.* 4. *PL* 183.353. Trans. from W. Stanford Reid, "Bernard of Clairvaux in the Thought of John Calvin," *WTJ* 41, no. 1 (1979): 142.
81. Bernard of Clairvaux, *Serm. Cant.* 23.15. *PL* 183.892. Trans. from George Stanley Faber, *The Primitive Doctrine of Justification Investigated*, 2nd ed. (London: Seely and Burnside, 1839), 157. English updated for clarity.
82. Bernard of Clairvaux, *Fest. omn. sanct.* 1.11. *PL* 183.459. Trans. from Faber, *The Primitive Doctrine of Justification Investigated*, 185.
83. Bernard of Clairvaux, *Epist.* 190.6. *PL* 182.1065. Trans. from John Mabillon, ed., *Life and Works of Saint Bernard, Abbot of Clairvaux*, trans. Samuel J. Eales (London: John Hodges, 1889), 2.580–81.
84. Ibid. *PL* 183.1073. Trans. from Whale, *The Protestant Tradition*, 46.
85. St. Bernard as recorded by William of St. Thierry, *S. Bern. vit. prim.* 1.12. *PL* 185.258. Trans. from Alban Butler, *The Lives of the Fathers, Martyrs, and Other Principal Saints*, vol. 8 (Dublin: James Duffy, 1845), 231. English updated for clarity.
86. Bernard of Clairvaux, *Serm. Cant.* 22.8. *PL* 183.881. Trans. adapted from Franz Posset, *Pater Bernhardus: Martin Luther and Bernard of Clairvaux* (Kalamazoo, MI: Cistercian Publications, 1999), 186.

ACKNOWLEDGMENTS

Special thanks to my colleagues, Michael J. Vlach and Kelly Osborne, for their help in the course of my research. Thanks as well to John MacArthur, Nick Needham, Stephen J. Nichols, Carl R. Trueman, William Webster, and Steve Lawson—both for their kind endorsements and insightful feedback on the manuscript.

I am also grateful to Drew Dyck, Kevin Emmert, and the entire team at Moody Publishers, who worked diligently to make this project possible. As the developmental editor on this project, Kevin, with his expertise in Reformation studies, proved especially valuable in refining the final product.

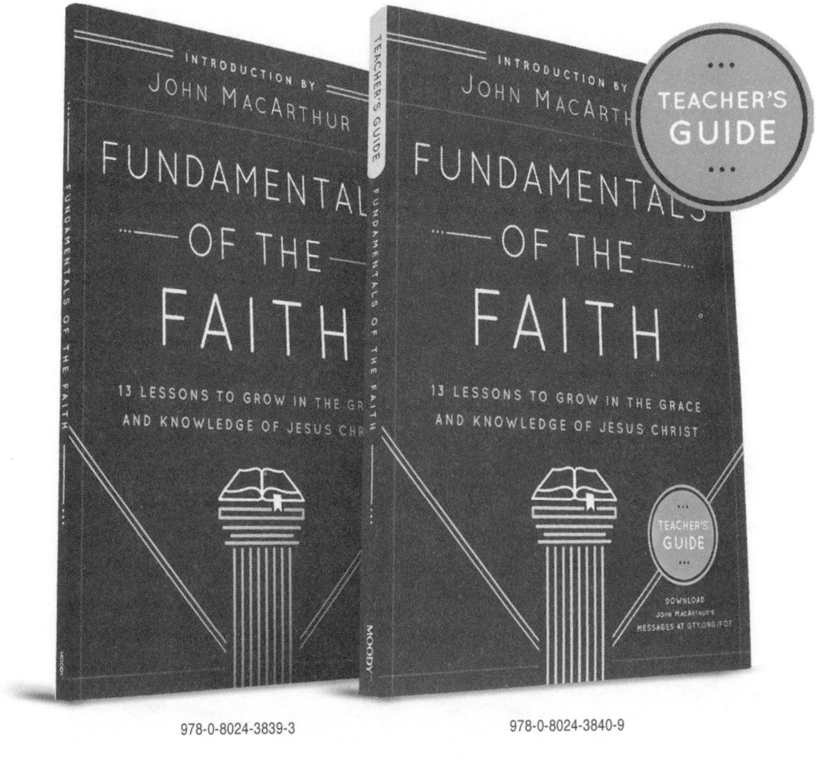